What Others Are Saying ...

"Dr. Butterfield writes the same way she lives her life. If you're interested in breaking the bonds that hold you back, unleashing your transformative leadership powers, and making a real difference in this world, read this book right away!"

Debra Ball, SPHR Vice President, Human Resources
St. Luke's Hospital

"A must-read for any woman in healthcare (or any organization) who wishes to understand and use the subtle art of achieving results by bringing all the players to the table as equal and valued contributors."

Steven M. Joyce, MD, Clinical Professor of Surgery
Division of Emergency Medicine, University of Utah

"This work is wonderful—so very needed! It speaks to the challenges most people grapple with every day and makes very clear that looking inside is the only sensible thing to do."

Janine Moon, Master Certified Coach
Author of *Career Ownership*

"Paula has identified the new form of power emerging in our organizations. If you want to engage your strengths as a woman and become a transformational leader, read *In Our Right Mind.* You will get the powerful coaching questions and ideas you need to create amazing results."

Marcia Reynolds, PsyD
Author of *Wander Woman: How High-Achieving Women Find Contentment and Direction*

In Our Right Mind

THE TRANSFORMING POWER OF WOMEN IN HEALTHCARE

PAULA S. BUTTERFIELD, PH.D.

PUBLISHED BY PEPPERNIGHT PRESS
COLUMBUS, OH

Peppernight Press
PO Box 164024
Columbus, OH 43216
www.peppernightpress.com

ISBN: 978-0-615-34924-4

Cover design and text layout: Michael Laning
Editing: Jane Sherwin, Jan Tremaine
Production supervision: Green Venus Design
Printing and binding: Malloy, Inc.

We have a strong commitment to protecting the environment and using sustainable resources that are responsibly harvested. This book is printed on 30% PCW paper.

Special discounts are available to corporations, associations, and educational institutions for quantity purchases. Contact Peppernight Press for more information.

Library of Congress Control Number: 2010921458

For Jeannette

1916-

Contents

Acknowledgments

Many of the people who contributed to this book are people I know only through their books. Exploring their ways of seeing and making sense of the world has kept me on the steep edge of the learning curve and continually revising and expanding my own worldview. To them I owe a deep note of thanks. You'll find some of their names in the pages and bibliography of this book.

I also am grateful to the many people I've crossed paths with in workplaces over the years. Some were stellar examples of what's possible when we put service ahead of self-interest. Others taught me how *not* to be and to them I am especially grateful. They awoke in me the desire to seek ways to create kinder, more compassionate and courageous workplaces.

The clients I have coached are a different source of inspiration and appreciation, for it is through working with them that I regularly glimpse what is possible when we support and challenge one another. I hold a special place of gratitude for the colleagues whose work has helped give direction and depth to my own work: Bob Anderson, Jim Anderson, Barbara Braham, Dan Holden, Virginia Macali, Janine Moon, Barbara Sliter, and Dave Womeldorff.

In the five years of this book's gestation, dozens of colleagues read chapters and gave generously of their time and insight. I wish I'd kept the lists of readers of the early drafts so I could thank them all by name, but I did not. You know who you are. Please also know how grateful I am for your support.

My partnership with Jane Sherwin, an editor *par excellence*, took the book in a new direction. When it comes to asking powerful questions, Jane raises the bar. And my thanks also to Denise Hollerich for guiding me through the production process and having patience above and beyond the call.

A handful of people have suffered the going-ups and coming-downs of life with an aspiring writer on a regular basis. Malcolm "Duffy" Parsons, who was always there with a glass of wine and "How can I help?" tops the list. He alone knows how many times I hit the wall. My colleague and fellow aspiring author Barbara Sliter has been on the phone monthly for years now, providing exactly what I needed, when I needed it: a safety net, a reality check, a simple reflection, a brilliant reframe. To them I owe a special note of thanks.

And to my son Michael, whose faith and trust have helped guide us both through the dark as well as the light.

Introduction

I came to this book via disparate routes, first as a student of English literature, then as a practicing psychotherapist, and later as a healthcare manager and leader. In 1998, my career path turned in the direction that led to this book. I was having dinner with a friend at a neighborhood pub. We were lamenting the corporate "restructuring" efforts that had put many of our colleagues and now us out of work. I glanced down at the cardboard coaster under my wine glass. It said, *Good leaders are scarce, so I'm following myself.* I took the coaster home and tacked it above my iMac. My business as a leadership coach and professional speaker was born within the month.

Fifteen years of corporate work had taught me that the real challenges in organizations were not traditional business challenges like the ability to interpret trends in spreadsheets, tweak another 2% out of the hospital's operating costs, or raise the pass rates for resident physicians taking board exams. The real challenges were relationship challenges: getting people engaged and committed and bringing all of who and how they are to what they do, helping them adapt to changing circumstances in an unpredictable and ever changing world, translating their potential into sustained high performance and a sense of satisfaction.

My early clients were not in healthcare. I was burned out on hospital systems and intensely curious about how other industries were approaching leadership in a rapidly changing world. I read voraciously, pursued coaching clients in a variety of different industries and sectors of the economy, and discovered that new models of leadership were arising based on collaboration and partnership, growing awareness of organizations as living systems, and new knowledge about optimal human functioning. Within a few years, I returned to working with healthcare leaders with a deeper understanding that they were struggling with the same challenges as leaders everywhere else.

I also was drawn to working with women. Their effectiveness as leaders was often complicated by the male-dominated, hierarchical cultures within which they worked—cultures that did not value women's strengths. These were highly talented and experienced women who often struggled to fit their round strengths into square holes and judged themselves harshly when the two didn't match.

The more I observed and worked with leaders and systems, the more appreciation I had for the complexity of life at both the individual and the organizational levels. Are there simple solutions to complex problems? Yes. But they're not found where we've been taught to look.

I recall a Sufi-inspired story of a man who lost his keys one night. He was searching diligently around a streetlamp when another man approached and offered to help. After several fruitless minutes, the stranger said, "Are you sure you lost your keys out here?" The man replied, "No, I didn't, but this is where the light is." Most of us prefer to stay where the light is, even when what we are seeking is elsewhere.

Finding our way beyond the streetlamp requires a different perspective on leadership. Historically, our perspective has been soaked in patriarchal images: leaders as heroes or protectors or saviors. I prefer to view leaders as fellow travelers: individuals who want to create deeply meaningful work and futures for themselves and others, help people adapt to the complex challenges and demands they encounter in pursuing such work, and partner with them to strengthen their capacity to learn and grow and stay resilient along the way. Leaders like this exist everywhere in organizations, not just in traditional positions of power and authority.

While *In Our Right Mind* was written for women, it really is a book for anyone interested in creating a more collaborative, nurturing, and service-oriented work environment and a resilient and highly committed workforce. Creating such an environment requires us to move out of the light and back to where we know the keys are. This means moving away from the familiar top-down command-control streetlamp we've been gathered around for years and back to the essential purpose of any organization: serving others in meaningful ways.

So for you, the reader, *In Our Right Mind* invites you into the world I share with my coaching clients. It invites you to suspend what you think you know about leadership and today's hospital systems in order to begin noticing and learning from things *as they are.* It is designed to set you on a path of thinking about what you think about and to introduce you to different ways of framing what you do and why and how you do it. It is also designed to assure you that while the world is changing dramatically, you are fully capable of staying in the flow and changing with it. The journey just requires access to your own wisdom and courage.

Throughout the writing of this book, my challenge has been to balance the inner personal work required of leaders—the work that most people overlook and that is often at the heart of coaching—with the organizational work that most people equate with getting results. In order for an organization to change, its leaders must change. To paraphrase Alfred Einstein, we cannot solve problems using the same kind of thinking that created them. We need to broaden and deepen our thinking in ways that capture the complexity and interconnected nature of the systems we have created. We need to realize that many of the so-called "problems" we're trying to fix are, from a broader perspective, simply part of something bigger and more integral.

We also need to appreciate that the wisdom we need is not just in our heads; it is in our hearts and bodies. By learning to observe ourselves *in the moment,* by learning to be fully present to what is occurring, both internally and externally, we can reconnect with ourselves and those around us in powerful ways and unleash our own capacity to transform the world in which we live and work.

I've tried to capture the complexity of this work in the book's title: *In Our Right Mind.* First, it's a reference to the value of right-brain "feminine" qualities like intuition, synthesis, connectedness, and contextual associations. We need them to complement and temper the left-brain linear logic that has dominated organizational life for years. The title is also a reference to trusting that the worldview we bring to work isn't "crazy" or "wrong"; it is simply different and its differentness is legitimate. Finally, "right mind" is a reference to the importance of being open and aware—mindful—of what is unfolding right here, right now and of laying aside our judgments and interpretations so that we can learn and grow from direct experience. On every page, you'll find the importance of balancing left- and right-brain, masculine and feminine, direct and meandering ways of being echoed in the design of the text, with its margins of "flush left, ragged right."

On the window sill above my kitchen sink sits a perfect acorn. It was the gift of an industrious squirrel who was burying everything he could find in the flowerpots on my back porch. The nearest oak tree is more than a block away, yet the squirrel brought this perfect seed to my door. It sits on the sill to remind me of the vast potential that lies within: the acorn holds everything necessary to create a mighty oak. It also sits there to remind me that life is unpredictable: we never know what will show up next or who the messenger will be. But when we trust that the right thing will arrive at the right time, we open ourselves to a powerful world beyond the world of logic.

How the Book Is Organized

Part 1, which comprises the first four chapters, is about building a strong foundation for leading during rapidly changing and difficult times. Chapter 1 highlights the value of women's ways of working, introduces a set of self-coaching tools that can help you explore and expand your perspectives on the events unfolding in your life, and offers an opportunity to assess some dynamics of your own leadership style.

Chapter 2 addresses the challenge of learning to think differently. We can learn new knowledge and skills lots of places, but that doesn't mean we can translate what we know into actions that produce the results we want. What often get in the way are our own thoughts and beliefs. So this chapter highlights some common beliefs driving our behavior, introduces the importance of mental models for working differently, and puts a few of those coaching tools to use.

Chapters 3 and 4 set the stage for getting work done with and through others. Getting people focused on creating a meaningful future and holding an environment that supports them in identifying and adapting to what they encounter as they pursue that future calls for a firm foundation from which to work. Chapter 3 explores the power of purpose as the orienting center for leading and Chapter 4 looks at the glue that holds people together in pursuing a lofty purpose: a set of core values or principles that inform how people work together day to day. Women can bring much to both of these endeavors.

Part 2, which comprises Chapters 5 through 11, delves into more specific ways that we can use our natural strengths to create environments of curiosity, compassion, and caring. The ideas here are neither prescriptive nor exhaustive. They are simply examples of how people can organize and work in increasingly more adaptable and satisfying ways.

Chapter 5, which is anchored in the belief that the real power in organizations comes from the nature of our relationships with one another, offers guidelines for building webs of inclusion as a means of creating great experiences for patients and customers. Chapter 6 is about getting people aligned and engaged in fulfilling a shared purpose, which is much different from the more common activity of strategic planning. Organizations need both and women's relational strengths are particularly well suited for nurturing alignment.

Chapter 7 reframes the common fear of 'not knowing' into a strength that can be leveraged to create everything from powerful new employee orientations to guidelines for shaping an adaptive, highly responsive workplace and great patient experiences.

Information is the lifeblood of adaptive organizations, so Chapter 8 highlights the importance of sharing information as a way of fueling people's capacity to respond creatively and appropriately to whatever they encounter. It also addresses a very specific form of information sharing—meaningful feedback—and offers a perspective on it that's consistent with women's natural preferences and conversational style.

Chapter 9 explores the notion that when people know what they want to create, they can be brilliant at figuring out how, especially when they have a few purposeful guidelines for giving structure and direction to what they do and the freedom to find their own way.

Our lives are steeped in stories and storytelling, so Chapter 10 examines the power of stories and metaphors to influence others and offers a number of techniques to help you deliver stories with confidence and credibility.

If you're like many women, self-doubt is your middle name. Chapter 11 shows you how to embrace it as a path to greater self-awareness and use it to find new ways of working from the core of your own wisdom and experience.

YOU CAN ALSO IMAGINE THE BOOK ORGANIZED LIKE THIS

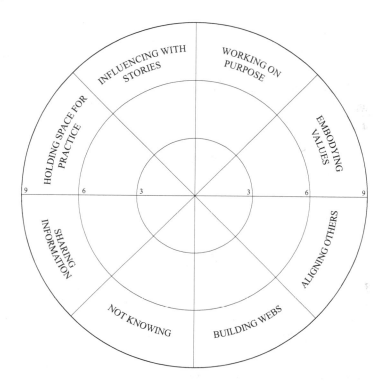

Notice how you respond to the shift from a linear, left-brain narrative to a graphic, right-brain image. What feels different about the two? Which do you prefer and for what reasons? One isn't better or worse than the other. They're simply different ways of conveying a message, just as women's ways of working are often different from men's.

Note also that you can use the wheel as a self-assessment tool. When you finish a chapter, determine your level of satisfaction with your *current capacity* in that area and mark the level on the circle. The higher your satisfaction, the higher the score. When you finish the book, connect the score marks. What do you notice about your "wheel"?

Using a different colored pen or pencil, you can also mark your ideal levels. Chances are, you'll have some gaps between current and ideal. Pick one or two specific areas to develop and begin working with the exercises and practices in that chapter. You can return to other areas at a later time. Note that ideal scores don't have to be at the outer edge of the circle in order for you to be effective.

I

Organizations are social structures. They serve us, they shape and give meaning to our lives, and they precede and succeed us. They also cannot exist without us, for we are the ones who create and sustain them—a fact that we easily forget.

Our standard model of organizations is patriarchal, steeped in hierarchy and tradition. We live it and reinforce it every time we catch ourselves complaining about the politics, struggling to meet the expectations of someone higher on the food chain, hunkering down in an effort to hold things together, or resenting yet another meeting about milestones, dashboard metrics, or poor performance.

We also live in moments. Those moments offer us an endless source of opportunity to shape and reshape our experience and, in turn, to affect the experiences of others. In any given moment, we have the opportunity to choose how we are, who we want to be, and what we want to pursue with one another. And therein lies our power.

Women have not had an easy go of it in patriarchal structures, and many of us have chosen to sideline our own strengths in order to get along. When we choose this path, we lose sight of the small but significant impact of those moments of contact with others. Even when we constitute a majority, as we do in healthcare, our oft-told stories about "the way it is" keep us tethered to the past.

Fortunately, times are ripe for a different way of *being* in organizations, and women are poised to lead the way. The question is whether we are willing to stand in our own strengths and bring them forth as legitimate alternatives and complements to commanding and controlling.

In the dawn of the 21st century, we have the opportunity to transform our organizations into communities of care and service, harmony and belonging. They are living systems, not machines, so the seeds of transformation are already within. At the 20,000-foot level, the task seems daunting. At the level of daily experience, it unfolds in very simple yet powerful questions like these: What am I here to contribute? How do I want to engage others along the way? How do I limit myself and what is the cost to those I serve? What commitments and promises am I—and are we—willing to make to create an organization that reflects what we most deeply value?

The journey starts in the world behind our eyes, with a strong foundation and a commitment to embody, at the level of one, what an organization of many is capable of embodying for all.

1

If Not You, Then Who?

OPPORTUNITIES TO FIND DEEPER
POWERS WITHIN OURSELVES COME WHEN LIFE
SEEMS MOST CHALLENGING.

Joseph Campbell

Why Women, Why Now?

The world is changing in ways that are creating remarkable
challenges in the workplace. Some of the changes are readily
visible. We're more connected, for instance, and have access
to more information than ever before. Think of the impact that
household access to the Internet has had on patient awareness
and expectations. Or the speed with which healthcare providers
and administrators have become married to their Blackberries
or iPhones, or the volume of information now available at a
patient's bedside with the single click of a mouse.

The world is also more complex and interdependent than
ever before. We encounter it every time we talk with someone
in Manila or Bombay about a travel reservation or a credit card

balance. We're exposed to it every time a news anchor runs a story on global warming or our retirement account drops 5 points because of events half a nation or half a world away. We experience it on a more local but no less complex scale at work every day.

Take a look at Figure 1. It's a quick and incomplete list of the people involved in getting a single patient through a single surgery, from admission to discharge, in a single hospital. And this just includes people within one degree of separation from the patient!

Figure 1

One patient + one surgery = a high degree of complexity and interdependence

* The primary care or referring physician and his office staff
* The surgeon and her office staff
* The presurg registration greeter
* The registration clerk
* The coordinator
* The phlebotomist and others involved in presurgical testing
* The nurses and aides
* The OR surgical staff supporting the surgeon: anesthesiologist, technicians, nurses, house staff
* The PACU staff
* The hospital transporters
* The unit clerk
* The floor nurses
* The postsurgical phlebotomists and/or lab techs
* The dietary staff
* The case manager
* The discharge planner

These are just the people who have immediate contact with the patient. If we broaden the circle one degree, we find more people who are less directly but no less importantly involved in the process:

* The persons who schedule the OR
* The persons who schedule the OR staff
* The OR housekeepers
* The laundry personnel who assure sterile linens
* The materials manager who assures the availability of durable and disposable products
* The sterile processing personnel
* The radiology staff
* The laboratory staff
* The chaplaincy staff
* The quality assurance and performance improvement staff
* The IT staff who support the complex electronic scheduling, materials management, patient record, and purchasing systems for supplies
* The medical affairs credentialing staff
* The peer review staff
* The vendors who supply the OR tools, equipment, and medical devices
* The third party representative who authorizes the procedure
* The financial people who handle payables for everything related to the procedure
* The financial people who handle receivables for everything related to keeping the OR open and running.

And we have not touched the thousands of people whose efforts have combined to educate and train everyone buzzing around the patient or those who have contributed to designing, making, and delivering each and every durable, disposable, and ingestible good involved in the patient's care.

The workforce is changing dramatically, too. Healthcare planners, for instance, are struggling to retain skilled nurses and recruit new ones into a profession that needs a major facelift in order to rejuvenate its public image. Hospitals already have an estimated 120,000 vacancies for registered nurses and will face a projected shortfall of nearly one million a decade from now. Young physicians are choosing "lifestyle" specialties or practice options that offer greater work-life balance, while seasoned clinicians are opting for early retirement or alternative careers that offer greater satisfaction and fewer regulatory and administrative headaches.

Complicating the situation is a whole generation entering the workforce with a whole different set of values and expectations than those held by the four—count 'em—*four* generations still actively employed. Unlike their predecessors, this new generation was educated in open classrooms, shaped by the human potential and self-esteem movements, and advised and encouraged to follow their passion. They grew up with cell phones, instant messaging, social networking websites, and multiplayer online role-playing games that run 24/7 in real time and often require *and* teach important leadership skills. They are energetic, hard working, impatient with dull or routine work, and expecting to make a contribution from the moment they walk in the door of your organization. Being connected is this generation's way of life, and they are entering the workforce *en masse*.

Factors like these—increasing connectedness, greater complexity and interdependence, changing expectations, instant access to information—plus the sheer pace of change are posing significant challenges for organizational leaders. What worked in the past is often no longer sufficient or, at times, even necessary for succeeding now or in the future. If we are going to adapt effectively to both the pace and nature of change, especially in an industry as inundated with daunting challenges as healthcare, we desperately need different ways of working and leading in our organizations.

We need people who know how to develop and sustain networks and partnerships that share a common purpose. We need people who can think and work in flexible, egalitarian ways who willingly take the lead one moment and take instruction the next. We need people who can sense the emotional tenor of human interactions and intervene in ways that move both human effort and the human spirit forward, especially during stressful times. And we need them at all levels in our organizations.

Behavior flows from thinking, so we also need different ways of framing how we think about work. Metaphors, for instance, are common "frames" that we use. They help us understand complex or new things by linking them to things we already know. The traditional management metaphor is that of the machine, with its emphasis on equilibrium, prediction, and control. It was an apt metaphor when this country was developing mass production processes and ways to control output by reducing variability.

Human beings, however, are living organisms. Unlike machines, we learn, we adapt, and we both affect and are affected by the world around us. In that regard, we're continually engaged in a complex—and improvisational—dance with the environment. In fact, the lack of equilibrium, prediction, and control is what triggers and fuels our adaptive capacity. We and the organizational systems we create are dynamic, not static. So we need metaphors that reflect both the highly complex, interconnected, and interdependent nature of work *and* the adaptive capacity of the living beings *doing* the work. The machine metaphor is simply insufficient for capturing either.

Similarly, the traditional masculine metaphors of military and athletic competition were sufficient for business in a simpler time. What we need now are metaphors consistent with the key themes of 21st century business: win-win rather than win-lose, collaboration rather than competition, partnership rather than patriarchy, adaptation rather than autocracy.

In short, the answer to "why women, why now?" is that our organizations desperately need what women have to offer: ways of working and leading that are circular rather than linear, lateral rather than top down, adaptive rather than rigid. I am not saying that men are incapable of working this way; many are very capable. Nor am I saying that one style is better than the other. Today's work environments need the strengths of both masculine and feminine ways of working and being.

I want to highlight how women's natural strengths are particularly well suited for leading in changing times and to help women step forth and use those strengths more fully than ever before. Historically, women have had few models to serve as guides. This book is one step toward filling that gap.

ORGANIZATIONS DESPERATELY NEED
WHAT WOMEN HAVE TO OFFER:
WAYS OF WORKING THAT ARE
CIRCULAR RATHER THAN LINEAR,
LATERAL RATHER THAN TOP DOWN,
ADAPTIVE RATHER THAN RIGID.

Chapter 1 offers a toolbox for the work that unfolds in later chapters. In the next section is a story to illustrate how women often misplace their own power and how a shift in perspective can lead them back to it. The story also sets up the following section, which describes several common coaching tools that I use throughout the book to help you explore and expand your capacity to lead yourself and others through changing times. You'll also find a self-assessment survey to use as a baseline for getting started and some suggestions for getting the most from your own self-development efforts.

If you are looking for a book that tells you how to change *other* people, this is not the book for you. In my experience as an executive and leadership coach, the work is not about quick fixes or "outside" answers. It is about uncovering and pursuing what matters most to you and those you serve. It is about exploring your own thinking in ways that reveal how you shape and are shaped by the networks within which you live and work, and how you may unwittingly contribute to the challenges you encounter at work. The more you recognize your own contribution, the more choices you have for alternative courses of action.

The work is also about learning to trust that your strengths as a woman are valid and valuable, especially in the complicated and very human domain of work. By offering models, stories, and an array of coaching exercises to expand how you think about what you do, my goal is to help you transform your natural strengths into an expanding capacity to adapt, thrive, and get great results in complex, rapidly changing, and unpredictable times.

Looking for Leadership in All the Wrong Places

You're probably familiar with Albert Einstein's remark that we can't solve problems with the same thinking that created them. Complex problems like those we face today demand different thinking, which requires broader and deeper levels of awareness. When we can step back and see complex problems as part of something bigger, we can discover new options that we were blind to before.

Think of the simple question, "Is the glass half empty or half full?" Traditional thinking holds that persons who see the glass half full are optimists, while those who see it as half empty are pessimists. If we answer either way, we're working from a forced-choice perspective and missing the bigger picture: at any given moment, the glass is both half empty *and* half full. *One cannot exist without the other.* What creates the "either-or" quality is *not* the fluid or the glass but our *perception*. When we're in a forced-choice mindset, we completely miss the "both-and" alternative.

The same is true for the problems we encounter in life and at work. They arise from our perceptions. As Mark Twain said, he had a lot of problems in his life, most of which never happened. So while we think about, talk about, and often experience problems as being "out there" "in the real world," they more accurately are born and raised in the world behind our eyes.

That was the case with my client Sara, who left a large, mission-driven nonprofit organization to take a position in a for-profit company serving the healthcare industry. She was hired to create a department of training and development and to set a strategy for developing the organization's employees, starting with its regional directors. She quickly discovered that the company had no clear vision for the future and no strategic plan. For several months she struggled, first with the executive team's lack of interest in setting a vision and then with the lack of direction she felt in her own work as a result of having no leadership from on high.

During this same time, Sara was also reaching out to the regional directors she was hired to serve. She interviewed them to learn about their jobs and what they needed in order to be effective in a rapidly growing business. She shadowed them to learn about their relationships with customers and the challenges they faced in serving those customers. And she used what she learned to create training programs and materials. She was also coaching individual directors, teaching staff how to develop their direct reports, and facilitating dozens of conversations about new and different ways to serve customers. Yet her own morale was falling. She was doubting herself, feeling increasingly directionless and disengaged, and becoming cynical. More importantly, she didn't know how to halt or reverse the downward slide.

Essentially, her glass was half empty.

So we began examining her perspective. We started by identifying some of her key assumptions. She assumed, for instance, that the CEO and executive team should set a clear vision for the company and create a strategic plan to realize it. And she assumed that without clear direction from them, she was directionless. She also assumed that her way—getting a vision and strategic plan from on high—was the "right" way, which automatically made the executives' laissez-faire way "wrong" and led to some tense conversations between them.

We began making distinctions and reframing her assumptions in order to create a bigger picture. For instance, when we distinguished between what she *wanted* the executive team to do and what they were *actually doing*, she saw that her cynicism and disengagement were being fueled by her own unmet expectations, *not* by their behavior. In order to see a bigger picture, she had to begin suspending those expectations.

This did not mean that she stopped believing in the importance of a vision and a plan. It meant that she was beginning to see a more complete picture: she thought that vision and plan were important, *and* the CEO and executive team did not share that thought, *and* she was waiting for something that likely would not come, *and* she did not need to wait.

So we devised some personal practices to help shift her focus, alter her mood, and keep her grounded in her own wisdom and knowledge. In particular, she practiced suspending judgment and simply attending to what was actually occurring in the moment. As a result, her whole experience at work began to change.

She discovered that she already knew what mattered most: patient safety, helping company customers serve their patients, and helping in-house staff serve company customers. She did not need the CEO or anyone else to "give" her a vision. While she thought she wanted the CEO to agree with her approach and "set a vision and a plan," what she really wanted was his approval. Recognizing and letting go of the need for approval freed her to pursue what she already knew needed to be done.

She realized that she was already doing the exact same work she'd be doing if she had a strategic plan. Because she asked questions, didn't assume she knew the answers, listened to her stakeholders, and combined what she was learning with great knowledge and content expertise, her work was already strategic. She had moved beyond strategic planning to strategic doing.

As she reflected on her own history, she realized that she had always defined her competence in terms of producing a tangible product. In time, she recognized that the product she was producing was often another person's *experience* rather than a deliverable program or plan.

One day when she was complaining that "daily fires" kept the company from "moving to the next level," I asked her what the next level looked like. She thought for a moment, then said, "Engaged staff, which ties to staff retention, which leads to client retention." When I reminded her that her coaching, training materials, and in-services were already energizing staff and drawing great kudos from them, she realized that her natural ways of *being* with others were already moving them to "the next level." The acknowledgement shifted her focus immediately and prompted her to tell me about a new project that she and her team were working on. "And," she said with a burst of enthusiasm, "we're having a ball!" In a span of 10 minutes, her tone and mood shifted dramatically.

Here's the important point in Sara's story: *the CEO and executive team did not change.* What changed was how she viewed them. Her frustration and negativity were arising not from her colleagues but from her own stories about what she needed and what they should do about it. As her stories changed, her experience changed, from cynicism and self doubt to enthusiasm and self assurance.

CHANGE OUR STORIES

AND WE CHANGE OUR REALITY.

By learning to observe herself *in the moment*, she began to see her own self-limiting assumptions. By learning to be fully present to what was occurring, both internally and externally, she discovered that she not only had the capacity to transform her world, she was already doing it. She was just so steeped in traditional ideas of leadership that she couldn't see her own strengths or the powerful and positive influence she was having on people.

You Already Have What You Need

A main theme of this book and the central note upon which each chapter is tuned is this: you already have what you need in order to create what you want. This doesn't mean that you have all the skills and/or knowledge you need. It does mean that you already have within you the capacity to imagine an inspiring future and the capacity to overcome whatever obstacles you encounter along the way.

Most of us are so far removed from this capacity that we no longer remember how to tap into and work from it. As Sara's story suggests, it often is buried deeply beneath the unexplored assumptions and beliefs we hold about life and work.

So how do we gain access to it? By learning to use our own experience in new and different ways. I start with self-awareness, since it is the source of all the data we need. The questions in the box are examples of what Sara and I used to expand her self-awareness. Chapter 2 will explore this process in much more depth. Notice that the questions have little to do with Sara's colleagues and much to do with how she interprets and responds to what she encounters.

What can I learn about the world behind my eyes?

* What assumptions am I making about who and how I should be in the workplace?
* What assumptions am I making about how others are or should be?
* How are these assumptions furthering or hindering my capacity to take the lead in shaping the kind of environment I want?
* What would I lose if I let go of the assumptions that are hindering me?
* What does the idea of doing that evoke in me?

On the surface, these questions may seem simple and easily answered. But the goal of a self-awareness question is not to find a quick answer that works and then dart to the next question. The goal is to see our experience from a whole new perspective: to see, like Sara for instance, when and how we are standing in our own way so that we can find new ways to move forward.

To make this book more useful and to give you some practical ways for accessing your own wisdom, I rely on the common tools of the coaching profession:

* *Powerful questions* and *distinctions* that suggest new possibilities.
* *Self-observations* that can expand your self-awareness and the choices available to you
* *Practices* that help you test new ways of being and doing, including ways to use your body and emotions as well as your thinking brain to guide you on the journey.

Here is a brief description of each.

Powerful questions are questions that stimulate thought and reflection, surface underlying assumptions, refocus our attention, and invite us to ask more questions. They generate curiosity, encourage deeper exploration, and open the door to deeper understanding and meaning.

Distinctions highlight the differences between two or more things that we normally treat as interchangeable. They help us frame a concept or a perception differently, thus opening the way for new options. For instance, in Chapter 6 is a distinction between strategic planning and purposeful alignment; the former is a form of control while the latter is a form of connection. When we understand the difference, we have a whole new set of options available for getting the results we want.

Self-observation is a way to expand our self-awareness. The goal is to separate our behavior, which is what others experience, from our stories *about* our behavior by shifting our attention from what's going on "out there" to what's going on internally. Self-observation is grounded in our remarkable capacity as humans to be engaged with others while simultaneously floating above the interaction and observing what we're thinking, how we're feeling, and how our actions and reactions are shaping the event. Noticing what we're actually experiencing *in the moment*, cognitively, emotionally, and physically, helps us separate our behavior from the much more complicated world of our inner experience. When we can see our behavior "objectively" and as others experience it, we get an "aha!" that opens the way for a whole new range of responses.

One of my clients summed up the process like this. In preparing to talk with a direct report about a thorny performance issue, she said, "The challenge for me will be to just ask open questions and not color them with my own assumptions about what's going on. I have to participate in the conversation *and* simultaneously float above it, observing it like a third person." The examples later in the chapter illustrate how this works.

Practices are how we apply new awareness. As noted above, when we change the way we look at things, we often see new courses of action. When we select and experiment with one of those, we're engaging in a practice. New practices produce new results, which then become the fodder for new learning: *what happened? What did I get that I didn't expect? What did I expect and not get? What might I do differently the next time?*

Practices help us test the effectiveness of new behaviors and zoom in on those that work well. They push us beyond what's comfortable and familiar, so they help us become more flexible and adaptive. They help us learn. In short, they take us into the world of discovery.

The key point to practice is that *knowing* something—having a flash of cognitive or intellectual insight—is useless unless we can translate it into *doing* something that yields new and different results. So learning to translate knowing into doing is the real work.

When we are in the role of leading, this distinction becomes even more important. Leading is not about transferring knowledge to others. It is about nurturing their capacity to rise to whatever challenge they encounter as they strive to make a meaningful contribution to the world. And that requires skills far beyond the mere ability to tell others what, when, or how to do something.

"I Don't Have Time!"

Unlike *distinctions*, which are cognitive sound bytes that people grasp quickly or *powerful questions*, which invite different thinking, *self-observation exercises* and new *practices* are actions. When I suggest to clients that they observe themselves in the moment and keep a written log of their thoughts and feelings, they often say, "I don't have time." They are up to their eyeballs in problems and projects, and want a quick fix because they already feel like they're out of time: time to attend the next performance improvement meeting, act on sagging patient satisfaction scores, stay abreast of ever-changing regulations, keep referring physicians happy, and dance to the beat of the system leaders' financial chorus.

So if you hear that internal voice whispering *I don't have time*, then try telling yourself this: *I'm just going to disengage autopilot and pay attention to what is.* Self-observation doesn't take time so much as *attention*—a shift in focus—and a willingness to examine what we're actually experiencing in the moment: our physical self, the emotions guiding our behavior, the self-talk defining our story about what's going on. The second part of the exercise, note-taking, requires only a few minutes.

Similarly, new practices also require mindful awareness. Again, this is a shift in focus, a willingness to disengage our automatic responses and try something different in order to produce a different result. So it does not take more time, it takes more awareness. If what you have been doing is not producing what you want—either "out there" or deep in your heart—what do you have to lose?

The Challenge Is to See Through New Eyes

As our awareness expands, we begin to see the world through new eyes. Beth, another client of mine, is a great example. She was intensely frustrated with Carl, one of her direct reports. She was a 3-star extravert and he was a dyed-in-the-wool introvert. They often attended the same meetings together. She wanted him to show more leadership in these meetings. For her, that meant initiating discussion, soliciting everyone's input, providing direction, summarizing key points, and so forth. She had talked with him several times about taking the lead and was frustrated and angry that he was not heeding her advice.

I suggested she keep a written log of her frustration and anger, focusing on basic events like what she was doing when she got upset and what others were saying and doing at the time. Her task was to separate the observable experiences and events from her *interpretation* of those events, and to record both.

A few weeks later, she telephoned me. She had co-chaired a meeting with Carl earlier in the day. Like several other meetings in the recent past, it had triggered intense frustration in her. She was scribbling down her left-column thoughts when—bam!—it hit her: *she was the very obstacle standing in Carl's way!*

She said it was like a flash of light, this realization. What brought it on? Her willingness to slow down and observe what was unfolding in the moment, both internally and externally, both physically and mentally. She often worried about others' opinions of her, so she had a whole set of critical standards for herself, including things like starting meetings on time. She discovered that when the clock struck the start time for the meeting, if nothing was happening, her anxiety level took flight and a strong press for action swept over her. Her hands began to sweat, her mouth dried up, her mind began chattering about what others were thinking; within a minute, she was drumming her fingers on the table and could "hear my heartbeat in my ears!"

Since she was an extrovert, anything more than about 30 seconds past the start time seemed like an eternity to her. So what did she do? She jumped in and took the lead, in order to allay her own anxiety. For Carl, an intense introvert, 30 seconds seemed like the wink of an eye. He was barely settling into his seat before she was leaping into action.

As she sat observing and logging what was actually occurring in the moment, she also saw that she was expecting him to behave *exactly as she would* in this situation. She thought she'd been encouraging him to develop his own style of leading. That was her "story" about herself. But becoming aware of her expectation for him to do it her way led her to realize that she had little idea of *his* natural strengths and talents. She'd been too absorbed in getting him to do it *her* way.

> WHEN WE ASSUME THAT
> OUR WAY IS THE RIGHT WAY,
> WE BECOME THE OBSTACLE
> TO THE OTHER PERSON'S PROGRESS.

This new awareness of how she was responding to Carl led her to try an entirely different approach to developing her staff. She shifted from prescribing how they worked to defining the outcomes she wanted them to achieve. This practice, shifting from emphasizing process to defining outcome, was a critical shift for Beth because it opened the way for Carl and other staff members to find their own best path to the results she wanted.

She also began looking for her staff's strengths rather than dwelling on their limitations, and helping them explore ways to capitalize on those strengths. She discovered, for example, that

Carl was gifted at listening and summarizing people's concerns in ways that invited deeper discussion of key issues. He asked questions about people's emotional concerns and was open to whatever surfaced. Other direct reports brought other talents to the table. As Beth learned to let go of the need to have the answers, seek others' approval, and "be the leader," she saw a dramatic shift in their performance.

This was not an easy process. Beth struggled for months with the push-pull between wanting things done her way and honoring others' talents and gifts. She had to examine her own beliefs and assumptions about what "being the leader" meant and begin embracing a different definition. She had to befriend the anxiety she felt when things weren't going her way and treat it as a signal that something she valued was on the line rather than reacting to get rid of it. Letting go of having the answers and embracing others' differences took great courage for her. Yet she had everything she needed to lead in ways that fully engaged others. And, in the end, her willingness to do so created the space for others to shine.

What Are Your Ways of "Being" in the Organization?

We all come into organizations with a set of assumptions about what it takes to fit in and to succeed. We rarely treat them as assumptions because most of us translated them into behavioral strategies that became "fact" long ago. So let's see what your strategies are. [*]

---

[*] The theoretical framework from which this exercise and the subsequent discussion is based is the seminal work of Bob Anderson. Bob is the founder and CEO of The Leadership Circle and a Founding Partner in the Full Circle Group. Bob has developed the most comprehensive and integrated framework for leadership development in the field and out of that framework has developed The Leadership Circle Profile. This 360 leadership assessment is the most powerful assessment of its kind that I have ever used. For more information on Bob's work see www.theleadershipcircle.com.

Using the following scale, mark each item based on how you usually think and feel in situations. There are not any right or wrong answers, so work quickly and go with your gut response.

1 = usually true   2 = occasionally true   3 = rarely true

_____ 1. I prefer to play by the rules

_____ 2. It's important for me to appear competent and confident even though I don't always feel that way

_____ 3. I withhold my opinions in order to avoid conflict

_____ 4. I strive to do everything perfectly

_____ 5. I want others' input and approval before I take action

_____ 6. I push myself as hard as I push others

_____ 7. I set safe rather than risky goals

_____ 8. I have trouble taking direction from others

_____ 9. It's hard for me to challenge others' performance

_____ 10. I am critical when others don't meet my standards

_____ 11. I get along well by conforming to my organization's norms

_____ 12. At times, people have described me as intimidating, although I don't see it

_____ 13. I'd rather commiserate with like-minded colleagues than speak directly with people I disagree with

_____ 14. If I'm not getting what I want, I jump into action

_____ 15. I feel responsible when things go wrong

_____ 16. It's more efficient to tell people how to do things rather than wait for them to figure it out

_____ 17. I'm not good at changing the way things are

_____ 18. I'm ambitious and try to excel at whatever I take on

_____ 19. I delay making important decisions until I have all the necessary information

_____ 20. I am sensitive to disapproval or criticism of my work

_____ 21. I take action based on how I think people will respond

_____ 22. I usually share information only on a need-to-know basis

Now score yourself. Add up your scores for the odd-numbered items and write the total here:_____. Then add up your scores for the even-numbered items and record the total here:_____.

These two scales indicate the degree to which your behavior is guided by the desire to stay safe and protect your sense of self-worth or by the capacity to nurture a shared commitment to purposeful work.

The lower your score on the odd-numbered items, the greater your tendency to protect your relationships and your self-image by complying with group norms and others' expectations. If your score is less than 25, your tendency is to protect yourself by being cautious, not standing out, and earning others' approval. Such a stance is likely hampering your ability to dream big for the future and to work strategically toward the results you want. A score of 11 to 16 suggests that your sense of self worth is so closely tied to others' opinions that it's very difficult for you to take an unpopular stand on something important, make tough yet strategic decisions, or openly address problem areas lest you offend others. Your need to be liked, to please, to belong inhibits your ability to nurture a strong sense of purpose, commitment, and accountability.

The lower your score on the even-numbered items, the greater your tendency to stay safe by controlling situations and putting results over relationships. If you scored less than 25, your tendency is to protect your self-image by micromanaging in order to get results that make you look good. A score of 11 to 16 suggests that your sense of self is so closely tied to personal power, achievements, and results that it's very difficult for you to delegate responsibility, develop others' potential, or see the world in collaborative terms. Your need to do everything perfectly, to be in control, and/or to have everything done your way overshadows others' contributions and likely impairs your ability to nurture strong networks.

Going along to get along and micromanaging are survival strategies, ways to look good and feel okay about ourselves. We develop them early in life as a means of meeting basic needs and, later, they become ways to protect our sense of competence and worth as we grow into adulthood. But they do not help us or our organizations to *thrive*.

More than anything, leadership is about who and how we are in the world. Playing safe—whether by complying or controlling—is playing small. Your staff, your organization, and most importantly, your patients are counting on you to play big. Only by stepping into your own power can you pave the way for others to do the same. You start that process by becoming increasingly aware of what triggers your stay-safe strategies and how they show up in your life, and then experimenting with ways to move through and beyond them.

Use Yourself as a Learning Lab

In another life, I was a student of literature and an amateur painter. So throughout this book you'll find metaphors, stories, images, and frequent invitations to step back and observe the patterns and overall composition emerging in your own work life. It is the way of the artist, working between the easel and the viewing bench, changing the focal point in order to see something different. Only when we know how to step back and observe the emerging whole can we get a clear sense of the next step.

Toward that end, I encourage you to get a small spiral notebook or journal to carry with you. Many exercises in this book call for you to observe and log your experiences in the moment. As I mentioned earlier, it is a technique that helps expand your self-awareness and create new perspectives on your own stories and self-talk. By logging what you're actually experiencing, both internally and externally, you're shifting your attention and creating small opportunities to observe yourself from a different and broader point of view. Many people run on autopilot so much that they are unaware of their own thoughts and feelings. Just slowing down and recording what is actually occurring internally often creates new awareness and a new perspective. New perspectives, in turn, create new options.

Here is an important caveat. The temptation to think you already know what is going on—and, therefore, do not need to write it down—is powerful. The thinking mind, with its lightning-fast justifications and rationales, will outsmart you every time. Guaranteed. The only way to disrupt its chatter is to capture your thoughts and physical and emotional reactions *as they are occurring.* So if you are serious about growing yourself, get a journal and use it.

There is another reason for slowing down and examining your own experience. One of the most common questions clients ask me is, *"How?* How do I fix this … how do I change that?" I typically turn the question back, usually by setting it within the larger context of "what is it you really want?" I do that for two reasons. First, asking "how" reinforces the belief of many of my female clients that the answer is "out there" in another person, another seminar, another article, so it fuels their self-doubt and their tendency to defer to others.

Second, getting them to slow down and think seriously about what they want—in the long term, for themselves and for those they serve—reconnects them with why they went into healthcare in the first place. When was the last time you put down the to-do list and examined whether what you are doing is what you really want to be doing? If it has been a while, you'll have a chance in Chapter 3 to spend some time with questions of purpose, which is a central organizing principle that you'll encounter throughout the book.

Help Others Do the Same

We come by this common question of "how" quite legitimately. For years, our academic and organizational approach to learning has been built on telling others what we think they need to do and how to do it. We know intellectually that adults, like kids, learn best from doing, from discovering for themselves. And we know experientially that *telling* does not work.

What does work is an approach that helps people clarify what's meaningful for them, get into action, and then reflect on and learn from what they're doing in ways that move them closer to what they want. That is the heart of coaching and of leading, and it is naturally aligned with how many women prefer to work, which is in lateral and egalitarian relationships.

This approach unfolds via listening, modeling, and compassionately questioning rather than directing and telling, so it encourages people to discover what works best for them as they pursue a shared purpose and encounter unexpected obstacles. In the long run, it supports them learning from their own experience and becoming increasingly self-directed and self-correcting. As living systems, one of our greatest capacities is to adapt in ways that allow both the individual and the collective to grow and thrive.

As you work through this book, invite others to join you on the journey. Leadership is a community endeavor in the sense that it unfolds within systems of human activity that are interdependent, complexly intertwined, and always part of something bigger. The myth of our culture is that we're autonomous. The truth of our experience is that we're integrally connected with one another across both time and space. So find kindred spirits.

Think of Leading as a Creating Art

One weekend, I was listening to some of my son's friends playing in a band. Most of their music was improvised and even when I could discern a familiar tune, the variations were rich, eloquent, melodic, and highly original. Those kids knew how to work from the inside out, how to let go of the rules of music theory or the notes in someone else's song and embrace their own spontaneous expression. And the results were extraordinary.

As Scott, a member of the band, told me,

> We often start with music that's already written. While you may be able tell the melody, sometimes you can't. That's the beauty of it. It's just a frame and you use it as the foundation for your own music. Everyone has music inside. Some express it through instruments, some through art, and some through their work. Everything is music. A dog barking, the sound of typing, every sound you hear is music, the creative spirit coming alive.

Scott knows that the creative spirit is not limited to artists. It lies in all of us. The real work is to find our way back to it so that it can flow freely and naturally through us and into the world. How do you create a powerful environment of healing for patients? How do you find new ways of working with those pesky physicians or rules-is-rules regulators? How do you engage fully without tethering your identity and well being to the outcome? How do you grow your own creative process from a flash of insight to a way of life?

To answer questions like these, we must step out of the world of management techniques or leadership theory and into the richly paradoxical world of living beings. What we seek is not found in another healthcare system or management seminar. It is found by traveling through the world of our own experience, learning to be fully present to body and mind, exploring how the world behind our eyes frames and colors our experience.

Most of us have been gazing through the same frames for decades. And even when we get a glimpse of other perspectives, habit and stressful circumstances can snap us back to "reality" with remarkable speed. Yet knowing that being stuck is part of the creative process can give us the courage to persevere. Appreciating that our limitations are also the source of some of our greatest gifts can help us stay the course.

When we bring forth our nurturing nature, we call forth the best in others. When we make the purpose of work the patient rather than politics or turf protection, we create a space within which people at all levels can make meaningful contributions. When we trust in the power of networks to support human beings through the stress of adapting to major challenges, we open the way for them to generate fast, flexible, highly adaptive interactions at the point of patient or customer contact. When we are in our right mind, intention and action conspire to support us.

So let's get to work.

| IN OUR RIGHT MIND

2

Start in the World Behind Your Eyes

FIND THE RIGHT FRAMEWORK
AND EXTRAORDINARY ACCOMPLISHMENT
BECOMES AN EVERYDAY EXPERIENCE.

Rosamund Stone Zander and Benjamin Zander

Work from the Inside Out

Nearly every one of us has come up through the ranks of hierarchical organizations, so we have strong and often unconscious beliefs about how organizations operate and what our roles are. Those beliefs constitute our mental models, or a collection of deeply embedded assumptions, images, and rules that shape our understanding of how the world works and how we function within it. Mental models typically function in the background, like the operating system of a computer, helping us make sense of events while filtering our perceptions and directing our behavior.

Most of us are acutely aware of the work life around us. We know who our allies and adversaries are, where to go to for answers, and who'll assume or avoid responsibility. We know the quarterly patient satisfaction and financial targets we're expected to meet and the complex strategic plans, goals, and objectives we're expected to execute. We have the vision and values statements posted on the wall.

Yet most of us know little about our own internal mental models. We're too besieged with problems, projects, quarterly indicators, and looking good to dedicate much time to slowing down and reflecting on the mental models or frames through which we're viewing the world. And even when we slow down, those mental models are so much a part of our experience, they're so deeply embedded in our minds that, like Sara from Chapter 1, we think of them as *reality* or *the way it is* rather than as one of many possible ways of viewing the world.

We also wrestle with those nagging questions that keep forcing their way into awareness. Why do projects to grow service lines or improve physician relations take so long and rarely yield the results we want? Why do carefully planned, elaborately rolled-out efforts to improve patient loyalty fail to budge the patient satisfaction scores? Why doesn't increased training in patient safety have a more significant impact on the numbers of incident reports? Why don't patients whose lives are threatened by serious illness comply with treatment regimens or alter their lifestyles?

The answers lie in the world behind our eyes, where those mental models reside. Discovering new possibilities can only happen when we can find new ways of seeing, which lead to new ways of doing and, more importantly, new ways of being.

This is a challenge for anyone in a leadership role. Old management styles simply aren't sufficient to handle the pace at which changes are occurring and the complexity within which health care now unfolds. Women have additional challenges.

We've spent years trying to fit into the classic top-down model when our natural style is much more akin to a circle or a web. We've dragged hard-earned lessons into the workplace from our childhood and youth, and they no longer serve us well. In fact, they hold many of us back.

If you want a different hospital culture, different results in your department, or different team dynamics at the interface of patient care, you must do it from the inside out, by exploring and changing what goes on in the world behind your eyes. You *are* the culture, the results, the dynamics of your team and, as a woman in healthcare, you are clearly in the majority. The sooner you realize this, the sooner you can begin creating what you want.

So we start this chapter by looking at some of the most common beliefs or assumptions about the workplace and people's roles within it. Many of these beliefs do not support the natural strengths that women bring to work, so you'll find some self-observation exercises to help loosen your frames of reference and begin looking at your natural ways of being through a different lens. You will also meet a model that can reset your entire experience of work because it speaks to the remarkable creative and adaptive powers that lie within us.

Who Is the Leader?

Let's start with the most basic of questions: who is the leader in your organization? Chances are, you flashed on the name of your organization's chief executive officer. It is a natural response and it is the tip of one of your mental frames.

The traditional model for healthcare organizations is hierarchical: a top-down structure in which the few at the top pick the tunes while the many below wait to dance. It came out of the early 20th century and is responsible for much of this country's economic success. It is also a *management* model, not a *leadership* model. Until the 1980s, people did not make much distinction between the two. But as the speed of change accelerated, some organizations shot ahead while others struggled to keep pace. And leadership emerged as a critical variable for success.

If you define leaders as those at the top, in positions of power and authority in an organization, you are looking right through the lens of one of your own mental frames, the top-down frame. And if you're in any position other than the "top" in your organization, then you are likely waiting to dance or, at the very least, waiting for the *real* leader to affirm that the dance you're doing is the right one, because *that's the way it is* in top-down organizations.

Hierarchies are also patriarchal, so they evoke in women a dynamic that stretches back to our childhoods, where authority typically rested with daddy. Many of the women leaders I have coached behave differently around bosses and authority figures of either gender than around anyone else. Some have a driving need for the boss's approval and either will not take action without the latter's okay or cannot feel good about their work unless the boss acknowledges or supports it. Others get so tongue-tied and anxious that they have trouble thinking clearly and acting purposefully in the presence of a significant figurehead. Still others bristle with resentment when they encounter paternal behavior.

If you respond differently to people in positions of power and authority than you do to others in your organization, and if you want greater comfort and ease in working with those people, then try the self-observation exercise described on the next page. Keep your journal with you so you can keep notes on what you're observing. They'll be invaluable for you later.

A self-observation exercise

* Pick an authority figure around whom you're uncomfortable. Pay attention to your physical and emotional reactions when you are in that person's presence. How is your behavior different? What are you telling yourself? Write down what you observe. Don't judge or try to change your behavior or self-talk. Simply write it down.

* Then pay attention to how you personalize this person's behavior. Who are you reminded of? What does the person's presence or style trigger in you? Chances are, s/he evokes in you old patterns of behavior that were useful when you were much younger but no longer serve you well.

* Observe simply for the purpose of expanding your self-awareness, not to confirm what you already think you know; you're after a new perspective here.

* When you can see the old pattern being triggered and can feel yourself slipping into a familiar old reaction, practice just observing it wiithout any effort to change, get rid of, or act on it. See what it has to teach you. Then take a deep breath and remind yourself that what served you well in earlier years is now holding you back.

* Reframe your emotional reaction—be it anxiety or anger or fear—as a source of energy. Then direct that energy, first to listening actively to what the other person is saying and then to shaping the response you want to make now, in the moment, as a competent adult.

* Hold this distinction between a *reaction*, which is automatic, and a *response*, which is thoughtful and deliberate, whenever you are aware of patterns that do not produce the results you want.

What you're doing with this technique is loosening the frame that says power and authority are at the top of the pyramid. Most of us have lived with this model for so long that we don't stop to question it. Sure, we may wish that our organization were different; many of us would love to work in more inclusive, web-like organizations that encourage collaboration, authenticity, and mutual regard. But until we can see that "power at the top" is just a mental frame—one of many that are possible—we'll continue to act and react within the confines of top-down thinking, and nothing will change.

You do not have to be at the top to be a leader. You do have to recognize that your natural strengths as a woman are precisely what healthcare organizations desperately need in order to serve patients with compassion and care and to call forth in every employee the desire to do the same.

What Do Leaders Actually Do?

Think about this: what do leaders actually *do* when it comes to fulfilling an organization's mission? Very little! Their role is really to fulfill the mission through the efforts of others. Ben Zander, conductor of the Boston Philharmonic, realized this one day when he recognized that an orchestra conductor makes absolutely no sound; the *musicians* do. And the realization led to a dramatic shift in what he paid attention to. He stopped worrying about how good he was as a conductor and began wondering what it takes to engage and unleash the talent of his musicians. The result? He began looking at ways to enable musicians to "play each phrase as beautifully as they were capable" (Zander and Zander 2000, 69).

For most men, this is a major shift. They learn from an early age to distinguish themselves, focus on their performance and success, and get to the top. Their world is typically the world of goals and objectives, allies and adversaries, winners and losers. Paying attention to how they can maximize the performance and success of others isn't high on their priority list unless it's within the context of a competitive endeavor like team sports.

For many women, helping others develop and succeed comes naturally. We ask a lot more questions about what others want and need, seek more feedback about what's working and what isn't, and take pleasure in watching others do well.

What often stands between us and our effectiveness as leaders is our reluctance to distinguish ourselves and honor our own ways of being as valid and valuable contributions to our organization's culture and success. Distinguishing ourselves takes many of us back again to childhood, when we were taught not to stand out, to put others' needs ahead of our own, and to be appropriate and nice.

We know how to cultivate relationships and help others, but when our relating style is compliant and self-effacing, we come off as soft and insecure. When we strive too hard for consensus and democratic decision-making, it comes back to bite us as being indecisive and wishy-washy. When we lean too much on our tendencies to take responsibility for everything, confess all of our weaknesses, and avoid conflict, we get labeled with low self-esteem. When we take on the mantle of control and begin micromanaging and issuing orders, we earn the infamous title that rhymes with "rich." And it's not just men who pass these judgments on us. We do it to one another all the time. Why? I suspect it's because we're so accustomed to working in top-down, patriarchal environments that we just automatically judge feminine behavior through a lens of masculine standards.

When we can balance our strengths—cultivating relationships and networks, inviting and exploring others' perspectives, handling the details while holding the big picture, helping others succeed—with a deep trust in the value of our own ways of being, we begin to step into our own. We discover, for instance, how to make and deliver tough decisions by speaking from the heart in ways that are both empathic and aligned with the welfare of those we serve. Or we begin to challenge misaligned behavior by stepping fully into the role of engaging others in fulfilling the organization's purpose and embodying its values, even in demanding times.

Distinguish Managing from Leading

While most hospital managers are women, I find that few see themselves as leaders. So let's start with another basic question. What distinctions do you make between the purpose of managing and the purpose of leading? Note that this is a different question than asking what kinds of *activities* you associate with each. Before you read on, jot down what you think is the purpose of each on the lines below.

Managing_____

_____

_____

_____

_____

_____

Leading_____

_____

_____

_____

_____

_____

Here is a distinction I use: management is about *sustaining the status quo* while leadership is about *safeguarding the future.* Management attends to the short-term *what is* while leadership always has an eye on the long-term *what can be.*

Management sustains the status quo through results-oriented tasks like planning, budgeting, staffing, monitoring key quality and performance metrics, and so forth. It's the world of detail, follow-through, and day-to-day activities in service to next month's or next quarter's reports. Most women I've worked with are quite comfortable with the demands of management. They're expert at juggling multiple short-term tasks, picking up the slack when others don't follow through, and taking care of the next fire in the hallway or the next item on the to-do list.

Leadership, by contrast, safeguards the future by keeping a focus on the organization's purpose and direction, engaging people in fulfilling that purpose, and nurturing their capacity to learn from and adapt to whatever they encounter along the way. Leading is the world of connection: it connects today with tomorrow, individual efforts with the big picture, personal interests with organizational and community needs. In a simpler time, leadership was about authority and control. In the world of vast networks of connections, leadership is much more about influence and adaptation—qualities that women have used for years to navigate corporate hierarchies.

Yes, there is plenty of overlap between managing and leading, and successful, high performing organizations need both. Most organizations, however, are over managed and under led.

With this distinction in mind, try some self-observation. Begin by paying attention to when you manage and when you lead. Simply observe yourself and take notes in your journal. Select a question from the highlighted list or create a question of your own and live with it for a week or two. Write it at the top of a page in your journal and, as you move from conversation to conversation, record what you're experiencing *in the moment.*

Questions to live with

* When do I lead? When do I manage? What internal cues do I use to decide?
* What is my focal set point? How narrow or broad, detailed or conceptual is the range of perspective within which I typically work?
* When and how do I introduce new ideas or directions in meetings? When do I refrain from doing so? What do I tell myself about the difference?
* When do I question my peers and those senior to me about the strategic implications or wisdom of their decisions? When do I not speak up? How do I explain the difference to myself?
* How do I feel when I'm not getting the results I want? Do I use them or do they use me?

Don't try to *be* different. All you're doing here is getting a clearer picture of how you respond to situations in the moment. After a week or two of observing, read over your notes and see what patterns emerge. Remember, do not rely on your memory to answer these questions. You will automatically fall back on your stories *about* "the way it is." Those stories include not only the "facts" but also your assumptions, interpretations, judgments, expectations, and so forth.

So *live* with the question. Let it accompany you into meetings and conversations. Then write down what you observe. Don't be surprised if answers start bubbling up from your subconscious when you least expect it. Remember that the reason for doing this is to learn something new about how you experience or view the world. Once you discover something new, new options will naturally open up for you.

Invite Emotions to Work

Stepping into a leadership role often evokes fear and anxiety in women. It forces us to confront and step beyond some of our most deeply embedded beliefs about who and how we are in the world. Keep in mind that fear and anxiety are simply indicators that we're working at the edge. We can shrink back from them and stay with what's familiar or we can embrace them, learn to use them to our advantage, and step into the world of possibility.

The notion of embracing our own fears is just one variant on the theme of emotion in the workplace. We have heard for years that emotion has no place at work, yet organizations—especially healthcare organizations—are brimming with it. And well they should. Emotions are our energy source. The roots of the word are from the Latin *to move* and the Old French *to excite*. They fuel our motivation, our passion, our commitment to people and projects. They also are the source of our knowledge about what we most value, what most moves us inside. Without them, we have no way of determining the value of anything.

Yet we have been cautioned for years about the dangers of being emotional at work. Traditional management is steeped in Cartesian rationality, which separated mind and body and put us on a coarse of dualism that we're still recovering from, and Newtonian physics, which gave birth to the man-as-machine metaphor.

In the world of logic, emotion has no place. So we struggle to reduce everything to its component parts in a desperate attempt to understand, control, and predict outcomes. We create complex tables of organization to show who has power and authority over whom, and often are frustrated by our inability to control those surly physicians and third-party negotiators who are beyond the table. We divide work into clinical and support service lines, which often creates redundancy and turf wars. We devote hours to writing detailed job descriptions that committed employees don't need and mediocre employees hide behind. We import Six Sigma techniques from manufacturing to better control clinical processes, and we continually revise thick policy and procedure manuals to cover every imaginable contingency or infraction. And precious little changes.

THE DANCE IS BETWEEN EMOTION AND LOGIC,
PASSIONATE INTENSITY AND REASONED CAUTION.
GREAT DANCING REQUIRES BOTH.

Logic makes people think but emotion is what makes them act. If you want to be an effective leader, you need to invoke the intelligent use of emotion. In the 1990's, Daniel Goleman popularized the work of several psychologists when he published *Emotional Intelligence* (1995) and *Working with Emotional Intelligence* (1998). He was affirming what we have all known for years, that high IQ doesn't determine a person's success; high *emotional* intelligence does. Our success is contingent upon our ability to recognize and manage emotions—our own as well as others—in effective and productive ways.

Emotions in and of themselves are neither intelligent nor unintelligent. They are simply adaptive responses to various stimuli. But when emotion meets cognition—when we begin to process and manage emotional information in order to get a positive result—now we step into the realm of intelligence. Emotional intelligence arises from the interplay between our emotional and cognitive selves. It takes two to tango.

So the dance is between emotion and logic, passionate intensity and reasoned caution. Great dancing requires both. When raw emotion takes the lead, the dance can spin out of control. When pure logic takes the lead, the dance is barren and uninspired. As women, we bring to the workplace a natural affinity for and comfort with emotion. Our challenge is to surface and manage it in ways that enrich and enhance our organizations and the people we serve.

In order to create an environment rich in commitment, compassion, and creative juice, we must venture into what the Irish poet William Butler Yeats called the foul rag-and-bone shop of the heart. Rather than direct people with logic, we must help them find something they are passionate about. With some, we can do it simply through conversation aimed at discovering what's most important to them and then helping them find ways to embody it in their work. With others, especially those who've lost heart, the starting point often must be our own mental model and the behavior that it drives.

So let's take an extreme and common example from healthcare—heart disease—and use it to explore not only how our mental models shape our feelings and behavior but also how an entirely different model can yield entirely different results.

Change the Frame and You Change the Picture

Heart disease is this country's number one killer. For years, physicians and nurses have admonished cardiac patients about the hazards of lifestyle choices that aggravate their disease. Yet the vast majority of patients who've had coronary bypasses continue to smoke, overeat, not exercise, and be stressed out. Over time, physicians and nurses adjust to the reality that very few patients do what they need to do in order to survive. Many clinicians get frustrated and even cynical about patients' inability to change, even when their very life depends on it.

Now let's shift gears and turn to our mental frames and

models. Common sense tells us that scaring the wits out of people with facts and data about impending death, especially when they're in a crisis state, is the way to evoke change. But experience and a mountain of research data tell us that *it doesn't work*. So what do clinicians do? They continue to issue scary facts and data, hoping that this time it will make a difference. And what do patients do? They continue to smoke, overeat, avoid exercise, and be stressed out.

Several years ago, Dr. Dean Ornish, professor of medicine at U.C. San Francisco, teamed up with Mutual of Omaha to study an entirely new approach to working with patients with heart disease. His program, outlined in a *Fast Company* article titled "Change or Die" (Deutschman, 2005, 94) is radical and his success rate is high. What does he do differently?

He reframes the issue, first for himself and then for his patients. Starting from the assumption that patients' lifestyles are designed to help them cope with emotional troubles, he works backward to the conclusion that "'Telling people who are lonely and depressed that they're going to live longer if they quit smoking or change their diet and lifestyle is not that motivating. Who wants to live longer when you're in chronic emotional pain?'" So rather than scaring people with facts and data about what will kill them, Ornish engages them in the "'joy of living,' convincing them that they can feel better, not just live longer" (2005, 59).

His program requires radical changes in diet and lifestyle and supports patients with ongoing meetings and partners. According to Deutschman, 77% of the 333 patients in the study stuck with the lifestyle changes in Ornish's program, thereby avoiding further angioplasty or bypass surgery and saving Mutual of Omaha about $30,000 each, for a total of $7.7 million (2005, 58).

WHEN WE SHIFT THE LENS
THROUGH WHICH WE VIEW PEOPLE'S BEHAVIOR,
A WHOLE NEW WORLD APPEARS.

What is key here for our purpose is not just the existence of a successful model for helping cardiac patients heal themselves but the fact that bright, educated clinicians continue to rely on methods that don't work and continue to see noncompliant patients as the problem. It's a variation on that well-known phrase, "If you continue to do what you've always done, you'll continue to get what you've always gotten." Clinicians use the same ineffective approaches, patients use the same ineffective coping behaviors, and both feel powerless to effect any long-term change. But when we shift the lens through which we view people's behavior, as Ornish does, a whole new world appears.

One of my core beliefs is that all behavior is purposeful and driven by good intentions, even when it looks otherwise. Starting from that assumption, the self-destructive behavior of cardiac patients begins to raise interesting questions. What purpose does smoking, overeating, or numbing out in front of the TV serve? They are all forms of self-soothing. So what needs to be soothed? What internal turmoil or pain is gnawing away at this patient? When we begin asking these kinds of questions, what we once interpreted as resistance to clinical "wisdom" now becomes a brilliant expression of good intention: the desire to self-soothe.

It is a good illustration not only of the power of our mental frames but of a deeper, more universal truth about our human experience, namely that the structure or pattern of our belief system is what defines the results we get. The whole notion of using fear to motivate people flows from a structure designed to get rid of or move away from something we don't want. We do it to our patients with threats of suffering and death; we do it to our kids and employees with threats of punishment; we do it to ourselves with fears of looking foolish or incompetent.

The cycle is predictable and self-reinforcing. A problem arises that we don't like: we can't zip our favorite jeans, 3 West failed to get their patient sat scores up, Dr. Smith is threatening to gather up his scalpels and head down the street to another facility. The problem generates an emotional reaction in us: *this is terrible, I don't like this, I have to fix this.* Seeking relief from the emotion, we jump into action.

In the short term, our behaviors often work. The cardiac patient follows orders for a few months after an attack, the diet makes the jeans a little looser, the 3 West scores go up for a quarter, Dr. Smith cools his jets. But the relief is only temporary. The patient returns to his old lifestyle, the self-sacrificing diet gives way to self-indulgence, the 3 West scores slide again, and Dr. Smith is back on the warpath. So over time, a pattern emerges: we jump in to "fix" the "problem," it goes away, we move on to something else, and then—*wham!*—it's back, usually bigger and brighter than ever.

As anyone who has worked in a traditional organization more than a few years knows, these ups and downs bring with them those familiar inner monologues: *here we go again, I thought this was taken care of last year, this place is impossible, nothing I do seems to make a difference.* We are just like the clinicians, using the same old tactics, getting the same old results, and eventually feeling powerless and ineffectual.

What we fail to see is that the underlying pattern of how we're operating is what's keeping us stuck. Moving away from what we *don't* want takes us in a much different direction and produces much different results than moving *toward* what we *do* want.

When the initial trigger for action is a problem—like mediocre results, adverse incidents, falling revenues, or high costs—it evokes negative emotions like dissatisfaction, frustration, anxiety, even anger or fear. Those emotions are what drive us into action. We think we're trying to eliminate the problem, but we're also trying to eliminate the unpleasant emotions. Since those are the real driver, when they go away, so does our motivation.

But what if we let go of the driving need to fix or solve or get rid of, and shift instead to creating the kind of work environment we deeply want? What if we start with a strong desire that anchors us in what we most deeply value and that evokes our enthusiasm and passion? That's what Ornish did by creating a program that pulls patients *toward* a joyful life rather than pushing them *away* from suffering and death. They were now in pursuit of a dream.

The structure works at any level. When I pick up a few pounds, I know that putting myself on a diet does no good; I throw myself at the refrigerator with reckless abandon. But when I take up rowing two nights a week and am exhilarated by the challenge, my jeans start getting looser. When you help the staff on 3 West to clarify and pursue what they want their patients' experiences and their own work life to be like, the patient satisfaction scores rise steadily. When you can hear with an open heart Dr. Smith's feelings of isolation at being left out of decisions affecting clinical care, you open the way to deeper understanding and a collaborative rather than an adversarial relationship.

In each of these cases we are changing mental models. We are switching to a model that anchors us in something we want, something that really matters. It triggers a much different emotional response—excitement, anticipation, passion, the warmth of inclusion—which fuels action that pulls us closer to the dream. The more committed we are, the more passionate we become, which deepens our motivation and sustains us through thick and thin.

Trust that People Already Have the Wisdom They Need

We can only change our mental models when we are aware of them: when we can see the beliefs and assumptions that are shaping our everyday actions as choices we make in the world behind our eyes rather than as external realities. In the next chapter, we'll talk about the importance of identifying and staying focused on the patient's experience. For now, let's look at the importance of recognizing and reframing our most basic assumptions so they are aligned with creating empowering and purposeful work environments.

Tim Gallwey, author of the *Inner Game of Work* (2000), tells a wonderful story about being asked by AT&T managers to help operators improve their "courtesy" ratings without increasing the time they spent on each call. Gallwey agreed to the challenge on one condition: that the program did *not* have to be about courtesy. Reluctantly, the AT&T managers agreed.

Now think about this. You are a hospital director who wants to improve patient or physician satisfaction scores on your units. You ask a knowledgeable outside consultant to help and she agrees on the condition that the program she delivers doesn't have to be about patient or physician satisfaction. What are you telling yourself right now? To get the most from this story, pull out your journal and write down your self-talk. How would you respond to the consultant's position and what is the reasoning behind your response? Do this before reading on, then compare your thoughts and logic with Gallwey's.

The first step Gallwey took was to observe what the operators' work life was like. He discovered three things:

* The work was intensely boring and mechanical because of its routine nature
* It was highly stressful because operators' productivity and courtesy were continually monitored, and
* Operators' work was so prescribed by supervisors and procedural requirements that they felt treated like school children.

So he proposed a program to help reduce stress and boredom and to increase the enjoyment they got from their work. He also insisted that the program be voluntary. The proposal was met with a lot of skepticism but many signed up anyway.

His approach was grounded in a significant assumption: he assumed that telephone operators *already knew how to be courteous*. So rather than leap into corrective action to "fix" their lack of courtesy, he engaged them in a series of simple awareness exercises. First, he had them pay attention to and make distinctions about the caller based on the caller's tone of voice. Did they hear stress? irritation? anger? warmth? Then he had them practice altering their own voice qualities.

The real experiment began when he asked them to combine awareness of the caller's tone of voice with their own voice tone. They quickly discovered that by altering their own voice, they could influence how the caller was responding. Speaking through a smile could soften an angry caller. Matching the caller's pace could calm the latter's frustration. The guideline gave the operators "a small but tangible impact on a great number of people" (2000, 38). The result? Courtesy ratings exceeded management's expectations, stress and boredom went down 40%, and operator enjoyment went up 30%!

As human beings, we already have the wisdom we need to provide great service. We are all customers. We all make major purchases, occasionally end up with lemons, want someone to appreciate our suffering, and resent the callousness we encounter daily with most customer service systems. Similarly, we all have been ill, struggled with the loss of functional ability, and wanted someone to appreciate our suffering. But the wisdom of our own experience can easily get lost when we're under seige on the operator's end of the phone or the manager's side of the bed.

So review the notes you jotted down earlier. What do your thoughts reflect?

* A deep belief in people's desire to have an impact?
* Curiosity about what life is like for employees at the front line?
* Faith in their abilities to discover what works and to self-correct?

Or the more common assumptions that employees are the problem and the manager's job is to get the problem fixed?

What leads us astray when we're thinking like managers is that we're often seduced into traditional control-it, fix-it thinking, like the AT&T managers. They prescribed so many procedural requirements and monitored productivity and courtesy so closely that their operators were stressed and resentful. Was this their intention? No. Their intention was to provide more courteous service to customers. So while a fix-it frame is rooted in great intentions, it often actually interferes with our ability to create an empowering environment.

Gallwey started from a positive assumption that operators already knew how to be courteous and that something in the nature of the system was interfering with their ability to do what came naturally. His assumption created a space that allowed the operators' natural courtesy to emerge.

Ornish's radical approach to treating heart patients is based on a similar belief in the natural ability of human beings to adapt. When he abandoned the traditional tactic of scaring patients with facts and data and engaged them in the 'joy of living,' when he traded logic and fix-it thinking for emotional engagement in a lofty and desirable goal, the results were stunning. By reframing patients' lifestyle behaviors as coping strategies for getting rid of emotional discomfort, he treated them as intelligent, adaptive, living systems rather than as machines. The sheer act of attributing a positive intention to what most people consider dysfunctional behavior helped unleash the adaptive powers of patients to create a life they genuinely wanted.

The important point in these examples is that when we operate from a positive base—when we trust in the capacity of human beings to adapt to their circumstances in self-enhancing ways and when we create an open, accepting environment for that to occur—we allow their natural powers to surface. This is not easy work because of the sea of assumptions we float in. Most of us are awash in reactive, fix-it thinking; our to-do lists are filled with the urgencies of the day and our minds are scanning the surface for some solid solution to land on.

So in the coming days and weeks, pay attention to your own assumptions about your role, the purpose of your work, why the nurse manager on 3 West is always blaming her staff for their low patient satisfaction scores, or why the house staff continually discuss patient cases in public elevators, and observe your responses. What are you assuming about their behavior or about what is expected from you?

If you want to get more concrete, look at your daily calendar. How much of it is devoted to fixing problems or meeting scorecard indicator targets? How much of it is devoted to nurturing people's natural abilities and creating an environment rich in commitment, compassion, and creative juice? Is the balance where you want it to be?

What Are Your Self-Limiting Stories?

Let's look at your own life and work. Are you dancing at the edge of your capability, maximizing your own potential, enjoying the dance, having fun, and enhancing the well being of those you work with and serve? Or do you have a gnawing sense that you could be contributing much more *if only*...?

Complete the sentence with whatever fits for you:

* If only my boss ... or the higher-ups at corporate ... or the board chair ... would let me
* If only I had more power ... more authority ... more resources
* If only I had more leadership support from on high ... or less pressure to dance to someone else's tune ... more committed staff ... or fewer slack-offs.

If you are caught in the world of *if only,* you are caught in another of your own mental frames.

Yes, you've had a lot of help from the outside. Top-down cultures have bred a mentality of dependence and compliance for years. They encourage men and women alike to trade autonomy and honest expression for safety and security. Yet if you think about it, when was the last time, honestly, that someone who was truly effective at getting great results in your organization, someone who supported and mobilized others to excel, was rewarded with a pink slip? I'll bet you cannot think of an example.

So if you're not working at the edge of your capability, if you are not passionate about what you're doing, if work is no longer fun and fulfilling, what is holding you back? What stories are you telling yourself that are limiting your possibilities?

* That you need others' approval before you take a stand on something important and potentially controversial?
* That you'll look foolish because those around you seem to know the next steps or know more about "how"?
* That you must be invited to contribute rather than be the one extending the invitation?
* That you'll be chastised, or worse, for not following orders?
* That the golden handcuffs have become too valuable to risk losing?

Revisit the scores you gave yourself on the survey in the previous chapter. Do they suggest that your style is to avoid what you don't want, like others' disapproval or failure to get results no matter what? Or do they suggest that you're willing and able to embody what you most deeply value and to help others do the same?

Every barrier we encounter arises from our mental models. Every barrier to creating a different culture, getting different results, becoming a different organization arises from mental models about how people—ourselves as well as others—work and how our organizations are supposed to be. Find the right model—the one that supports what you most deeply want—and extraordinary results can become commonplace events.

3

Play Big and Play On Purpose

Start with a Wide-Angle Lens

For years, men have outnumbered women in the executive suites of organizations, even in healthcare, where female employees outnumber males 6 to 1. My male clients are not afraid to tell me why: they think men have a better grasp of the big picture and a broader base of experience. In my experience, women are quite capable of seeing and appreciating a bigger picture, but it is a different picture, motivated by a different set of values and expressed in a different, more intimate way. Our way isn't better; it is simply *different,* and the workplace needs both. We are interdependent, so one without the other is incomplete.

This chapter begins by comparing these differences in style and perspective, and offers a distinction between two very different yet complementary definitions of "big picture:" one based in operations, the other in core purpose.

Purpose anchors work to the heart, so the next section is about clarifying your personal purpose. If you are like many women, you want meaningful work yet often wonder whether you're making a difference. The exercises in this section are the initial steps for putting what matters most at the center of your efforts.

The chapter then broadens to include organizational purpose, what working "on purpose" looks like in action, and ways to start working on purpose in your daily work life. Women's conversational style and comfort with creating inclusive networks are well suited for helping people explore questions of purpose and find deeper meaning in their work. By helping employees connect their own work with what matters most to the organization, you can create the conditions for deep commitment.

We end the chapter with an atypical perspective on vision, a prediction about the resistance you'll likely encounter in pursuing a purposeful work environment, and ways to respond that will help you stay the course.

* * *

Men run most organizations, including healthcare systems. They have grown up in the world of team play and ladder climbing. They often have 2-, 5-, and even 10-year plans for themselves. When they take a manager position, they're already thinking of their next step to the director level. When they accept the director position, they're setting their sights on a vice president slot. I've worked with several men whose ultimate goal was to become CEO of their own hospital, and I have no doubt that many will succeed at it.

Knowing where they want to go, they set out to accumulate

experience. They change jobs every few years. They make important connections. They mentor each other and learn early on to keep one eye on today's tasks and another on tomorrow's goals. They pick high leverage projects and make strategic lateral moves. As a result, they gain valuable experience and a wide-angle perspective on the great scheme of things. They get "the big picture."

By contrast, many women—especially those who grew up prior to the 1990s—have limited experience with team play and even less experience with mentoring and being mentored. They're accustomed to moving within small circles of friends and relationships. They're used to doing what they're asked, volunteering for whatever needs to be done, and staying within those familiar circles. They work hard as individual contributors and hope that someone will recognize their dedication and tap them for a management role.

When they move into management, they take that style with them. Some learn early on to trade it for a more effective style. Many find themselves up to their eyeballs in crises and current demands, all of which they feel responsible for, and end up feeling overworked, isolated, and alone. Others get frustrated, park their careers in positions that are comfortable but unchallenging, and become insulated from what's going on elsewhere in the organization.

I'm not saying that you must climb the ladder or have a 5-year career plan in order to develop a sense of the big picture. I am saying that if you want to develop your potential or influence the quality of your patients' experiences or your own work environment, you need a broad network of people who can support you. *And* you need a mental frame that does the same. The mental frame is the tough part.

While women can be masterful at nurturing relationships,

we typically treat them purely as social connections. We exchange the most intimate details of our personal lives, but we won't use relationships to make business connections or to learn more about business operations. We label such behavior as distasteful, inappropriate, even manipulative, so our exchanges about the organization are usually limited to complaints or "troubles talk," a term linguist Deborah Tannen (1990) uses to describe how women share troubles in order to bond with one another. Men, on the other hand, use the quid pro quo of work relationships to exchange favors all the time.

It's not that one style is right or better than the other. It's that most women and men operate from different mental frames of reference, which are manifest in different interpersonal styles. Our style is anchored in developing and sustaining close relationships and consensus. Men's is often anchored in negotiating their status in the pecking order. For instance, think about how many times you've struck up a conversation with a man at work about a mutual concern, and you get frustrated because he jumps in with a solution. You're trying to cement a relationship with conversation while he's trying to solve the problem. Or think about the times you've phrased your responses carefully to help a male colleague save face and he's hailed as the hero because he took decisive action.

In essence, our interpersonal world is lateral while men's is hierarchical. And how are most organizations structured? Hierarchically. So while we're busy forming small, intimate circles of connection, men are busy establishing position and status. Our desire for closeness often isolates us from the larger organization while their desire for position leads them to learn about the whole operation.

So if, like many women, you dislike using relationships for personal purposes, then it's time to reframe your thinking.

You need a frame that supports 'yes and' rather than 'either-or' thinking, a frame that lets you use your relationship-building gifts to create close connections with those near *and* distant in the organization.

* Consider changing metaphors. What about creating a lattice rather than climbing a ladder? Or imagining a structural network like a web, a crisscrossing framework than spans your organization and supports everyone connected to it? Notice how your mental image changes as you shift from ladder climbing to moving within an open, interconnected network.
* Or find another metaphor that gives you a wide-angle view, like gazing down from a tall building or an airplane.
* If you can't find an apt metaphor, then step outside your own story. For instance, if you prefer to give rather than to receive, then trust that other women feel the same way and reframe your story to fit that reality: every time you ask for help, reframe it as an opportunity for someone else to give and feel good about herself.

Here's the bottom line. This is not a question of gray matter; women are more than capable of seeing and appreciating the bigger picture. Nor is it a question of the good ol' boys' ladder blocking the way. I've coached numerous women who had no clear career aspirations yet rose through the ranks of their organizations by being sensitive to their own levels of engagement and letting their curiosity guide them into new positions and projects. Their careers weren't incremental or lockstep. Quite the contrary. Each of them took illogical leaps into new directions. The one constant for them was their deep desire for meaningful work. While their male counterparts were busy pursuing positions and fulfilling career goals, these women were busy contributing and fulfilling a sense of personal purpose. So ultimately, that is the question: what matters so deeply to you that you are willing to let loose the full power of your strengths to fulfill it?

You Need a Purpose More Than a Plan

We have been taught to think of "big picture" as a broad understanding of the scope of operations and the larger marketplace within which our organization operates. It is a valid definition, but a limited one. Big picture also refers to an organization's core purpose, its reason for being. This is a definition that many people, even those with leadership titles, often miss.

A few years ago, I was observing a 3-hour meeting of senior healthcare executives. Men and women alike were rushing to get through a jam-packed agenda. Halfway through the meeting and only a third of the way through the agenda, a subordinate presented a master list of space requests to be folded into the next year's capital budget.

"I have two more requests," said one executive.

"I have questions about where the outcomes people go," said another.

"I know the new VP is planning to submit a request for additional admin space," said a third.

They waded through a swamp of details until the president ran out of patience. "I've said this before. I'll say it again. This is a hospital. Anything within its walls should be for patient care. *Patients* belong here. Ancillary staff—outcomes people, Q/A people, marketing, legal—should go elsewhere. I've even thought of moving *us* out. We can walk back. It's only a block. Our business isn't our desk and the paper on it. Our business is patient care."

The president was a man; few women I know would ever make such a bold declaration. What he was talking about is the importance—and the difficulty—of working "on purpose." The big picture of operations and trends that's necessary to get ahead is different from the big picture of being purposeful. The former is about personal gain; the latter is about service.

Women are generally allergic to personal gain for its own sake but quite comfortable with serving others. Yet the women in this group lost sight of the patient just as readily as the men. So it's no surprise that few healthcare leaders, be they men or women, have been capable of creating and sustaining purposeful organizations, especially given the market dynamics of the past several years.

If you want to take a leading role—regardless of whether you're in the C-suite, in a department, or on a clinical floor— then train yourself to be purposeful, to keep one eye on daily activities and the other on what matters most. Purpose is the beacon that guides you in creating what you want. It also is the orienting center for leading others.

Being purposeful works at both the micro or individual level and the macro or organizational level. In healthcare, purpose often is framed in terms of organizational *mission*. For me, the terms *purpose* and *mission* are synonymous and I'll use them that way throughout the book. So we'll start with the question of personal purpose and then shift to the purpose or mission of your organization.

What Is Your Purpose?

When I was a freshman in college, one of my assignments was to write a paper answering the question, "What is your purpose in life?" I muddled through the assignment, but the question stayed with me for years. What was my purpose? What was I here to contribute? Not until my 40s did I realize that I was here to teach, to learn what life and others have to offer, and to pass it on.

It took several more years for me to appreciate that women and men have different expectations of work and that what we women seek is perfectly legitimate. As I suggested earlier, men often seem satisfied with moving up, earning fatter salaries, and having positions associated with power and respect. Women typically want a sense of fulfillment that's not defined by position or pay or power. We want to enjoy what we're doing, feel competent and worthy at it, and fulfill an inner need to contribute. In short, we want a sense of purpose, a clear gut feeling that what we are doing is meaningful and worthwhile.

What is your purpose? If you're not sure, and many are not, start with some self-reflective questions. Here is a coaching process that can be helpful.

Write one or both of these questions on post-it notes, and put them where you'll see them regularly: inside the notebook you take to meetings, on your computer monitor, on the bathroom mirror or the refrigerator door.

* What do I find myself drawn to?
* What naturally captures my attention and fuels my energy level?

Then live with them for several days. Use the notes as reminders to observe your attention and energy. Jot down what you think and feel as you move from one activity to another. Remember that with self-observation exercises, it's important to work quickly without censoring what emerges and to hand write your observations. Much more powerful material is likely to emerge.

If you find that few things attract and energize you, then try living with a different set of questions, like the ones below. Again, post them where you'll be reminded of them regularly. Reread them often so they seep into your subconscious.

* When in my life have I been so absorbed in something that the world seemed to fall away? What has drawn me in so entirely that I lost all track of time, and emerged feeling energized and renewed rather than drained and depleted?

* When has my concentration been so laser like that what I was doing seemed effortless?

As answers bubble up, simply record them. Don't monitor, judge, edit, or try to analyze them. Just stay open to whatever surfaces. When you have some material to work with —and, trust me, you will, even if it draws from childhood or adolescence—then spend some quiet time working through the following.

* What did those absorbing times have in common?

* What talents of mine did they tap? What skills did they demand of me?

* Which of those talents and skills—which of my natural and learned abilities—left me feeling full and complete when I exercised them?

Continue to observe yourself at work and at home. Pay attention to and record times when you feel drawn in and energized, when your talents are being fully utilized, and you're working for the sheer joy of it. Also pay attention to and record times when the opposite is occurring: when you feel drained and depleted, when your talents aren't being tapped, and you're merely going through the motions.

Then try another reflective session with your latest observations and questions like the following:

* What is motivating me in each set of situations?
* When am I driven by the need to conform or control?
* When am I driven by something much richer and more rewarding?
* When do I measure myself by external rather than internal standards?
* When do I measure myself by what's most deeply satisfying?

Many women become so engrossed in taking care of others that they fail to notice their own downward slide into despair. If you find work less and less rewarding, then explore the following questions with the same approach you just used. This time, go after the tacit internal assumptions that you've absorbed from working in top-down environments, using the questions in the box below.

If work is less and less rewarding ...

* How do I think I am expected to act? What—and whose—external expectations am I using to define my role?
* When do I find myself behaving in ways that are inconsistent with what I value? What competing needs are generating tension in me?
* What internal expectations do I hold for myself? Are they a burden or a source of energy?
* How do I define success for myself in this organization? When I succeed at something, does it give me a deep sense of fulfillment or am I left rushing to the next item on the to-do list and wondering why there's no Eureka at the end?
* How do I view my role? As someone responsible for organizing and planning work for others, telling them what to do, and monitoring their progress? Or as someone who believes deeply that others are capable of organizing and planning too, and that my role is to clarify direction and help link them with opportunities for personal growth and contribution?

* In tough situations, do I act in order to save face, avoid blame, and protect my own interests? Or do I seek to understand others' perspectives, take my share—and only my share—of the responsibility when things go wrong, and open myself to feedback in order to grow and learn?

As you become more clear about when you are being guided by purpose rather than driven by ego needs, you'll begin to experience a significant shift. Your work and daily activities start to be guided by your intentions rather than by others' expectations. What used to seem like an overwhelming list of activities begins to shake out into natural priorities: those that further your intentions and help you fulfill your purpose and those that don't. You begin to operate differently in the world.

I am not talking about intention in the sense of will or determination. It is much more akin to tapping into a universal force field or energy field. When we set an intention for ourselves that aligns with our sense of purpose, we tap into something that we cannot see or measure but that works on our behalf. We sense ourselves in the midst of something very potent. If you doubt the existence of such a field, try explaining—without relying on the concepts of gravity or magnetic fields—why bodies drop to earth or why certain metals attract and repel one another. Setting intentions is a conscious, cognitive activity, but it involves listening to that deep inner voice of purpose. Once your intentions are set, they will operate subliminally, helping to guide your behavior and decision making in self-enhancing ways.

If you want to accelerate the process, find two or three other women who want to develop their leadership capacity and form a learning team. Do these self-awareness exercises and the other exercises and practices described throughout the book.

Meet periodically to talk about what you're learning. Commit to helping each other discover your own purpose and align it with what's most meaningful in your organization. And commit to expanding your learning team by bringing other like-minded women into it, including women from throughout and beyond your organization.

Discovering your purpose does not happen over night. But the more attention you pay to slowing down and listening to what's deep inside, the clearer you'll become. The more time you devote to observing when your actions do and do not reflect this deep inner voice, the more decisive and directed your actions will become, and the more people will begin to experience you as someone they trust and want to emulate.

What Is the Purpose of Your Organization?

Historically, hospitals have been grounded in a deep sense of purpose. Caring for patients—the sick, the injured, the dying—was their fundamental reason for being. Nowadays, most hospitals are part of complex organizational behemoths with thousands of employees, hundreds of physicians, and dozens of facilities. And while hospitals still care for the sick, injured, and dying, one towering challenge for leaders is how to help individuals work on purpose each day, given the sheer complexity within which care unfolds and the vortex of non-direct care activities swirling around it: marketing, outcomes, quality assurance/utilization review, facilities management, strategic planning, foundation development, medical informatics, physician relations, medical staff affairs, risk management, legal affairs, training, human resources, and on and on.

So before you read any further, jot down your organization's purpose or mission statement. *No peaking at a wall plaque or file or home page to get the wording right!* Even if you work in one of the rare healthcare organizations that hasn't been through the mission drill, jot down what you think the mission is. Then consider the following questions, just as points of awareness.

* Do you know this mission like you know the Golden Rule? Do you see it embodied regularly in how people work and what they hold each other accountable for? Do you feel it when you walk the halls?

* Or does it have a noble ring that fails to translate into everyday action? Is there a discrepancy between the espoused mission and the one in practice? If a discrepancy exists, what do you think is the cost to the organization and to you?

* How do you think those farther up the hierarchy would answer these questions? What about those closer to the point of patient contact?

To illustrate the orienting power of purpose, consider the following story. One of my clients, a vice president, was appointed to a system-wide committee charged with integrating the IT network across several hospitals. The committee was asked to create a system that streamlined billing, medication delivery, patient record keeping, and hospital performance. It comprised senior-level operations people, IT staff, physicians, and quality assurance and performance improvement directors, all of whom met weekly. What I found most striking about the several hours of meetings I attended was that the patient's perspective and experience were not mentioned once!

Here was a group of highly paid experts working diligently on the periphery and paying no attention to the actual experience of the patients—those who received the bills, relied on the medications, had their data stored in the records, and were on the receiving end of "hospital performance." During these meetings, the group made little progress. My client was frustrated and unsure about how to intervene until we began discussing the purpose of this new IT network from the *patients'* perspective. With the patients' experience as the focal point, my client quickly generated a number of ideas for helping the committee move forward.

My belief is that the purpose of any healthcare organization is to help patients get what they need, when and where they need it. In many instances, that translates to timely care and services. In some cases, it translates to the capacity to allay suffering when the patient enters territory beyond the realm of medicine. Patients are the reason for any hospital's work. Without them, what is the organization's reason for being?*

Putting patients at the center of an organization's efforts requires that managers make a significant shift in both mindset and behavior, from being the person in charge of managing activities to being the person who supports, collaborates with, and does what's necessary to create optimal experiences for patients.

This is a tough transition for men because it requires letting go of the traditional assumption that those in charge are the ones with the answers and the power. It is a tough transition for women because it requires the same letting go of who's in charge *and* it calls for us to embrace on a grander scale our own power to pull people together into collaborative, purposeful networks. The upside is that when we make patients and

---

* I am aware that many healthcare organizations consider physicians rather than patients as their primary customers. It is a valid focus. For me, it generates more complexity than it resolves. Yes, physicians are the primary source of hospital referrals. They also serve patients, which makes them partners in care. Without the backing of hospital staff and facilities, physicians cannot help patients get what they need, when and where they need it. Expecting staff to serve two masters, patient and physician, muddies the water, especially when clinical issues arise. Think of situations involving standing or inappropriate orders, for instance, or negative reactions to treatment. When clinical staff are working as partners with a shared interest in what's best for patients, the nature of their relationship—and the mental model guiding their behavior—are much different than when one is subordinate to the other.

quality care—rather than individual success—the center of our networks, we begin to shape a different kind of organization: one that invites people to serve a common purpose.

What Working On Purpose Looks Like

When people are working on purpose, they have an energy and enthusiasm that's magnetic. They draw a deep sense of satisfaction from what they do. They often radiate joy. Their openness and authenticity are welcoming; you have the sense that what you see is who they really are. They give and receive respect and trust. When people are working on purpose, who they are is manifest in what they do. Purpose allows them to work with remarkably clear intention.

My most powerful experience with purpose in the workplace occurred many years ago in my first week on the job at a large healthcare system. Everyone I encountered, from cafeteria cashiers to janitors to floor nurses to vice presidents, was clearly aligned with the organization's mission and values. People in every corner of the place seemed happy, energized, and devoted to their patients and to one another.

I'd worked in other places that had mission and values statements. Usually they were cooked up during an executive retreat at an expensive resort, made pretty by the marketing people, then distributed to the common folk on laminated cards at a big kick-off event. Most of the cards were trashed before the hors d'oeuvre plates were washed.

This organization was different. The acronym for their values was SPIRIT and you could feel it in every corner of the organization. People lived it. They embodied it.

I asked one of the vice presidents, "How did you create this kind of devotion throughout the ranks?"

"We learned it from our CEO," she said.

"Really? What's his secret?"

"He educates people. He spends time, day in and day out, recognizing when people are living with SPIRIT. He has a deep respect for people. He keeps them informed. You'll see it at the next system-wide staff meeting. He gives out financial and operational data that most CEO's keep close to the vest. He sends people to other organizations to learn new ways of *being*. And he holds every one of us to the same standards. You can't work without SPIRIT and stay here very long."

This man did not just respect people; he seemed to have a deep and abiding belief in the greatness of every single person in the organization. The hospital had over 5,000 employees, and he knew an amazingly high number of them by name. A walk with him through the halls always took three times longer than usual because he'd stop for short chats with everyone he encountered.

The quarterly manager meetings had small agendas and big blocks of time to answer any questions that emerged. And questions flowed like water. He shared his thinking on virtually everything with the belief, I suspect, that even if a manager passed on "trade secrets" to someone in another hospital, the latter wouldn't be able to replicate the invisible qualities that made this system stellar. His commitment to the people in that organization was palpable and it paid high returns.

Purpose became a source of both energy and personal power for people throughout the organization. It wasn't created at an executive retreat and made part of a corporate rollout to get employee buy-in. It was discovered from within and embodied in the hearts and actions of people willing to step into what gave great meaning to their lives and work.

The CEO left the organization a few years later and within six months the atmosphere changed dramatically. His successors were far more focused on the hospital's financial performance, even though the hospital had been doing quite well, and they spent far less time roaming the halls and maintaining bonds with staff. The open release of information at system-wide meetings was replaced by a need-to-know mentality. Gone, too, were the rituals of caring and connection that had opened and closed each meeting. A new set of values, which I suspect were established during an executive retreat at a pricey resort by the hospital's new leadership, resulted in a new acronym that quickly became the brunt of countless staff jokes: FEES.

I believe the new leaders' intentions were similar: to run the hospital according to a clear mission and set of guiding values. But they simply were not capable of operating at the level of personal awareness that the former CEO embodied or that is required for creating a great service organization. They had the big picture in terms of operations and market share. What they could not see was the big—yet invisible and immeasurable—picture of working *on purpose*. My guess is that their own needs to protect their sense of security, competence, and self worth prevented them from nurturing the same in others. It wasn't their "fault." They just didn't know better.

Many managers followed the lead of those at the top. They reacted by adopting the new mentality and letting go of the rituals, the open sharing of information, the continual emphasis on living and working with SPIRIT.

But several managers had the courage to continue leading as the former CEO had. They set aside time in their own departments to maintain the rituals of caring and connection. They continued to share financial information with their staff, to create opportunities for staff to learn what was going on elsewhere, and to hold them accountable for embodying the values most important for sustaining a caring, compassionate workplace.

If you were in this situation, which choice would you make? Would you follow the lead of those at the top or would you follow your heart and stay on purpose? There is no doubt that it takes courage to act differently, to pursue what is most meaningful rather than what is most expedient. I was with the organization for 18 months after the first CEO's departure. And not a single manager who chose to follow the heart was dismissed or demoted. In the end, our only leverage point is right where we are, and when we work on purpose and from a deep commitment to those we serve, the results are powerful.

Get Yourself Aligned

The managers who continued to work purposefully in this organization had a powerful model in their CEO. You may not have such a model. You may have to find your own way. You can do so by looking at your everyday activities and decision-making through the lens of personal purpose and the purpose of your organization. For instance, my coaching clients often complain that they have no time for new or different activities. Since most of them spend large amounts of time in meetings, I ask them to make a list of all the meetings they attend and then answer the highlighted questions below.

Making more time in the day

Answer the following for every meeting you attend:
* What is this meeting's purpose?
* How does it help fulfill the purpose of our organization?
* What is my role here?

* How does my presence help fulfill my own purpose and further the purpose of the organization?
* What would happen if I did not attend this meeting?
* Is my response to this last question one of playing small by contracting and pulling back, or is it one of playing big by embracing my own purpose and potential?

Try this yourself. Chances are, you'll discover that you're unclear about the purpose of most meetings. It's not a fault or a weakness. Lots of meetings have been in existence and running on autopilot for years; others are called simply because *that's the way it's done* and we don't question it. Still others, like the committee charged with creating an integrated IT network, are not oriented around the larger purpose of the organization. In addition, women tend to be process oriented and compliant, and both distract us from staying true to our purpose. We think that if we're invited to attend a meeting, then we should accept. If we're asked to take on a new assignment, like being the department representative on a standing committee, we automatically agree, even if we know it's a dead-end task.

I've had countless female clients, including executives, who are stellar at planning, organizing, and implementing projects, juggling multiple tasks and details, and generally doing—and even excelling at—what they've been asked to do. And their careers languish. It is the proverbial trees-versus-forest dilemma. Our natural tendency seems to be one of taking a tactical rather than a strategic perspective on our daily activities. We want to please. We want to be helpful. And it costs us.

When we are clear about both our own purpose and the larger purpose of our organization, we can use that understanding to make better-informed, more purposeful decisions on a daily basis. One of my clients, a vice president, simply couldn't get the word "no" out of her mouth. As a result, she was swamped with projects and committee assignments that had little relevance to the strategic goals she was responsible for. She was working longer hours than any of her colleagues, yet was passed over for a significant promotion because, according to her boss, she was "too tactical." Translation: she had a vice president title but was functioning as a support person.

When she stepped back and clarified her purpose, she was able to determine the value of each activity she was involved with. As she practiced saying "no" to low-priority or no-priority projects (yes, it was hard because "no" had not been in her vocabulary) her days became more focused and she began accomplishing more while working less.

Put Purpose into Practice Through Conversations

A few years ago, I was speaking to an audience of nurses and ancillary care personnel in Paducah, Kentucky and wanted some fluorescent lights removed from the front of the room so that people could see the slides. The talk didn't start until 9:00 a.m., so at 7:30, I tracked down a nice young maintenance man named Matt and told him what I needed. "I'd be glad to help," he said, "as soon as my supervisor says it's okay."

Of course, his supervisor wasn't due for another hour, so I pressed Matt to just pop the bulbs out on his own. "Oh, no, ma'am," he insisted. "I couldn't do that without his approval."

So we agreed that he would return as soon as he had his supervisor's OK.

At 8:50, he came by to say that his supervisor still hadn't arrived. Frustrated, I took a deep breath, reached for a gentle tone, and said, "Matt, we have 100 people in this room and a lot of material to cover in the next 6 hours. I'm sure that part of your job is to take care of customers, especially when you have this many of us in one place. What's the consequence for not taking care of customers?"

Fear flashed across Matt's face. He began to fidget.

I turned toward the door and said, "I'm going to make one last trip to the ladies' room before we start. I trust that you can help us, Matt."

Five minutes later, I returned and the lights were gone. Matt was exiting the room. I rushed up to him and asked, "Did your supervisor arrive?"

"No," he muttered, "I decided to do it myself. But please, *please* don't tell anyone. I don't want to get caught. I *need* this job!"

Imagine fearing the loss of your job for serving a customer! I felt badly for Matt and wondered about the levels of stress he must feel regularly in trying to serve two masters.

Chances are, you have your own Matt-like employees. How do you help them get beyond this line of thinking and engage them in working on purpose? You model the way. As a leader, you must breathe life into your organization's purpose every day, in every action you take. You must embody it at every turn, like the CEO who worked with SPIRIT.

You start, quite simply, with conversations. Begin with your colleagues and direct reports. Use the approach and questions I discussed earlier for discovering your personal purpose and use them to help define the organization's purpose.

* What are people drawn to?
* What naturally captures their attention and fuels their energy level?
* When are they so engaged that their work seems effortless?

* Which talents and skills leave them feeling full and complete?

Take the mission statement off the wall and into staff meetings. Invite people to explore what it means to them and what it looks like in action in their corners of the world. Help them tie their strengths and talents, their daily activities and decisions to the quality of the patient's experience. Treat the mission statement as an outline that they can color in with what's most important and meaningful in their worlds. What you're after here is a deep, shared understanding of what purpose in action looks like—at 2 a.m. on a step-down unit, on a Saturday night in the emergency department, when pushing a meal cart or cleaning a room or writing copy for a new service-line brochure.

We often shy away from conversations like these because we have been taught that they are too touchy-feely, too removed from getting the work done. But I have yet to meet a person who, deep in his or her heart, did not want meaningful work and an opportunity to make a contribution. And when people grasp the notion of purpose, they start working differently, like the vice president who learned to say "no."

YOU DO NOT NEED TO HAVE THE ANSWERS.
YOU NEED TO HAVE THE COURAGE
TO POSE THE QUESTIONS AND LISTEN CLOSELY.

Sometimes it's helpful to ask people about images and metaphors that capture the essence of their work. One team I worked with skipped the words and opted instead for the image of an aura cast over their work. They wanted to envelop others in it as well, so they began treating every action as an opportunity to pull others into the light. Similarly, a rehab group wanted to create a web of healing within which they were tied to their patients and to one another. Several months later, one of them commented that she'd not realized how much suffering the staff were experiencing until she began looking at her relationships through the lens of a healing web. In both of these instances, the metaphors became guidelines for people's work.

With this approach, you do not need to have the answers. You just need the courage to pose the questions, listen closely to the responses, and begin making the linkages that women are good at making. Ask people the same question that I ask executives: "What is the purpose of our business?" The cynics will pipe up with something about making money. Don't let them off the hook; even in the for-profit sector, leaders are learning not to confuse purpose with profit. Having a reasonable margin is essential for an organization to survive but it is not the organization's reason for being.

Others will answer with statements about the services you provide. Post their statements someplace where everyone can see them. Push people. Ask them, *What's significant about those services? Why are they important?* Drill down more. Try the "Five whys" approach, which is to keep asking, "Why is this important?" for five iterations (Collins and Porras, 1994, 226). The mere fact that you keep pushing for more depth will convey to people that you're serious about working differently. And if you keep at it, you will find that a hundred, even a thousand different answers distill into just a few core principles reflecting your organization's purpose or mission. Many are already living it. Others will begin to grasp it. Make yourself a hub through which your group develops a greater respect for and shared understanding of what's most meaningful and significant in each person's work. Make purpose the orienting center.

You don't have to be at a senior level to do this. You can identify a clear purpose for your unit or department. One nursing director I worked with got tired of having no direction from on high beyond a set of target metrics. So she took the lead and engaged her staff in defining their purpose and a set of guiding principles for their unit, a general surgery service with high numbers of elderly and nursing home patients. It became known as the "high touch" unit. Eight months later, she said, "The whole tone here has changed. We're working from a deep commitment to our patients and each another. And we're consistently meeting our numbers. It's happening naturally. I don't have to push anymore. Our staff turnover is low—way below other units in the hospital—and I have people from other units asking me to let them know when we have an opening. They want to be part of this."

And What About the Value of a Vision?

The business literature of the past 20 years is filled with articles and books on vision, and consultants have made millions helping executive teams write vision statements. Vision is different from purpose or mission and leaders and managers often confuse the two. Envisioning the future is a *creative* process, while identifying your organization's purpose is a *discovery* process. The former comes from imagining what your organization is capable of becoming; the latter comes from exploring the significance of what you already do.

Collins and Porras talk about vision as a 10- to 30-year BHAG, or Big Hairy Audacious Goal (1994, 232). It has an end point, requires remarkable effort, and is inspiring and achievable. John F. Kennedy's call for "A man on the moon before the end of the decade" is a prime example. It fired up science teachers across the country and likely gave NASA engineers a case of sustained heartburn since they had to create a whole new generation of technology to accomplish it. But with a clear vision of what could be, they did it: they achieved what originally had seemed impossible.

The main point here is that Kennedy had a clear purpose driving his vision. He wanted to rebuild America's prestige as a scientific leader. Russia had launched Sputnik in 1957 and sent a cosmonaut into space in 1961, and American morale was waning. So his vision, anchored in a powerful purpose, became a dramatic call to action that built on America's core values and boosted American pride at a time when both were sorely needed.

In my experience, the sheer act of creating vision statements often leads healthcare leaders astray. Visions of "what can be" are meaningless unless they're connected to and driven by a deeper sense of purpose. And while the purpose of a healthcare organization may seem obvious, if you're running the marketing department, directing business development, overseeing facilities management, or heading up any of a dozen other non-clinical activities, it's remarkably easy to lose sight of your organization's core purpose. Until a shared sense of purpose echoes throughout your unit, department, or organization, efforts to get people fired up about a BHAG usually fail.

IN HEALTHCARE, A GOOD VISION IS HARD TO FIND.
SO PUT IT AWAY AND SET OUT TO DISCOVER
THE MISSION YOU'RE ALREADY ON.

When you step into a leadership role, people will be looking to you for guidance. The higher you are in the organization, the more they will expect you to have a vision and a plan for realizing it. That's one of the measures people use in determining your credibility as a leader.

But in healthcare, a good vision is hard to find. How do

you inspire caregivers to seek a big, hairy, audacious goal when the real value of what they do is at the patient's bedside every hour of every day? When was the last time you read a vision statement for a healthcare organization that left you saying, "Wow! Now *that* is something worth pursuing"? Unless your vision is so compelling that you and all the people you work with are consistently fired up to achieve it, it is probably not serving your purpose. So put it away and set out to discover the mission you are already on, both personally and organizationally.

I know this runs counter to the prevailing views of a leader. Leaders are supposed to be visionary, and people have been trained to want and expect direction and plans. Yet most women I have worked with struggle with trying to create a vision. They wrestle with concepts and then with word-smithing. They try to make it acceptable to everyone and end up diluting it beyond recognition. Instead of getting people fired up, it leaves them yawning.

When we are clear about purpose, we are grounded in what is already deeply meaningful. We know what we stand for. Our stance now becomes one of inviting others' ideas about what to create and how to create it. Now, creating a vision becomes another means of orienting people to a core purpose, like the nursing director who engaged her staff in creating a high-touch unit or the group that created a web of healing.

INVITE OTHERS' IDEAS ABOUT WHAT TO CREATE.
SOME WILL RESIST,
OTHERS WILL CRITICIZE YOU FOR HAVING NO VISION.
DO NOT TAKE IT PERSONALLY.

Here is where women's desire to nurture lateral, inclusive networks can work to our advantage. By refusing to embrace the notion that vision comes from on high and by inviting everyone to contribute, we can begin to break down some of the common assumptions that keep top-down structures in place and that fuel high levels of disengagement and frustration throughout the ranks.

When you take this approach, you will be met with resistance. People in large organizations are accustomed to being told "Here's where we're going" and "Here's what you need to do." It's the lead-follow mental model and it is well ingrained. In fact, most people have no experience with the notion of articulating their own purpose or creating a vision for their work unit or organization. So those who are disengaged or who protect themselves by pointing the finger of blame may feel threatened at being asked to take an active role in defining the future. They may accuse you of being weak and criticize you for having no vision or plan. To them, you must be able to say, "Even if I had a vision and plan, I'm not willing to assume that they are right for everyone in this department, much less for our patients. Anything I create on my own is bound to be far less than what we can create together. Your experience and your ideas are as valuable as mine. I'll lead the process but I won't unilaterally determine the way."

You'll find that some will welcome the opportunity to co-create a vision that's anchored in the organization's mission. The majority will wait to see if you are serious and a handful will actively resist. Stay grounded in your purpose. Hone your skills for pulling people together by actively listening, valuing participation, and encouraging diverse perspectives. And *do not take the resistance personally*. Resisters must let go of their beliefs about how it *should* be before they can embrace how it *can* be. Those unable to let go may leave. That's okay. As those who remain come to trust your motives and feel more secure about their ability to contribute, their negativity will subside and they'll start to re-engage in new ways.

Remember also that excellence of care can vary across hospital units and across arenas of care delivery, so one vision may not fit all. The factors affecting excellence on an obstetrics unit will differ from those on a pediatric or adult surgery unit. Similarly, factors affecting care in a home health agency will differ from those in an inpatient facility. The challenge is to help people think globally and act locally, and you do that by inviting them to translate—through conversations—the broader purpose of the organization into daily, purposeful behavior directed at defining and realizing their vision for serving patients or customers in their own work environment.

Transfer the Power from People to Purpose

The beauty of working on purpose is that it opens the way to transferring the power in a group or organization from people to purpose. When purpose is clear and people are dedicated to fulfilling it, no single person or group of persons runs the show; it is a partnership built on the contributions of each individual. Everyone plays together in a dynamic performance that calls forth the gifts of each player.

When purpose is running the show, decision-making can occur anywhere, responsibility is shared, and the interplay of people's strengths and talents yields amazing creativity. Small successes reverberate quickly through the system and mistakes become fonts of learning. Functional silos give way to collaborative playing fields. Given the chance to self-organize, people become increasingly flexible and, in turn, the system becomes increasingly orderly and stable over time.

Many people in your organization are already working on

purpose, like the nurses in the high touch general surgery unit or those in the rehab web-of-healing unit. Every day, in every corner of the organization, they are embodying what matters most. So draw attention to what working on purpose looks like.

Gather and share the stories of those who are doing it. They convey what working on purpose looks, feels, and sounds like in ways that scripts, classroom training, and wall-mounted mission statements can never capture. Trust that when people connect emotionally with what working on purpose looks like, they will want it for themselves.

When the purpose of every action is linked to personal purpose, and when personal purpose embodies a greater shared purpose, people are free to bring more of who and how they are to what they do. And the sheer diversity they bring is the fuel the organization needs to adapt and thrive in innovative, self-renewing ways.

4

Speak To and From the Heart

IT'S NOT HARD TO MAKE DECISIONS
WHEN YOU KNOW WHAT YOUR VALUES ARE.

Roy Disney

PEOPLE SHOULD KNOW WHAT YOU STAND FOR.

THEY SHOULD ALSO KNOW

WHAT YOU WON'T STAND FOR.

Unknown

Quick! Grab a pencil and jot down the four or five values that guide and direct your behavior and decision-making every day, in every interaction. Give yourself 30 seconds.

1 _____

2 _____

3 _____

4 _____

5 _____

Now look over the list. Were these values easy to identify, or did you struggle? Do they *really* guide what you say and do, or are they more akin to a "should" list that doesn't have much bearing on your actual behavior or decision making? Would the people you work with say that you embody these values even when the going gets tough? Or are they more likely say that you go with the flow or take the path of least resistance?

Identifying what we value sounds simple, but it is far from easy. We all have values that guide our behavior, yet few of us know, clearly and confidently, what those values are and how they shape our lives day by day, action by action. The more aware we are of what we value, the greater the opportunities to align and direct our actions accordingly.

That alignment is the essence of integrity, which, in turn, is one of the most important qualities people seek in leaders. When our personal values align with those of our organization and we embody them on a daily basis, we're in a powerful position to earn others' trust and to inspire and engage them in helping to fulfill the organization's purpose. When employees take the organization's values to heart and embody them with one another and with those they serve, values become the source of the organization's integrity.

As I said earlier, organizations are living systems. They are complex networks of human activity. Many of the difficulties we encounter as we thread our way through an organization arise from differences in values. Resolving those differences is not a matter of figuring out who's right and who's wrong. It is a matter of having a framework of core values that guide everyone's behavior, especially in difficult times. Women are well suited to the task because of our sensitivity to the importance of community and egalitarian networks in serving others.

The first half of this chapter offers a framework for thinking about values and several exercises for clarifying and using them in your everyday work. The second half gives you some practical tips for creating a values-guided organization through conversations and practices that model the way. So let's take a deeper look at the power of values, of speaking to and from the heart.

Behavior Has a Backseat Driver

Imagine a vertical continuum, as in Figure 2, that starts at the top with our behavior and ends at the bottom in our beliefs and values. Behavior is visible to everyone, so our level of awareness is often high: we can readily observe our own and others' behavior.

Figure 2: Beliefs to behavior: a continuum

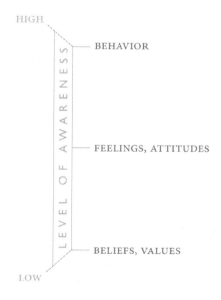

Behavior is driven by feelings and attitudes. When I am angry or upset, my behavior looks different than when I am excited and involved. Typically, our awareness of feelings and attitudes—our own as well as those of other people—is less than our awareness of behavior. And while we can *infer* what someone else is thinking or feeling, unless we confirm it by asking, we're merely running on assumptions.

Recall, for instance, the last time you gave a presentation, noticed someone staring out the window or scowling as you spoke, and were bothered by their behavior. What did you tell yourself? *He's bored. He thinks I'm an idiot. She's not paying any attention to this at all. She doesn't like what she's hearing.* Any or none of these might be the case. Unless you took the time to ask, you were running on assumption rather than accurate awareness.

Feelings and attitudes don't spring out of the blue. They are driven by deeper beliefs and values. Beliefs are mental ideas that we hold to be true, while values are principles or qualities that we think are worthwhile. Beliefs and values lie closer to our essence than feelings, attitudes, and behavior. Few of us dip into this deeper world. It's like the operating system in our personal computer, humming away in the background and making things happen. Only when something jolts us into awareness—like a system crash—do we begin to pay attention to it. And even then, we may just want to "fix" the problem rather than use it as an opportunity to gain a deeper level of awareness and understanding.

Because many of us are unclear about our personal values, our beliefs often take the driver's seat. If I believe, for instance, that I must have all the answers in order to look good and get ahead, I'll behave much differently than if I believe that we all have something to contribute or that questions unearth much more wisdom than answers. We've talked in earlier chapters about the importance of identifying and examining our beliefs and mental models. In this chapter, we add the importance of aligning our beliefs and behavior with what we most deeply value.

Listen to the Sounds of Experience

Our feelings—both physical and emotional—often send us important messages about our deeply held beliefs and personal values, if we're willing to listen. Several years ago, while waiting to board a flight in Washington D.C., I was paged by the gate agent. Normally, I'd simply respond. But this page made my heart pound, my mouth go dry, and my imagination kick into overdrive.

At the time, I was a single parent living on a shoestring. On off-parent weekends, I often took cheap round-trip flights to Washington to visit friends. This particular week, they had invited me for a weekend of sailing starting Friday morning. I had a supersaver non-redeemable, non-transferable ticket for later in the day and was too poor to pay a full fare upgrade. So early Friday morning, I went to my hometown airport, feigned an elaborate "I'm late" ruse, got past the gate agent, and made it onto the early flight.

When I heard my name booming through the speakers in Washington two days later, I feared that I'd been discovered and it was time to pay the piper. Not only was my body alerting me to something awry, but now my mind was racing. *The airline's going to charge me a gazillion dollars to get home ... WORSE ... I won't even get home ... Children's Services will take custody of my son ... they'll bring me up on charges of neglect, abandonment, utter failure as a parent....*

When I heard my name a second time, I slithered up to the gate. The agent, a dour fellow whose eyes never left the computer monitor, barked at me, "We have a SITUATION."

He paused, clicking away at the keyboard. "When we have a single mother traveling," he muttered, leaving me to think, *how does he know I'm a single mom?* "...We prefer to seat them together in the bulkhead ... where *YOU* are seated."

He paused again, eyes locked on the monitor. "Are you willing to accept a first-class upgrade to accommodate them?"

Whoaaa!! I was shocked back to the outer world. Here I was, drowning in guilt, and this guy was offering me a free upgrade to accommodate another mother traveling with kids!

Everything in me knew I had violated my own values by slipping onto that Friday plane without paying additional fare. And everything in me was letting me know: the pounding heart, the dry mouth, the guilt and embarrassment for what I'd done, the irrational self-talk about what was coming next. This event was a jolt of awareness that became a turning point in my life. I began paying much more attention to how the decisions I made affected my state of mind and my sense of well-being. Instead of letting feelings just influence my behavior, I started treating them as sources of information that reflected what was going on deeper down.

The more aware I became of those feelings as both mediators and messengers, the clearer I became about what I really valued and how I wanted to live. And that clarity shaped—and continues to shape—my life.

"Personal values," says Daniel Goleman, "are not lofty abstractions, but intimate credos that we ... *feel*. Our values translate into what has emotional power or resonance for us, whether negative or positive" (1998, 57).

He is right. Yet many of us never probe beneath that felt

sense. When something resonates positively with us, we usually want more of it. And when something resonates negatively, we automatically react by trying to get rid of it, even though reacting without awareness rarely serves us well.

If we are going to lead, we need to interrupt the automatic reaction and attend instead to what has emotional power for us. We need to know what energizes and depletes us, what we stand and won't stand for, what inspires and disgusts us. The deeper our awareness, the better we become at making sound choices, staying energized, and staying focused on creating what we want.

As leaders, if we want employees to invest their hearts in what they do, if we want them committed to serving patients and one another with compassion and equanimity, we need to be beacons of consistency at the center of the effort. When we can model the way, we make it possible for others to do the same.

Know What You Value

To nurture engagement and commitment among the people in your organization, you have to start in the foul rag-and-bone-shop of your own heart, by knowing what you most value and living in ways that reflect it. Then you can help others do the same.

This can be a significant challenge in cultures that reward action and results, not self-reflection and personal inquiry. While values are what guide our behavior, many people never take the time to think about what they really value. And while women are often more comfortable than men with emotion and its expression, we often are so absorbed in responding to and meeting others' emotional needs that we overlook our own needs and ignore what our own emotions are telling us.

So if you had trouble identifying five values in the opening exercise, here is an exercise to get you started. If you already have a clear set of personal values, live by them in bad times as well as good, and can stand firm even when afraid, you might find this section and the next two, on living what you value and practicing courage, helpful in guiding others to become similarly grounded.

Write down in your journal 8 or 10 values that represent who you are and what's most important to you. You can add to what you wrote earlier or use the list in the box below to prime the pump.

What do you value?

achievement	financial stability	optimism
adaptability	fitness	patience
balance	freedom	peace
challenge	fun	personal growth
change	happiness	recognition
collaboration	health	relationships
compassion	honesty	resilience
competence	humor	respect
creativity	integrity	security
curiosity	justice	spirituality
empathy	kindness	success
enthusiasm	learning	tolerance
excellence	love	tradition
faith	loyalty	wealth
family	meaningful work	wisdom

Next, read your list of words out loud, pausing after each one. Which ones *sound* like you? Which ones *feel* like a quality you want to be known for? Which ones resonate with that *felt sense* mentioned earlier? Now pick the five that feel most authentic, most genuine. Rank order them by importance, starting with #1, and write them in the left column below or in your journal.

<u>What I value ...</u>

1 _____ _____

_____

2 _____ _____

_____

3 _____ _____

_____

4 _____ _____

_____

5 _____ _____

_____

Now write a brief description in the right column of what each value means to you. Avoid dictionary definitions. Just write down the personal meaning each has for you. For example, "happiness" may mean "loving what I have" or "appreciating all that my life has to offer" or "being with those I love."

Finally, ask yourself, *How do these values show up in my daily life?* Write down three important behavioral examples for each. If tolerance is an important value, one example might be that you listen to differing views with an open, curious mind and a willingness to be influenced or changed by what you hear. If you value family, then maybe you show it in your work calendar with blocks of time set aside for daily gatherings and important family events and occasions.

How these show up in my daily life

1 _____

2 _____

3 _____

4 _____

5 _____

When you have finished, write your top five values on post-it notes and put them where you'll see them regularly. Then for the next few weeks, make a point of spending five minutes at the end of each day recording—yes, writing down—how you did or did not honor what you value in your daily routines. The sheer act of paying attention to how well your behavior and values align will likely trigger some subtle changes in your behavior.

Keeping a daily log is invaluable in helping you discover patterns over time. Maybe you are great at aligning behavior and values so long as you are not under much stress. Maybe your alignment shifts depending upon the person you're with. As you observe yourself in action, you may discover other values surfacing that you hadn't been aware of. You might discover, for instance, that in comfortable situations you value collaboration but in stressful situations you really value control. Or when you are around people senior to you, your behavior says you value safety or their approval.

The point here is to begin some simple self-observation and reflection for the purpose of learning more about who you are at the core, what matters most to you, and how—and whether— you express that true side of your nature in daily life.

Embody What You Value

While the above exercise is a start, what we value is far wider than the exercise suggests. Living by our values requires ongoing attention. When our values and behavior are out of alignment, the result is emotional static that makes life uncomfortable for us, like the guilt and shame that I felt in the airport. How often have you felt guilty going to the soccer game because you should be meeting with the cardiologists, or felt guilty being with the cardiologists because the soccer game started 20 minutes ago?

After you have clarified some important values and observed them in action, try the following exercise. Take a few minutes to jot down some examples of how your values and activities are *not* aligned. Maybe you say you value fitness and health, but your 70-hour workweeks and the pile of fast food bags and empty Starbucks cups in your car say otherwise. Maybe you say you value your family above all else, yet your calendar says the hospital is your first love. Or maybe you value meaningful work, but trudge off each day to wither in an unsatisfying job or organization.

What these examples illustrate clearly is that many times we have *competing* values. We want to be fit but feel compelled to work. We want to be with family but want to avoid being labeled 'not a team player.' We want to love what we do but feel overwhelmed by the fear of what we might lose if we moved to something else.

Sometimes what we think is a personal value driving of our success turns out to be just the opposite. How do we know? By the nature of the feelings we experience. When who we are and what we do are aligned, we feel good; when they're not aligned, we feel bad.

Take Katherine, for example. She rose through the nursing ranks to become chief operations officer of a community hospital. She saw herself as deeply committed to quality patient care and credited it as the primary driver of her success. When she got feedback from a 360 leadership survey, she was shocked to find that others experienced her as critical, highly controlling, and driven by her own personal agenda rather than by concern for others.

In a discussion of the 360 results, she told me that one reason she left patient care was because she felt tremendous pressure to avoid mistakes at all cost. The thought of causing suffering or harm to someone already ill or injured was more than she could bear. In fact, she could recall every clinical mistake she'd ever made. Yet she had virtually no memories of the hundreds of patients who'd thrived under her care.

Her intense commitment to quality care, which she carried into her managerial work, began to look different through the lens of others' experiences of her. She began to see its dark side: the need to avoid any mistakes and, in turn, the criticism she feared mistakes would provoke. Her fear was evident in myriad ways, from the tension she carried in her tiny body to the rare smile that graced her face, from the pressure she put on direct reports and colleagues around quality issues to the difficulty she had with trying anything new.

When I asked how much energy and enjoyment she got from her work, she began to sob. Acutely aware of the need to excel, and exquisitely sensitive to her own shortcomings, she'd found less and less enjoyment in either patient care or management. "Some days," she said, "I have to drag myself out of bed, and the idea of facing another day simply drains me."

Katherine's emotional world was giving her powerful messages: she was driven by fear and the desire to *avoid* mistakes and criticism, not by what she most deeply valued.

In the following weeks, I asked her to pay attention to the people she most admired. What did they embody that she valued? Observation taught her that it was their kindness and open acceptance of themselves and others. So we created a plan that called for her to practice both of these and to make a daily written note of what she'd done to embody them herself.

The work was not easy for her. It took time, focus, energy, and the courage to accept and let go of an old strategy for protecting herself against her own fears. The shadow side often reared its ugly head. But in time, she discovered that kindness and acceptance, including the willingness to let go of being perfect, led to deeper, more meaningful connections with others and to a newfound sense of energy and enthusiasm for her work.

Of course, she still had an intense desire to provide quality care to every patient in her hospital. What changed was her base of operation. No longer driven by the need to perform—and to have others perform—flawlessly, she was free to use her work as an outlet for expressing what she most valued. As her expectations and behavior changed, so did her relationships and results. Work became a source of joy and satisfaction. And her openness created the space for others to explore and experiment with new ways of improving quality of care. This is the kind of transformation that's possible when we anchor work in the heart.

So if what you think you value isn't producing energy and a sense of fulfillment, you may need to do what Katherine did: observe yourself in action, pay attention to what you admire in others, and then create a practice for yourself of embodying those qualities.

Trust the Wisdom of Your Body and Heart

We have several domains of experience: mental, emotional, physical, spiritual. They are interconnected. So we can enter and alter the cycle at any of those points. Katherine started with the mental or, more specifically, with the cognitive. My airport experience started with the physical.

Any time our behavior leads to negative feelings, we're likely caught—as Katherine and I were—in a mismatch between what we're doing and what we really value. So pay attention to your energy level, using questions like these:

* What energizes me?
* When do I feel open, compassionate, and expansive?

* What depletes me?
* When do I feel the need to circle the wagons and protect myself?
* What do these experiences suggest in terms of a deeper appreciation of what's important to me?

Embodying what we value is energizing; protecting ourselves or playing safe depletes us. While our minds can drift into the past and future, our bodies only know the present. So tune in to the ebb and flow of what you're experiencing physically at any given moment and name the feelings. They'll take you where you need to go.

When the physical feelings are negative—throat tightening, tears rising up, hands sweating, body feeling flushed—they often are the thin film separating us from our inner fears: of not being perfect, of not being enough, of lacking support or love or ability. As tough as it is, when these feelings occur, slow down and give them your full attention. Simply observe and experience how you are in that moment, and see where it takes you. Let your awareness expand.

When you can sit with a negative feeling without judging it or trying to change or get rid of it, a remarkable thing happens. The feeling begins to transform into something deeper, something more sensitive and expansive. Anger can give way to compassion, defensiveness can transform into acceptance, fear can dissolve into curiosity and wonder. Who you actually *are* begins to emerge. It is a moment of presence, and it is powerful.

Sometimes, just interrupting an automatic response and becoming aware of what is occurring in the moment can create a new choice for you. For instance, what public face does your fear wear? Simply observe yourself in action. When you're afraid, do you become cold and controlling? Passive and accommodating? Defensive? Dismissive? What values does your

behavior—*independent of your intentions and explanations*—
say are important to you? Put your story aside, let go of the need
to justify, and ask yourself, *What values am I modeling?* Then
step back into your story. Are the two consistent and congruent?
Does your behavior reflect your story of what you say is
important?

When your public face is out of synch with how you want
to be known, then you can choose, as Katherine did, to practice
being the way you want. Doing so may be scary because you're
trading a familiar protective posture for a stance that is much
closer to the heart. So if you find fear arising, pay attention to
it. Give it a name. Ask yourself, *What is on the line? What part
of me is feeling threatened or is at risk of being exposed?* Then
remind yourself that this is just one small part of you and that
you have a choice: to pull back and stay safe or to stand firm and
ground yourself in what you most deeply value.

You can also reframe your notion of fear so that it has
positive rather than negative connotations for you. Technically,
fear is a biological feeling of risk or danger, whether real or
imagined. It's a defensive response that motivates us to escape
to safety. So when we get butterflies or a dry mouth or pounding
heart, we immediately sense fear and often react, without
awareness, to eliminate it or escape from it. Yet in modern times,
most of what we fear is imagined, not real; it arises from our
self-talk. The more willing we are to slow down, acknowledge
the fear, and reframe it as a source of energy rather than a scary
scenario we're spinning for ourselves, the more purposefully we
can respond.

Actors, athletes, and other performing artists can teach us a
lot about reframing our response to fear. James Lipton, dean of
the New York Actors Studio, was interviewing the actor Andy
Garcia. Lipton asked, "When you read a script and it scares you,

is that an invitation or an impediment?"

"Fear is good," said Garcia. "The challenge is what makes me excel." Take a moment and think of a situation at work that scares you. Get the scenario clear in your mind. Then try on Garcia's interpretation. It requires that you suspend judgment about the situation and begin viewing it instead as a challenge to help you excel. Are you willing to make the shift?

In another interview, Michael J. Fox told Lipton, "When you walk through the fear of what people will think, something happens. We don't know what'll happen, but there's at least a 50-50 chance it'll be good, and that's enough for me." Those are powerful words from a man whose career was cut short by Parkinson's disease.

Courage Comes from the Heart

It helps to remember that fear is always, *always* rooted in the future. We can handle what's right here, right now. It is our fear of what might happen *next* that scares us. When we treat what *might* happen as if it were reality and back down from it, we miss the opportunity to grow into what we're really capable of becoming. Remember that old acronym from the 1980s: FEAR is only False Evidence About Reality.

Think about the times when you wanted to speak up in meetings but held back, only to hear someone else voicing and getting credit for expressing the same ideas. Or the times you observed managers or clinicians behaving badly but didn't want to raise questions and risk damaging the relationship or incurring their wrath. Most likely it was your fear of what *might* happen that was holding you back.

These and hundreds of situations like them call for us to be mindful of who we are and what we want, and to act with courage. Courage is not just the quality we call forth in the face of fear. It is the willingness to stand up for what we most deeply value. The word "courage" comes from the Latin "cor" or heart. Acting with courage means working from the heart. The clearer we get about what we deeply value, the more grounded we become in the heart and the more easily we can work from a base of authenticity and wisdom.

Katherine learned to ground herself in kindness and open acceptance. The general surgery unit staff grounded themselves in compassion and high touch. The rehab staff grounded themselves in a web of healing. What tethers you to the heart and represents who you truly are? If you're not sure, this is the time to start the journey. Healthcare systems are engaged every day in issues of life and death, joy and suffering. Patients need caregivers who can bring empathy and compassion to the bedside, and administrators who can bring the same to their leadership. When the healthcare environment is filled with mixed messages about what's most important, the ones who pay the price are often those receiving care.

Your Organization's Values Are Always on Display

Like purpose or mission, values are not something that can be instilled in people through training classes or a motivational rally. They are not something we create, but rather something we discover through our own experience. In working with dozens of organizations over the years, I have learned that regardless of whether I am talking with an executive or a patient care aide, what the organization values always makes itself known.

In some systems, I notice patterns of cool respect or aloofness, in others I find a compassionate and friendly spirit, in still others I see patterns of caution, secrecy, or distrust. These reflect values in action, and they produce entirely different experiences, not only for those who work in an organization but for those who are passing through as patients or customers. Start observing meetings in your own organization, with attention to questions like the ones highlighted below.

Observe a typical meeting in your own organization.

* How do people interact with each other? What behaviors do you observe? What behaviors do you not see?
* What do people talk about? What do they not talk about?
* When do people speak freely? When do they fade into silence?
* When and how are differences of opinion surfaced and resolved?
* What values do you see being exhibited in people's behavior?
* Are they consistent with the organization's stated values?
* Are they consistent with your personal values?

While an organization's values may be tough to measure or quantify, they are clearly observable in people's behavior. It doesn't take long for employees to figure out what an organization's leaders really value and to start behaving accordingly. In organizations where leaders hold everyone accountable for treating one another according to a clear set of guiding principles, like the organization that valued SPIRIT, we find people willingly participating and shaping their behavior in creative yet consistent ways. In organizations where mixed messages are the norm, we find resignation, hostility, cynicism, and distrust.

So two high leverage behaviors for you in leading are to embody the organization's values and to help others align their own values with those of the organization. Doing both reinforces your commitment and gives you a powerful platform from which to work. In a study of over 2300 managers, Kouzes and Posner found that clarifying and articulating "personal values has a significant payoff for both managers and their organizations. [They found] that shared values

* Foster strong feelings of personal effectiveness
* Promote high levels of company loyalty
* Facilitate consensus about key organization goals and stakeholders
* Encourage ethical behavior
* Promote strong norms about working hard and caring
* Reduce levels of job stress and tension" (1987, 154).

Even if your investment fosters only half of these results, wouldn't the payoff be worth it?

The CEO who led with SPIRIT modeled, in every action, the values that he and the organization held dear. What I discovered was that those core values, embodied throughout the organization, gave it an internal stability that couldn't be matched by external rules, regulations, and structure. Frontline employees used the values to guide their day-to-day interactions with patients and one another. Managers used the values to guide their decision making and, when faced with tough decisions, to question themselves and one another about the emotional fallout of various courses of action. Operating from this core of shared values, anyone in the organization could respond quickly and appropriately to difficult situations or to new opportunities. The organization's SPIRIT guided decisions about everything from doing something unusual in serving a patient to selecting which new service lines to pursue.

Lots of organizations have values statements. What they lack is discipline and consistency in bringing those values to life in everyday practice. Perhaps it reflects the common masculine style of being results driven: get those values statements formulated and on the wall, check them off the to-do list, then tackle the next item on the list. Perhaps it reflects a patriarchal discomfort with talking about feelings and values in the workplace. The reason is not as important as the fact that creating a values-guided organization will not happen until people at all levels can talk about and hold one another accountable to a set of shared values or guiding principles. "Do as I say, not as I do" doesn't work with kids, and it certainly doesn't work with adults.

So step into the lead by making values-guided behavior the norm for you and those you work with.

Start and Keep the Conversations Coming

If your organization already has a set of values or guiding principles, take them off the wall and into the hallways. Invite people to discuss what each means to them and what it looks like in action. What do words like *compassion, integrity, service, quality, trust,* and *respect* mean to individuals? How do they look and feel in exchanges with patients? With physicians? With non-service providers? With subordinates and bosses?

This is not a one-shot effort. Let these conversations unfold over time. And keep in mind that there aren't any right or wrong answers, only different perceptions. The more people are invited to express and explore their perceptions, the deeper the pool from which you can draw shared understandings.

Don't be surprised when you find gaps between what people value personally and what they think the organization values. While leaders often have honorable intentions about being values-driven, they are also human and thus prone to espousing one thing while rewarding another. The discrepancy is not what's deadly; lack of awareness and the unwillingness to examine discrepancies are what lead to problems.

So as a leader, start by encouraging greater awareness. If people see gaps between the organization's stated values and what they observe in everyday behavior, then put aside the stated values and work with one another to describe what your organization or department or unit *does* stand for. As James Audubon said, when the bird and the book don't match, trust the bird.

If your organization has no set of guiding principles, then go in search of them. What do people want their relationships with each other and with patients to be like? If they're struggling to answer, then ask them who is already embodying values that everyone admires? Tread carefully here. People may be guarded and reluctant to speak openly. Values lie near the heart, so for those with years of experience in a controlling environment, speaking openly is risky business. It could take weeks or even months of conversation before people begin to trust what you're doing and open up. Stay the course.

Encourage people to voice their own experience and, when they offer it, simply acknowledge it. By anchoring discussions in the first person "I," you minimize the "us-them" shame and blame mentality that's rampant in a lot of organizations. You don't have to agree with them; you simply have to listen and acknowledge. In the workplace, people so rarely feel heard that the sheer act of listening and acknowledging helps strengthen the bond with them.

As women, we are often quite good at listening and acknowledging. It is one of the ways we cement relationships. When we treat these conversations as explorations of multiple points of view, all of which are legitimate, we not only enrich our understanding of what our organization or unit currently stands for, but we create a safe space within which people can begin to make significant shifts. Think, for example, of the times that a disturbing situation has rattled through your own brain for days on end and you finally shared it with another person. The sheer act of voicing it aloud to someone you trust often makes it seem less powerful, less threatening. So step into your own power and create for others a safe, non-judging environment.

Give People a Voice

Through conversation, we also give people opportunities to voice—literally—what is most important to them. Pay attention to and use this. It is a powerful way to intervene at a non-cognitive level. Recall the exercise from earlier in this chapter about speaking your own values aloud to see which ones sound and feel right. Ask people to speak aloud what they know and then describe how it feels physically. Have them experiment with speaking values—their own and the organization's—using different words. Many times when the words and the feelings fit, people experience a noticeable physical shift. For some, it is a sense of deep relief, for others, a sense of expansiveness. Whatever its form, it is powerful because it connects them with what's deeply true.

Several years ago, I conducted a research project that involved having nurses evaluate the humanistic qualities of resident physicians on their units (Butterfield and Mazzaferri, 1991). We were validating a tool for assessing how humane, empathic, and compassionate the residents were in interactions with patients. The project triggered a lot of animosity between nurses and residents, so a colleague and I met with both groups to better understand their perspectives (Butterfield and Pearsol, 1990). The nurses were angry because they thought that residents didn't respect their knowledge and experience. The residents were angry because they thought nurses lacked the technical skill to evaluate them.

When we brought the two groups together, one of the residents said, "We've spent years in medical school and know a hell of a lot more about medicine than most nurses. Why can't you *respect* that?"

"You're probably right," said one of the nurses. "Except we weren't asked to evaluate your *clinical* competence. We were asked to evaluate how you interact with patients. We're both working for the same thing—the best possible outcome for the patient. And while you're still learning medicine, we've been caring for patients for years."

She paused for a minute, and then said, "We're your allies, not your adversaries. We *want* you to do well because then our patients do well. You have to be competent. But you have to be sensitive to the patient as well. Sometimes, the best medicine you have is your compassion."

The room was silent for several seconds. The tension dissolved. Some residents hung their heads. Others just sat quietly. Finally, a third-year resident spoke up. "You're right. For two years, I've been terrified of killing someone. There's so much to learn, so much to juggle, so much to think about that it's easy to forget the human side." Giving voice to this shared value and the purpose driving it was a turning point for both groups.[*]

What you are doing when you ask people to voice their values is anchoring them in what they know to be true. From there, you can begin to generate shared understandings of abstract terms ["respect," "service," "integrity"] by defining

---

[*]I don't know to what degree gender differences fueled the animosity between these two groups and to what degree the animosity was related to differences in roles. I suspect both were in play. Gender differences do arise and when they occur, keep in mind the distinctions between how women and men use language. Remember that when men make statements that sound like edicts or jump in to fix the problem, they are tuned to the task message while women typically tune to the relationship message. We can acknowledge both without favoring either; more importantly, by acknowledging both, we avoid falling into the common pit of taking the other person's behavior personally.

what they look and feel and sound like in action. Most misunderstandings arise because people attach different meanings to the same situations and then treat their own meaning as "truth" rather than as one of many possible interpretations. Rarely have I met a person in healthcare whose intentions are malicious. Quite the contrary. Healthcare attracts people who want to help others. When conflicts or misunderstandings arise, it's almost always because people are working from their own personal—and undisclosed—definitions or interpretations.

Through conversations, you not only clarify what your core values mean, but you create opportunities for people to broaden their own perspectives, perhaps even to think actively about concepts they've taken for granted in the past. If your organization already has a set of values or guiding principles, these conversations set the groundwork for co-creating an environment that actually embodies them in everyday life. If your organization has no clear guiding principles, then these conversations invite people to discover and define how they want to work together. As they become more aware of how they want to be with each other and with those they serve, you can support their growing awareness by encouraging them to put into practice—and hold each other accountable for practicing—being the way they want to be.

Translate Conversations into Practice

Changing behavior requires high levels of self-awareness. Aligning what we *say* we value with what we actually *do* value takes time and self-reflection. You can model the way by asking others to let you know when your words and actions seem misaligned. Invite their feedback and then listen openly, with the intention of reaching a richer understanding of how different meanings assigned to the same values translates to different interpretations of behavior.

Yes, this is scary, especially when you are putting your own behavior on the line. But in time, with awareness, reflection, and a little help from your colleagues, you will learn how to embody your own and the organization's values in ways that set you up as a beacon of integrity.

Agree to support—and gently challenge—one another in learning to embody, in every action, the qualities you say you value. When everyone agrees to work by a set of shared values, each person now has both the responsibility *and the authority* to speak up in service to those principles. As women, we often are reluctant to impose our values on others or to confront inappropriate behavior. Think about the number of times you've observed someone behaving badly and not wanted to be the lone voice speaking up. When people agree to honor a set of clear and shared values, they are not only empowered to speak up; they now have a responsibility to the group to do so. Within this context, your speaking up becomes the model. As others find the courage to join you, you'll gain the leverage you need to effect change in other parts of the organization.

Start or end staff meetings with informal discussions about how people are translating values into action and the challenges they are encountering in doing so. Consider posting examples of values-driven behavior to reinforce it. By drawing attention to challenges and successes, you increase people's awareness of values-driven behavior *and* the likelihood that they will pull their own behavior into greater alignment around those values.

Also consider engaging people in conversations about the relative importance of organizational values. Values give people internal guidelines to use in making decisions. When we encounter situations in which we must choose between competing values, knowing the relative importance of each gives us greater guidance in making sound decisions.

For example, put yourself in the shoes of a manager in an organization with these four values: compassion, integrity, financial stewardship, and respect. Imagine that you have a direct report who often misses work. She has a disabled husband and a chronically ill child at home. Her absenteeism is costly to the organization and her co-workers, who often must fill in for her. Because she is often stressed, she has been rude and inappropriately short with co-workers on several occasions. You know that she is the sole source of support for her household and is a good worker when she's not weighted down by a crisis at home. As her boss, would you act from *compassion* for her plight? Or in support of *respect* for her co-workers? Or in service to *stewarding* the organization's resources? How would your own *integrity* be affected? While there is no "right" answer, the clearer you are about the relative importance of each core value, the more guidance you have in reaching a decision about how to act.

People at the front lines must make choices daily, and having a clear sense of the priority of multiple values gives them the freedom to act locally and responsibly. In addition, when you explore priorities, you are sowing the seeds for self-direction. Remember that organizations don't have values; *people* do. And people are living systems. Unlike machines, they are capable of self-organizing, of adapting in effective and self-enhancing ways. All they need are some guidelines. That is the value of values. When people know what is important, and when they have the authority and the responsibility to hold themselves and one another accountable for what's important, they will rise to the occasion.

Build Loyalty on Principles and Purpose

As women, we have the advantage of being more comfortable and familiar with the world of emotion than many of our male colleagues. The shadow side is that we often don't know how to harness our emotions in service to what we most value. Perhaps that is why the topics of values, purpose, and alignment of word with deed have often been treated as too soft and touchy-feely for the business world. They do not fit neatly into the kinds of managerial controls that we normally associate with bringing order out of chaos and that govern operations in most organizations.

Yet purpose and values are what bring clarity and meaning to our work. They are the foundation upon which all else is built.

The ideas and exercises in these first few chapters may seem far removed from the demands of your usual workday. So you may be tempted to ignore them and attend instead to the fires burning outside your office door. But they are the means by which you define the core of your organization's identity and with which you build, collectively, a solid foundation. They are the path of leading, not of managing.

In examining how leaders build lasting relationships, author Frederick Reichheld found that "To build loyalty, ... you must first be loyal to others by helping them build relationships on the right principles. Then, your leadership actions must not only reinforce these principles, but embody them" (2001, 18). When you are willing to model the way, others will follow. The cry for leadership these days, both within and beyond the healthcare industry, is loud and consistent. People want to belong to organizations that stand for something meaningful. They want to know that what they do and how they do it have meaning and merit.

I talked earlier about our desire for a sense of fulfillment from our work. When we ground ourselves and our relationships in what is most meaningful to us, we create an energizing force that pulls others into its field. "And when people follow your example," says Reichheld, "when they begin to restructure their own network of relationships according to your model, when they begin to place the interests of their partners and customers ahead of their own, watch out! You will have initiated a chain reaction with breathtaking consequences" (2001,18).

II

There is no formula for creating a stellar community of care and service, no algorithmic "if A, then B." More policies and procedures will not do it, nor will a set of best practices imported from elsewhere or a new strategic plan, no matter how detailed. Top-down approaches lead us away from where we need to go.

Transformi.ng an organization into a community of service is a journey, a way of being and working that supports the continual process of *becoming*. Our capacity to create already exists; it is part of our self-organizing nature as living creatures. What we need are work environments that support us in transforming capacity into meaningful contribution. Women can bring much to the nurturing of those environments.

In Part 1, we outlined the basics for the journey and our role as guides. Change the frame and we change the meaning. Explore our contribution and we find new opportunities to make a difference. Discover our shared purpose and we breathe new meaning into everyday activities. Speak to what we value and others will join us. We are not alone.

Part 1 also introduced the context within which the work unfolds: relationships and conversation. Relationships with our inner world and with each other are pivotal, not peripheral, to everything we do. Conversations are how we discover what matters, share what we know, and dream of what might be. They also are how we support, challenge, and inspire one another.

Part 2 delves into more specific ways of using our natural strengths to create a climate for contribution and discovery.

Build webs of inclusion and connection. Embrace not knowing. Value questions over answers. Hold a space for practicing and learning. Trust in the power of story and the wisdom of our own experience.

These are guidelines, not prescriptions, for engaging one another in an ongoing dance with information, ideas, and intentions. They are simple to understand and often difficult to do because they require us to stay mindful of the choices we have and make. Every action has the potential to affect the whole, regardless of our place in the organization. Hold a space for our own curiosity and we find new ways to influence and shape our world. Hold a similar space for others and our collective intelligence can yield high engagement, creative responses to the unexpected, and a remarkable capacity to thrive when times are tough.

5

Build Webs of Inclusion

JUST REMAIN IN THE CENTER, WATCHING.
AND THEN FORGET THAT YOU ARE THERE.

Lao-Tsu

Webs Are What We Do Best

Women have worked in patriarchal systems for years. We know
the political nature of making it in a "man's" world and the
emotional downsides of doing so. We've learned to survive in a
top-down world and navigate around the networks of exclusion
that men have used for years to get ahead and retain control.
But most of us prefer—and are better at cultivating—inclusive,
lateral networks that bring people together for a shared purpose
and that rely on a much less dominant and more supportive form
of authority.

During tough times, we humans adapt most readily when we
have a supportive environment combined with pressure to learn
and grow from our own experiences. While authority-driven

hierarchies give us the illusion of safety and protection, webs of inclusion give us the chance to become the authors our own lives.

Jenna's approach is a prime example of what this looks like in action. The head of quality assurance and performance improvement in a large community hospital, she spends much of her time on the floors talking with nursing and ancillary staff. When she works with a unit having problems, her initial focus is on listening and learning. What happens to patients that should not be happening? How do staff members want the unit to function? What ideas do they have about ways to work differently? What can they learn from their patients? Whose work do they most admire and what do they think is admirable?

Her approach is one of inquiry. She enters conversations with an open mind and a desire to learn about the experience of those on the floors, like Gallwey with the AT&T operators. If someone gets defensive, she drops all discussion of content and focuses instead on how the person is interpreting the situation. In this way she is able to drill down to the feelings and deeper issues that she senses have been triggered.

She steers away from talk about who did what or who said what and aims instead for a firm grasp of the other person's framework, the subtle meanings and assumptions going on behind the scenes. As she eases those assumptions to the surface, she helps reframe them in constructive ways and then encourages staff to test them in practice. She also asks regularly about what's working well, which focuses people's attention on positives and possibilities rather than on negatives and ruts.

I have observed her several times and each time the other person's feelings and position softened in ways that yielded a desire to move forward rather than against. How is she able to do this? She starts with an abiding belief that they are all in this together. "My job," she says, "isn't to go in as the answer woman and fix what's wrong. These people know far more about what's going on in their unit than I do. My job is to partner with them in ways that give us all a greater understanding of what's actually occurring and then use what we've learned to try something else."

In Jenna's world, competence is tied to asking questions that engage people and lead them to new options. Since her competence is not tied to being right, she does not have to defend or argue the merits of her position. She can stay open to others' perspectives. And when people get defensive, she doesn't take it personally and go on the offense. Instead, she dips beneath the surface to explore the deeper feelings being stirred. Since she works from the assumption that everyone brings valuable experience to a discussion, she can listen with an open mind. She also conveys the powerful message that others are competent and capable of making contributions too, which strengthens rather than weakens their emotional connection with her.

Finally, she takes a non-traditional path to finding ways that work. Rather than focusing on problems to solve, she focuses on the people affected by those problems. It is a subtle but powerful shift of focus. She encourages people whose units are having problems to talk with staff on high performing units, learn what's working well, and experiment with it on their own floors. She clearly knows what actions would make a difference, but she has a deep faith in their collective ability to find actions that work for them. She also knows that linking people in ways that allow them to discover different possibilities on their own is far more powerful than giving them directives. In short, the thrill of discovery gives people a jolt of positive energy, an emotional charge that directives miss entirely.

The people she works with love her, and she gets great results.

Jenna is an example of someone who operates in a web-like rather than a top-down structure, even though she works in a classic patriarchal system. At the center of her world is the patient, surrounded by a network of relationships Jenna has formed with clinical caregivers. She moves throughout the system making connections, linking people who otherwise would have little contact with one another, asking powerful questions, and supporting every effort to question the status quo when it is not serving patients in optimal ways.

Her story is our starting point for Part 2 because webs are the structural networks by which we pull people together and transfer power from people to purpose. This chapter hits some high points for building webs of inclusion across an organization, starting with examples of ways to involve everyone, clinical and non-clinical alike, in shaping patient experiences. These are not behavioral prescriptions; they're merely ideas to stimulate your own thinking and imagination.

Living systems abide by rules we cannot see. In top-down organizations, inviting people to work differently often triggers negative reactions, so the next section offers strategies for working through and beyond people's negativity.

Webs and lateral networks have a much different power structure than hierarchies. So the last few sections invite you to think of power through the broad lens of relationships rather than the narrow lens of control.

Involve Everyone. Everyone.

There are no "right" answers when it comes to creating webs and nurturing alignment in the workplace. You don't need a four-page plan or a RACI [responsibility assignment] matrix to get started. You just need to act with the intention of generating connections and a sense of belonging.

Use purpose and values as your context. Pick a point of entry that's meaningful for you: some aspect of service or the work environment that you want to be different in the future. Invite others to join you. Seed their curiosity. Ask questions and listen deeply to their responses. Get them observing, talking about, and imagining what *might be*. Let them participate at whatever level is most relevant for them. Above all, believe in them and in their capacity to make a difference, both individually and collectively.

Be patient focused

Being patient focused is different from being patient driven. The former helps employees retain a sense of the organization's purpose and identity while the latter can dissolve into trying to become all things to all patients. As women, we know how easy it is to slip into this be-all mindset. That's why being clear about purpose is so important; it becomes a gauge by which you can assess the relative merit of everything you do or are asked to do.

If you're in a senior position, consider examining your entire service process from the patient's rather than the provider's perspective. Set aside some days to follow a few patients through the house. Yes, this takes time as well as the willingness to slow down and observe what's actually occurring. It also takes the willingness to suspend belief in your own stories about the service process so that you can see the process with fresh eyes. Trust that in the big scheme of things, this investment will more than pay for itself.

So clear your schedule for a few days (yes, you *can* do it) and set out to experience your hospital from the patients' perspective. Wait while they wait. Eat what they eat. Observe. Listen. Take notes. Imagine what you would want for yourself and those you love. Use what you learn to guide what you do.

If you're in an entry-level or middle management position, look for like-minded people in other departments and start building collaborative relationships around the experience of the patient. Invite your counterparts in dietary and pharmacy to lunch. Learn what they do. Appreciate how their work complements yours. Explore with them how you can work together to create great experiences for patients. This may require the courage to challenge existing processes, but if you start with a beginner's mind and put the patient's experience at the center of effort, you'll discover lots of ways to influence the system. Chapters 7 and 8 offer some guidelines and examples for doing this.

Distinguish customer service from serving customers

Traditional "customer service" puts the in-house process at the center of activity and views those further up the hierarchy as the ones in charge. Managers issue the manuals and frontline workers carry out the processes. By contrast, serving customers—creating the best experience possible for them—puts the patient at the center of activity and treats those at the front lines of contact as the ones in charge. Modern-day "customer service" is about efficiency. Why else do we use automated phone systems that either toss customers into an electronic maze or route them to call centers half a planet away? Creating a great experience is about effectiveness.

Which mental model are you working from? Are you one of the many managers trying to manage in-house *processes* in order to create specific *outcomes,* or are you more aligned with the great service organizations who manage *expectations* in order to create great customer *experiences?* The mental model you work from will determine the results you get.

If you work in clinical care ...

Engage caregivers in exploring care from the patient's perspective and identifying ways of creating flawless experiences for them. Think big. Think interdisciplinary and interdependent. Get the emergency department staff talking with the bed management czar, housekeeping, inpatient unit managers, transporters, and discharge planners. It doesn't have to be formal; you can do it over meals or during breaks in a corner of the cafeteria. The point is to keep directing people's attention to the system as a whole until they get the message: what they do, even if it seems small, affects many others and extends across both time and place. They are more powerful than they realize.

Encourage people across departments to meet with and educate one another about the frustrations and successes they experience. Encourage your staff to work in another department for a week or two. The purpose is for them to taste firsthand what life in those departments is like. Yes, it's time away from your department. It is also time that pushes them to think more empathically about what others face and more systemically about how interconnected they are with people they rarely see. Set aside 5 or 10 percent of your own time to do the same. Debrief with your staff regularly so you can all learn what makes for seamless care and great patient experiences within a very complex system.

If you work in a non-clinical area ...

If you're in marketing or human resources, transcription or laboratory services, have your staff visit and interview people in the departments they serve to learn how their in-house customers view doing business with them. The purpose of these visits is twofold: to increase their awareness of how others experience them and to connect them back to the patient through the daisy chain of in-house customers.

Use a simple interview protocol like the one below to get the group started.

How do you experience us?

Ask in-house customers questions like the following:
* From your perspective, what does the actual process of doing business with our department entail?
    * You just want the steps here, not any interpretations or judgments.
    * Map the details—literally—so everyone sees what actions are involved.
* What is your experience of doing business with us using this process?
    * Now you're inviting interpretations and evaluation of the experience.
* How do you think this process affects the experiences of patients and their families?
* What could we do differently in order to create a great working relationship with your department?
* What else is important for us to know that we haven't covered already?
* What does the idea of doing that evoke in me?

When your staff have a clear and detailed understanding
of what it's actually like to do business with them, explore
questions like the following:

* Whose needs are each of our processes set up to serve,
   our own or our customers'?
* How do we want to be known by people in other
   departments?
* What would we have to do differently to create ideal
   working relationships with these other departments?
* What might we gain from developing closer
   relationships with in-house customers and having
   personal connections across the organization?

Work from Questions, Not Answers

It's easy to assume that managers are supposed to have the
answers because that's another part of the top-down belief
structure. But take a step back and think about how we women
naturally form and maintain personal relationships. We ask
questions. We listen to others' experiences with curiosity. We
share our own experiences. We readily admit to not knowing and
use it to deepen our exchanges with others.

Most of us know that having the answers and telling others
what to do doesn't produce what we want. So when we're
building webs, especially webs for holding people steady
through the tough work of finding their own answers in uncertain
times, questions are much more powerful ways of working.

Asking open-ended questions shifts responsibility back
to those doing the work. Asking questions that turn people's
attention to what they don't know pushes them beyond their own
expertise and into the realm of new knowledge and ideas. It's
also a great way to make learning more important than knowing.

Most discussions are dominated by people advocating their own positions rather than listening actively and deeply to one another. So practice asking questions that build on what someone else has said. It is a powerful act. It conveys respect for the person speaking and for the capacity of the group to generate a deeper and shared understanding of the situation. It also conveys respect for the power of listening in creating strong and trusting networks.

Expect the Negative and Work with It

If your organization is hierarchical and problem oriented, expect to hear a lot of negative comments as people begin to acknowledge and voice the degree to which inclusion and alignment are lacking. They will quickly drift into complaints and fix-it thinking, perhaps even blaming you or those higher up in the organization for their plight. It is a signal of their level of frustration and despair.

Don't take it personally, and don't let it stop you. One of the downsides to our relating nature as women is the tendency to personalize others' remarks and actions. Doing so keeps us tethered to others' expectations and approval when we need to be grounded in our own values, strengths, and purpose.

So when people rail against the system or other employees, don't get pulled into their story. Stay grounded in what you know. Practice listening and acknowledging their frustration. You do not have to agree with or share their perspective, only hear and appreciate it. Being witness to their experience, without the press to fix it or "correct" it, is powerfully affirming. It conveys to people a message they rarely get at work: *I hear you.* Not until they feel heard are they free to move forward.

Witnessing without taking action also keeps responsibility for their experience where it belongs, with them rather than with you. Webs are egalitarian networks. Within them, individuals take and share rather than relinquish responsibility, and that is what you want to nurture.

WITNESSING SOMEONE'S EXPERIENCE
—WITHOUT THE PRESS TO "FIX" OR "CORRECT" IT—
IS POWERFULLY AFFIRMING. IT SAYS
I HEAR YOU.

Sometimes people get stuck in complaint mode. They don't know how to move forward because they don't know how they are contributing to the situation. When their story doesn't change, listening unconditionally can become a form of collusion. To avoid colluding, stay outside the situation so you can see it from a broader vantage point and offer frames or perspectives that they can't see. When the frame changes, the story changes. The art here is to work with permission, presence, and heart.

Here is an example. A few years ago, I was doing a workshop with a group of healthcare managers, and they wanted to talk about "problem" employees. One woman raised her hand and said loudly and curtly, "So what do you do when someone repeatedly disrespects you and you have to work with him every day?"

The room went silent. I said gently, "I'm going to answer your question with another question. Do you think this man gets up in the morning, looks in the mirror, and asks himself, 'How can I disrespect her today? What can I do to set her off?'"

She paused for a long moment, and then answered, "Well, no, I don't."

"So," I said, "what other possible ways might you interpret his behavior that don't involve you and that don't leave you feeling frustrated and powerless?" It only took a few minutes for her to generate several possibilities. The more she spoke, the more her voice relaxed. The brittle, angry energy of her initial question melted into a lighter, more positive tone.

Setting her story within a larger context gave her a chance to disengage her "self" from the situation and explore some other perspectives. Any time we reframe like this, we're simply broadening the context or changing the meaning of a situation in order to create a more positive experience.

Reframing works best when we ask permission to offer a different point of view, especially when someone is emotionally entangled in a situation. Asking permission conveys respect. It does not assume that our opinion is the only one that matters, so it levels the playing field. It also honors the other person's right to say no—a right that is often disregarded in the workplace. Yes, asking permission has connotations that may disadvantage you in other kinds of workplace conversations. But in situations like this, it is a relationship builder.

If a person asks directly for input, I treat it as a request and step into the conversation, like I did in the situation above.

If a person is complaining and not requesting anything from me, I ask for permission before offering anything else. I might say, "Would you like a different perspective?" or "Would a different way of looking at this be useful for you?"

If the person says no, then I honor her decision. It tells me that she is not receptive to anything new at that moment, which is absolutely fine. If I were to offer a point of view without her consent, my words would likely be met with resistance or resentment. If she says yes, then she has given me an opening, an opportunity to make a difference. Now we have a connection that can move us both forward.

Working with heart is easy for many women. The challenge is to stay fully present and open to whatever arises. When we're hit with complaints and negativity, or anger and accusations, it is hard not to want to lessen the other person's discomfort—and thereby lessen our own in the process. But this work is not about avoiding discomfort. It is about helping people move through and beyond their self-limiting stories. So it requires that we get increasingly familiar and comfortable with our own emotions, whatever they may be, without reacting to get rid of or intensify them.

WE ARE HOOKED ON AN EMOTIONAL HOT SPOT
WHEN WE FIND OURSELVES WANTING
TO PROVE SOMETHING OR DEFEND OUR OWN POSITION.

The other tough piece is staying emotionally present and connected without being attached to either an outcome or a position. With a chronic complainer, the complaint story is hers, not ours, to change. When we assume that we know what is best or what will work for someone else, we blur the lines of responsibility. Like my client Beth, who got angry with her direct report for not being more "leader-like," when we assume that our way is the right way, *we* often become the obstacle to the other person's progress.

When a situation hooks us in one of our own emotional hot spots, we lose the capacity to stay present and unattached. We know that we're hooked when we find ourselves wanting to prove something or defend our own position. We get pulled into opinion swapping. We want to be *heard!* When that happens, we can no longer offer a broader, or neutral, perspective.

So if you get frustrated when someone is ignoring your sage advice or if your own negative emotions are welling up, look at what you're attached to. In the previous example, the woman was attached to a story about being powerless; the hook was in thinking that her co-worker's behavior was personal and intentional. My client Beth was attached to a story about being competent; the hook was in thinking her way was the right way and the only way. You might be attached to a story about being an outsider or being nobody special; the hooks are in thinking that you bring little or no value to the group.

One way to unhook or disengage from our story is to shift to a broader—that is, a more neutral and less personal—point of view. It's reframing turned inward. Here are two examples. See if you can come up with two more.

* Remind yourself that you are not the center of everyone else's world. Actions that may feel very personal to you—because of the powerful reactions they evoke in you—may have nothing to do with you, as with the woman above. It is a sobering yet freeing dose of reality, this reminder that the world does not revolve around us.

* Remind yourself that you are more than your role and that in the workplace, people quite often confuse the two. They react to what your role represents in their life rather than to you as an individual. Holding that distinction can help you stay present and deeply interested without getting personally attached. Note that this distinction between your role and the whole of you applies regardless of whether you are a senior executive, a middle manager, or a frontline provider or staffer.

Negativity wears down all but the most diehard optimists. When you find yourself in the midst of a negative conversation, what's important to remember is that the complainer's story makes complete sense to him or her. Think of negative people—pessimists, cynics, critics—as frustrated idealists who've lost their sense of personal power. Your job is not to dispute or deny the merits of their story, but to hold their plight with compassion and a deep faith in their ability to have an impact on their world.

Remember also that you are building a web and webs are powerful because they create the conditions within which people can surface, explore, and choose to move beyond their self-limiting stories. Your job, like Jenna's, is to stay both deeply engaged and personally unattached so that people can self organize to address whatever issues or problems are important to them. Those who do not want the responsibility that comes with working in flatter, more egalitarian webs of inclusion will self-select out. And that is okay.

Living Systems Abide by Rules We Cannot See

In 2005, my then-20-year-old son Michael awoke with abdominal pain and, within 15 hours, was giving up his appendix to a surgeon's laparoscope. We were home in less than 24 hours. Four small steri-strips held his skin together as his body went about the quiet but awesome business of healing.

This scene plays out daily in every hospital. Every living organism has a structure. When threatened, it expends energy to preserve and renew that structure, like Michael's body silently healing after the appendectomy. And while the structure is stable—he looks now just like he did before the surgery—the whole episode is a reminder that we are continually changing in unseen ways, guided by laws of order well beyond what is visible to the naked eye. Nobody gave Michael's abdomen orders to generate new tissue, absorb and dispose of toxins and waste products, or adapt to life without an appendix. His body simply did it naturally.

Organizations are living organisms, too, although our traditional management models do not treat them as such. They have a stable appearance, a wholeness, yet they are always changing and adapting internally, like a hospital system adjusting to a merger or new leadership team, or a critical care unit adapting to new equipment or JCAHO requirements. Individuals come and go, but the identity of the organization remains stable. The systems within our own bodies are interconnected, just as the units within a health care system are interconnected. When one is dysfunctional—like an inflamed appendix or a poorly functioning emergency department—the impact is felt throughout.

While the desire for stability comes naturally to us, we often confuse stability with predictability and control. We create rules and protocols to control processes and strategic plans to control growth and change. We write scripts to increase patient satisfaction scores, or create reward systems to enhance employee or physician opinion surveys, yet they fail to produce the results we want. So the irony is that the stabilizing structures we create are often the very things that hold us back.

Controlled systems, which impose structure and order on people as well as processes, limit our potential. Self-organizing systems, which are open and permeable like the human body or an ecosystem or high performing organization, abide by much deeper laws of order.

The surgeon removed my son's inflamed appendix and the self-organizing power of his body did the rest. Tim Gallwey removed the obstacles to telephone courtesy and the self-

organizing power of the operators' natural desire to help and
influence did the rest. Jenna removes the burden of judgment
from nursing units having trouble and the self-organizing power
of the nurses' desire to do well by their patients does the rest.
What do you observe in your own work life? Pay attention for a
few days to your own organization. The questions in the box can
help focus your attention.

We know more than we see

* What obstacles to self-organization exist in the structures, policies, and standard operating procedures of your organization?
* What has your own experience taught you about the dynamics of closed, tightly controlled systems and their impact on individuals within the system?
* What holds you back from acting on what you know?
* If you are a clinician by training, what do you know about the invisible forces that support or inhibit healing and renewal?
* How can you apply the lessons of patients and personal experience to your own work and relationships?

These questions lead us back to the mental models and
frames within which we operate. What if we traded our policies
and standard operating procedures for webs of connection and
more transient processes and structures that form in response to
specific needs—like task forces or small ad hoc groups with a
deep investment in meeting those needs—and then dissolve into
new structures and processes as other needs arise? What if we
allowed our organizations to operate as living systems?

Similarly, what if we trusted our personal experience of
how small, intimate groups can generate huge momentum? In
The Tipping Point, for example, Malcolm Gladwell describes
how small groups of women reading the same book put it on

the bestseller list (2000). Why don't we mobilize ourselves and others at work the way we mobilize in the community via efforts like the Komen breast cancer movement or the Pantene "Beautiful Lengths" program that encourages people to grow, cut, and donate healthy hair for wigs for women who have lost their hair to cancer treatment?

THE MORE WE TRUST WHAT WE KNOW AND CANNOT SEE,
THE GREATER OUR POWER TO INFLUENCE.

As women, our tendency is to play small. But the means by which we naturally work speaks to thousands, literally. Humans are, by nature, a social species. And the sooner we acknowledge that relationships abide by rules we know intimately but cannot see, the greater our power becomes to influence and effect positive change.

Power Is in Relationships, Not Individuals

Hierarchies are pyramidal. The seats of power are at the top, so if you want to make more money and have more power and control, the name of the game is to move up. You leave a staff position to become a manager, then a director, then a VP. And the irony, as any CEO knows, is that even when you're at the top of the pyramid, you're still not in control, even if you have more money and apparent power.

I remember an amusing story from author and organizational consultant Peter Block. He was meeting the powerful CEO of a large company in which Block and his colleagues had launched a major system-wide empowerment project. The CEO voiced his frustration at getting flack from his bankers and board chair, and then launched into a story of comparable frustration about how he couldn't get the kind of ketchup he wanted in the company cafeteria.

"I was stunned," said Block. "I had thought that the president of a company could have it any way he or she wanted it ... and here the chief executive officer was telling me he was caught in the middle like the rest of us. He found it difficult to please those above him, and giving orders to those below him provided no guarantee that action would be taken" (1987, 67).

What Block encountered over 20 years ago is still occurring today because most people are still working from the same mental models, including models that value hierarchical or positional power. Yet as Jenna knows, there is another, more potent, form of power that comes not from title or position but from relationships. It is energetic power, and it is magical.

Positive relationships generate positive energy; negative relationships generate negative energy. We know this experientially, but we easily lose sight of it when we get caught up in top-down politics and power plays. Pause for a moment to consider two questions:

* What would be different in your work life if you viewed power as a source of energy arising out of your relationships with others rather than as an external source of authority and control?
* How might that shift in thinking affect your behavior? Your sense of being?

I once worked with a hospital operations VP who wondered how he could "get more love into this place" in order to generate greater commitment. We bring more love into organizations through inclusion and the energy generated by relationships. We do it by conveying our regard for others' talents and roles. We do it by expressing our trust in their ability to seek creative responses to challenging situations. We do it by enabling people to make decisions about their daily work life and by our willingness to be influenced by them. We do it by recognizing our interdependence on them. And with every one of these actions, we are exercising power: the power to make a difference in someone's life.

Bruce Lipton, a cell biologist and author of *The Biology of Belief*, tells of leaving a faculty position at the University of Wisconsin School of Medicine and teaching cell biology at a Caribbean medical school (2005). When he arrived, the term was half over and two professors had already bailed. He began by giving students a quiz to see how much they'd learned. Most failed dismally. He saw the panic in their eyes and gave them a 10-minute pep talk in which he promised that via his teaching, they would understand cells by the end of the term.

After class, he realized "the enormity of the commitment I had made" (2005, 34). Doubt set in as he realized that many of these students weren't qualified to be in medical school and others were capable but unprepared. So he gave himself license to restructure his entire approach to teaching. He began using models and metaphors that he had thought about for years and that echoed the concept of living systems in the study of cell biology. The course turned out, he says, to be "the most exhilarating and intellectually profound period of my academic career" (35).

> After my call to arms, my class of misfits stopped acting like conventional medical students; they dropped their survival of the fittest mentality and amalgamated into a single force, a team that helped them survive the semester. The stronger students helped the weaker and in so doing, all became stronger. Their harmony was both surprising and beautiful to observe.

...I think a good part of the reason for my students'
success was that they eschewed the behavior of their
counterparts in the United States. Instead of mirroring
smart American medical students, they mirrored the
behavior of smart cells, banding together to become even
smarter.

I like to think that they went in that direction intuitively,
after listening to my praise of cells' ability to group
together cooperatively to form more complex and highly
successful organisms. ...I now believe that another
reason for my students' success was that I did not stop
at praising cells. I praised the students as well. They
needed to hear they were first-rate students in order to
believe that they could perform as first-rate students (47-
48).

Such is the power of relationships. The science of self-
organizing systems demonstrates this power. Whether at the
cellular level, the level of the human body, a small group of
humans, or an entire organization, strong, healthy relationships
and the power they generate are what produce healthy
functioning and sustained high performance.

When we can eschew the traditional top-down, command-
control model in favor of people banding together, they become
smarter. When we pair their capacity to learn and our own
capacity to nurture, we strengthen the webs of engagement.
When we transfer power from people to purpose, we move
beyond "survival of the fittest" to create a single force.

As women, we intuitively understand the power of
relationships in strengthening community. Our challenge, as

noted earlier, is expanding it from small, intimate circles to larger organizational units. We start, like Jenna, within our own sphere of influence. We experiment with relinquishing control and "knowing how" in favor of inclusion and discovery. We encourage open dialogue and challenge sacred cows and the-way-we've-always-done-it thinking. We trust in the innate capacity of individuals to rise to the occasion in service to a common purpose.

Some people will resist. Others will wait in disbelief. Our determination will be tested, and at times we will have to choose between staying the course and retreating to that familiar place of safety. That is why our networks are important. Finding kindred spirits with whom to build communities of commitment gives us a safety net for staying the course. We sustain and fuel one another. We are no longer a lone voice in the woods.

6

Align Rather Than Assign

Left-Brain, Right-Brain: the World Needs Both

Psychology and neuroscience researchers have confirmed what most of us know by now: that the two sides of the brain, the left and right hemispheres, function differently. The left is logical, linear and sequential while the right is intuitive, holistic and simultaneous. The left analyzes while the right synthesizes. The left is literal and anchored in facts and data while the right is metaphorical and rich in symbols and contextual association.

Our organizations are predominantly left-brained analytical, yet most women are more comfortable with right-brained synthesis. Our nature is to see things as interconnected and interdependent rather than as pearls on a bead chain or rungs on a hierarchy. We're more at home with webs of inclusion than with jockeying for position. When stressed, we "tend and befriend" those around us while our male counterparts are more likely to resort to "fight or flight." And since we typically work in organizations that are top-down, sequential, and analytic, we back away from the wisdom of our own experience, fearing that it is somehow deficient.

The best example I know is my own experience. For years, I thought of myself as a poor thinker. I was never able to sit down and outline anything sequentially, be it a magazine article or a plan for a new project. I struggled with the "if A then B" approach, which I thought was the hallmark of a good thinker— and a good manager. As a result, I continually doubted that what I had to offer was of value.*

But it wasn't just writing and planning that I struggled with. Because I did not understand or trust my own style, I often suffered from what psychologists call "impostor syndrome," or the dread fear that I had somehow lucked into success and would be exposed, any day, in all my ignorance. It was a terrible feeling. No matter what I accomplished, a voice inside whispered that I was a fraud and my accomplishments were little more than the product of dumb luck.

It took years for me to learn that I was measuring myself against external standards that operated differently from my own experience of the world. As an English major, I was accustomed to the world of metaphors and analogies, storytelling and narrative. But these were alien concepts in the literal, rational world of business. As a parent, I saw close similarities between raising a child and developing a direct report. But as a manager, I deferred to the mostly male business authors who frowned upon drawing connections between work relationships and

---

*This self-doubt lasted until I discovered mind mapping, an approach to recalling and recording information that mimics the brain's natural operations. If you want to try it, I recommend the work of Tony Buzan.

familial ones. As a psychologist, I found that the qualities I had valued and used as the foundation for practice—self awareness, collaboration, honest conversation, authenticity, personal accountability—put me at risk in management. Managers did not want honesty, especially when it ran counter to the party line. And they certainly were not interested in collaboration. Honesty translated to being a poor team player and collaboration was synonymous with sniffing around someone else's power base.

In short, as a woman who valued relationships, connection, and authenticity over power plays, status, and self-protection, I felt isolated and poorly suited for the business environment. I was a right-brained character trapped in a left-brained world, but I couldn't see it. I felt so out of place that I did not talk with any of my female colleagues, all of whom seemed to be adapting better than I. So this sense of isolation and ill fit continued for years, despite the confident "game face" I learned to put on in public.

Neuroscientists know that healthy functioning requires both sides of the brain working together. If injury or illness disrupts the operations of either side, the person's ability to function effectively is seriously impaired. Sounds like many of our organizations, doesn't it? They've been stuck in the upright and locked left-brain position for so long that they don't even know a right-brain counterbalance exists.

Fortunately, times are changing. When we study great service organizations like the Ritz-Carlton, SAS Software, and Southwest Airlines, we see that their phenomenal success comes from putting people and purpose first in a common dance that generates remarkable alignment and commitment and that consistently produces profitable results.

What these organizations have discovered—and what most women know intuitively—is that when we nurture people's spirits, when we honor their desire to make a difference, when we invest in their capacity to rise to the occasion in service to a greater purpose, when we invite them to co-create an environment that we all mutually value, we are setting the stage for a well-aligned organization and the pursuit of excellence.

WHAT WE BRING IS NOT BETTER OR WORSE
THAN WHAT MEN BRING. IT IS SIMPLY DIFFERENT.
ORGANIZATIONS NEED BOTH.

Essentially, these are all strategies for alignment. We have used them in our personal lives for years, every time we tape a child's drawing to the refrigerator or support the budding high school musician or listen attentively to a friend's ambivalence about her marriage or a spouse's dissatisfaction with his job. We are helping them navigate the world of emotion. We are holding a space within which they can grow and adapt. We are helping them discover and honor what's important to them and align what they do with who they are. For us, the challenge is to bring this capacity for nurturing engagement and alignment into the workplace on a larger scale than we are accustomed to.

Keep in mind that what we bring is not better or worse than what men bring. It is simply *different*. For healthy functioning, organizations need both left- and right-brain, masculine and feminine styles. Employees at all levels are aching to have a greater say, to be heard, and to be counted on to make a meaningful contribution. By embracing the notion of "yes and"—yes to the value of linear, analytic thinking *and* yes to the power of contextual associations and webs of inclusion—we can create an environment in which each individual is encouraged to participate at a deep level.

This chapter looks at the power of getting everyone in your organization engaged—emotionally as well as intellectually—in fulfilling its purpose. We start by distinguishing purposeful alignment, which is right brain, from the more common left-brain activity of strategic planning, and then examine several ways to generate alignment, starting with individuals and broadening to systems and processes.

Distinguish Strategic Planning from Purposeful Alignment

Like their counterparts in other industries, healthcare leaders expend considerable time and effort setting strategy for their organizations. For many leaders, that translates to strategic planning. Over the years, I've watched strategic plans grow from simple documents to elaborate charts, from narratives of intent to full-color maps that systematically detail the goals, objectives, deadlines, milestones, accountabilities, and actions flowing from a few sweeping scorecard indicators. I suspect such effort is a noble attempt to get greater clarity of purpose and accountability among the workforce by defining in detail how to organize people and resources to accomplish the organization's goals.

But the measurable results that these plans yield are not the same as the dynamic results that most leaders want: high engagement, loyalty, sound decision-making well out in the ranks, adaptability and innovation, creative responses to the unexpected, and service activity that generates great experiences for patients. Results like these don't flow from intricate strategic plans; they flow from having people and processes aligned with the organization's purpose and guiding values. They flow from having webs of connection.

Don't misunderstand me: strategic plans certainly have a place in organizations. But they lack the power to generate commitment and engagement at all levels of the organization. Full-hearted commitment comes not from issuing a sleek four-color strategic plan or assigning names to accountability slots on the scorecard, but from creating connections that engage people at a deep level of meaning and purpose.

Perhaps you've heard the old story of the three bricklayers at a work site. When asked what they were doing, the first said, "I'm laying bricks." The second said, "I'm earning an income to provide for my family." The third said, "I'm building a cathedral." They're all *doing* the same thing.

Now assume you are setting strategy for the bricklaying project. What are you doing? You're determining things like who surveys and prepares the site, when the bricks and mortar will be delivered, when the hod carriers and brick layers will get to work, and how the bricks are to be laid. Your planning relies on and reinforces the "silos" or functional activities of surveying, engineering, constructing, and detailing.

Setting strategy, however, does not touch the question of meaning that each worker attaches to the work. The bricklayer who's simply laying bricks will soon find his work dull and routine, no matter how elaborate or efficient your strategy. His level of engagement will be less than that of the bricklayer who defines work in terms of providing for the family. The greatest engagement will come from the worker who's building a cathedral, a sanctuary, a place that touches us all because of its connection to something deeply meaningful in our lives. His perspective includes laying bricks, providing for family, *and* creating something of significance.

Setting strategy starts with *who, what, when, how,* and is aimed at accomplishing the goals of the organization. It is a form of control. Historically, the word "strategy" referred to military operations and the planning and conduct of combat operations.

Strategy was a plan of action designed to *win*, and it still carries that connotation. In most organizations, those in command still set the strategy and those at the front lines carry it out, one brick at a time.

STRATEGIC PLANNING IS A FORM OF CONTROL.

ALIGNMENT IS A FORM OF CONNECTION.

Alignment, as mentioned earlier, is the process of getting everyone in your organization engaged—emotionally as well as intellectually—in fulfilling the organization's purpose. It is a form of *connection*. Alignment starts with *why* and generates a sense of personal power among employees by helping them see deeper layers of meaning: they are providing for others and building a cathedral, not just laying bricks. When people are clear about and deeply committed to the *why,* they can be remarkably adept at figuring out the *what, when* and *how.*

Strategic planning without alignment generates compliance in the form of workers who are merely laying bricks. Alignment—emotional connection to a meaningful purpose—is what drives the enthusiasm and passion that underlie great performance. Think about it: if you're heading into surgery, who do you want in the O.R., the care providers who are doing their eight and hitting the gate or the ones who are there to protect your life?

Getting people aligned is much different from getting them organized and assigning them tasks and performance targets. Of course, you need to organize and assign, and strategic planning can be an appropriate way of doing so. But these are management tasks. First, you need to align, and that is a leadership task. Fortunately, it is one that taps the natural right-brain strengths of many women.

Give People a Role, Not Just a Job

You cannot "fix" or manage your way to alignment. You create it by putting patients rather than tasks at the center of attention and then invoking each employee's desire to make a difference.

I remember waiting for a service elevator one day in the lower level of a hospital. A Vietnamese gentleman pushing a large laundry cart joined me. He flashed a big smile and silently nodded.

"Where are you headed?" I asked.

"To make bed comfortable for patients," he said in broken English. "Sick patient need nice bed." I had no doubt that every patient he tucked in was treated like a personal guest, and that his department manager was focused more on patient comfort than on linen inventory and laundry detergent. I tracked her down and asked how she got people so dedicated to taking care of patients. "It's easy," she said, "so long as your goal is the comfort of the patient and your staff appreciate their role in the process."

The key word here is *role*. A job is a set of tasks we do, usually in exchange for a paycheck. A role is a part we play in something bigger, like building a cathedral or creating a meaningful experience for others. Observe your own work. How much time do you spend addressing the tasks and metrics associated with people's jobs, and how much time do you spend on defining and drawing connections between their roles and the experience of those they serve? How do the results you get change with the approach you take? Which set of activities gives you a deeper sense of satisfaction? If you're not already thinking in these terms, try some self-observation for a few weeks to become more conscious of where you invest your time and energy.

Several years ago, I worked in a hospital that subcontracted cleaning services to an outside vendor. The manager ran the operation with an iron fist. He would sift through patient survey data for complaints about housekeeping and whack his staff regularly for not following protocol. If he saw fingerprints on the hospital doors or bits of trash in the lobby or halls, he'd march directly to the basement break room and bellow at whoever was around. As you'd expect, he had high turnover and consistently mediocre results, both of which he attributed to the mediocre quality of people applying for housekeeping positions.

The hospital CEO, dissatisfied with the hospital's appearance, negotiated with the subcontractor to replace the manager with Ted, an in-house vice president who obviously had no direct authority over the vendor's staff. Ted began holding meetings to talk with the staff about the importance of the hospital's appearance in shaping patients' perceptions of the quality of care they received. "People's first impressions of our hospital are in your hands," he said. "What would you like them to see?" By inviting the staff to help define a welcoming environment and by acknowledging the importance of their role, he began the process of getting them aligned.

Ted had other responsibilities besides housekeeping. But unlike most of his peers, who scheduled meetings in their own offices and rarely left the administrative suite, he regularly met with people on their turf. So he was frequently out and about in the house. Whenever he saw a piece of trash, he'd pick it up and carry it to a wastebasket. He'd straighten magazines in the visitor areas while he was waiting for an elevator. He kept a cloth handkerchief in his back pocket to wipe fingerprints off the glass doors.

He never mentioned these small acts, but the housekeeping staff took notice and, within weeks, the hospital was looking more cared for. He learned which housekeepers were responsible for what and started each staff meeting by complimenting someone about an area of the hospital that looked great as a result of their diligence. He was showing them, in very personal ways, how important their actions were in shaping patients' perceptions. The credibility he earned by staying focused on and modeling what he wanted paid off handsomely. Turnover dropped significantly and staff willingly aligned with his desire to create a facility that was clean, polished, and welcoming.

Ted understood the importance of giving people an important role to play. He understood that involvement helps people feel important and that feeling important is a powerful motivator. When people feel important, especially about something that's deeply meaningful to them, they do remarkable things. Think about how Ted did this. His style—inviting people to help define visitors' first impressions, focusing on their role in making it happen, recognizing their efforts—was quite consistent with how most women work: building consensus and support, and helping others feel important.

So regardless of whether you are a senior vice president or a team leader, you can nurture the ability to get people aligned by shining a light on the importance of their role. Start, as Ted did, by putting the experience of the patient at the center of conversation. Then build community around it by helping each employee find an important role in serving patients, even if they rarely see a patient. Build on practices like those in Chapter 5 by connecting non-clinical people with people working closer to the interface of patient care. Or take a page from the playbooks of wise basic science researchers who bring together lab personnel and patients at annual events like walks or runs for a cure or manufacturing companies that bring together employees and patients whose lives depend on medical equipment for annual meetings to honor one another. When a lab tech or a call center employee hears a recipient talk about walking onto a stage when 8 months earlier she was bed-bound, the employee's work is reframed in a heartbeat. Bricks become cathedrals.

Align In-House Processes to Support Your Purpose

No living system can survive and thrive unless its internal parts are aligned and working in ways that support its growth and renewal. In an organization, you need in-house processes that reinforce the behavior you want. What often happens is that busy people simply work around dysfunctional processes until an adverse event occurs. Then they or their managers jump into fix-it mode in an effort to restore the status quo without taking the time to explore and understand what really led to the adverse event in the first place.

Unfortunately, people are often blamed for errors and breakdowns. If we look closely and with an open mind, we usually find that systems and processes, not people, are the culprit. People are trying hard to do what they think is right.

Consider, for instance, this scenario. In 2008, my 90-something mother was hospitalized and needed a walker, so her physician wrote the order at 1 p.m. on a Friday afternoon. That evening and again the next day, I inquired about the walker. The primary care nurse didn't know what was causing the delay.

At 6 p.m. on Sunday, I again asked the nurse when the walker would arrive. She had no idea. By now I was frustrated, so I pressed the issue. We agreed that either one of us could walk to Central Supply, grab a walker, and have Mom touring the halls in less than 15 minutes, although doing so might breach some in-house policies. Within an hour of our conversation, the nurse—tired, perhaps, of my inquiries—went to another floor and "borrowed" a walker. Total time between the order and delivery of the walker: 53.5 hours!

As much as I appreciated the nurse's effort, it taught us nothing about optimal experiences nor about when and where the process was breaking down. Her best guess was that the delay was due to what she called "weekend staffing," which, of course, was handled by someone in another department. More importantly, the idea of providing a positive patient experience wasn't even on her radar screen.

On Monday and Tuesday, I endured a similar scenario trying to get a bedside toilet for my mom. It took 19 hours from time of order to time of delivery. When a third event occurred a few days later, I was suspecting a pattern.

Process breakdowns like the ones my mom and I encountered are the products of networks of people and activity stretching across time and space. Most people pay little attention to the complexity of these situations. They focus instead on what's immediate and expedient.

That's why it's hard to see intra-departmental misalignments; our focal point is what's right here, right now. It's even more difficult to see misalignments that reach across departments or functional units. Sometimes we get a glimpse of a bigger picture and can see that what we've been calling a "problem" is really just part of a larger system. Our perception is suddenly and strikingly reframed. When that happens, new options appear. Here's a non-clinical example.

My client Andrea, a business development specialist, was rewarded handsomely for attracting new physicians to her organization. She had a great track record, partly because she promised physicians things they valued like high-tech equipment and broad referral networks. But occasionally her promises generated expectations that the physician relations staff struggled to meet and when that happened, she found herself at odds with them.

She then accepted a promotion and became the director of physician relations. Three or four months later, she called me with a story to share. She'd been arguing with one of her former business development colleagues. He had made some big promises to two new staff nephrologists that her staff were unable to honor. As the argument unfolded, she heard herself saying things that the former physician relations director had said to her when she was in business development. Suddenly she saw the misalignment: she was being rewarded for *retaining* physicians while her former colleague was being rewarded for *attracting* physicians. In that moment, she realized they both were working hard and with good intentions, but the organization's compensation/reward system was pulling them in opposing directions.

Andrea brought the misalignment to the attention of her boss and they worked with the human resource (HR) department to realign the compensation system so that the people recruiting physicians and those retaining them were working in concert rather than at odds with each other. Because Andrea and her boss recognized this as a systems breakdown, they didn't get pulled into blaming people. Because they approached HR with a positive intention—creating a well-aligned system that supported hospital relations with physicians—people readily engaged in the endeavor. The success of their efforts led to the realignment of several other internal systems the following year.

So if you're not getting the results want, look at your organization's internal systems and processes through the lens of alignment. This is especially important when people rather than processes are being blamed for problems. While it is wholly appropriate to hold people accountable for results, if the systems they are using do not align to support them and their purpose, they'll have a Sisyphean challenge on their hands.

These days, many healthcare organizations have performance improvement efforts in place to identify and resolve clinical process misalignments. But clinical activity is only part of a patient's experience. If you want organizational alignment, you need to think in terms of whole-system experiences. So here are some common non-clinical sources of misalignment:

* Patient satisfaction: is your system aligned to improve your scorecard indicators or to enhance the actual experience of your patients?

* Risk management: is your system aligned to deal with claims and law suits post hoc or is it a proactive, early warning system that minimizes patient suffering and maximizes on-the-spot learning and improvement of clinical processes?

* Billing: is your system aligned to accommodate cumbersome software and incompatible platforms or is it generating a single, easily-understood bill for patients?

* Housekeeping: is your system aligned to serve the department's scheduling and staffing practices, or is it structured around the needs of patients and the units taking care of them?

The irony of misalignment is that the people at the front lines have remarkable insight into what's working and what's not. Moreover, they always have simple and highly effective alternatives. Unfortunately, in top-down organizations, they are rarely asked for their input.

So regardless of how your organization is structured, if you want to identify and tackle process misalignments, invoke your female instinct for inclusion. Invite everyone, not just people in supervisory or management roles, to express and explore what they experience. Listen with a different ear to complaints. Treat them as veiled statements about what's important to people, not just as observations about what isn't working.

Listen openly and you'll find simple yet elegant ideas at the front lines, like this one from a San Antonio teaching hospital. To minimize turnaround time between when an inpatient bed was vacated and when it was ready for a new patient, the staff devised a system using two jars at the nursing station, one for clean beds and one for dirty. When a patient was discharged, the nurse wrote the room number on a piece of red paper and dropped it in the "dirty" jar. When the housekeeper finished cleaning the room, she removed the red slip from the "dirty" jar and put a slip of green paper with the same room number in the "clean" jar. In a glance, the unit clerk could tell if a clean bed was available (HFMA, 2006, 3).

Get the Dog Wagging the Tail

Healthcare organizations are so complex and many workers and managers are so far removed from patients and the point of care that they see no connection between what they do and its impact on those they serve.

In these situations, helping people discover the connection is an important first step. Many times, the tail is wagging the dog. People in one department are unaware of how their actions affect those in other departments. They only know the tasks they are expected to perform. They may know the function of their job, but they don't know why they do what they do.

Getting the dog wagging the tail—creating alignment within a complex system—starts with a consistent and repeated focus on the "why" of people's efforts. Four-color strategic plans, mission and values statements that never leave the wall, and directives delivered at staff meetings won't cut it. Neither will a barrage of e-mails or memoranda. You need to be out and about, creating connections and nurturing involvement.

In 2005, our old family dog, a gentle, saintly Sheltie named Peppernight, became seriously ill, and my son Michael and I chose to end his life rather than prolong his suffering. It was a tearful time, and the veterinarian and staff at The Ohio State University Veterinary Hospital were wonderful, even honoring Michael's desire for Peppernight to die outside on a beautiful summer's evening. Three days later, a package arrived from the hospital. Inside were a plaster cast of Peppernight's paw print and a sympathy card with handwritten notes from each of the people who had taken care of him the previous weekend. Also in the mail was a sympathy card with handwritten notes from our regular veterinarian and her assistant.

I immediately called my elderly mother. Had she received anything like this following my father's death a few years earlier? "No," she said. "All I got was a stream of bills from umpteen different departments and a patient satisfaction survey three weeks after your dad died."

I was appalled! In the following days, I talked with several friends who had lost loved ones. None had heard anything from their physicians or hospital caregivers and two had received patient satisfaction surveys after their loss.

If we assume for a moment that hospital personnel want to be sensitive to the suffering of others, then how do we account for such egregious behavior? As I mentioned earlier, the culprit isn't a person with poor intentions. It's a focus on setting up internal systems to control and track activities without being mindful of the larger system and how new processes align with or interfere with people's ability to work on purpose in serving their patients and one another.

THE MORE COMPLEX THE SYSTEM,
THE GREATER THE OPPORTUNITY
FOR THINGS TO BE MISSED.

In any situation, what typically gets attention is what's personal and immediate. The healthcare systems I've worked with run patient satisfaction surveys through their marketing or human resource departments and outside vendors. Names pass through the system as electronic data points and are pulled at random to receive surveys. So for someone working in the department responsible for generating patient satisfaction scores, what's personal and immediate is the importance of getting those scores generated in a timely fashion. The more impersonal and distant challenge— translating those electronic data points into patient needs, for instance—is beyond their scope.

If we take a step back, we begin to appreciate that people in one department often have little understanding of how their efforts affect people in other departments and, ultimately, how they affect the patient. The more complex the system, the greater the opportunity for things to be missed. Ambiguity arises around who's responsible for what, and people's tendency is to do what is most expedient: simply work around problems and get the tasks done.

In a top-down, fix-it world, managers as well as workers become complaint-driven problem solvers rather than co-creators of environments designed to serve patients. Had my elderly mother complained to the hospital about getting a patient satisfaction survey following my father's death, the letter probably would have gone from the president to a vice president to the head of marketing (or whoever was responsible for patient satisfaction data), who likely would have felt powerless because he's just running on data provided by the finance department, which is faster at churning out discharge information than patient records, which is struggling with either a mountain of data to get into the charts in 30 days or an electronic system with glitches that Information Systems hasn't been able to resolve.

As with most situations, we have well-intentioned people trying to do good work at every level in every department. But addressing complaints puts us in the classic reactive mode of getting rid of something we don't want. It blinds us to the alternative of creating the kinds of experiences that patients need and want. As a result, the same problems keep cropping up, year after year.

BE CURIOUS. ASK QUESTIONS.
LISTEN TO THE SOUND OF LIFE AND FOLLOW IT.

Remember that a key function of leading is to help people figure out how to provide quality care in a complex world. You cannot do the work for them. But you can create opportunities and hold an environment within which they begin to think differently about what they do, for whom, and why. You want thinking about the whole dog, not just the tail.

You can seed the process in staff meetings and one-on-one conversations using broad, open-ended questions about what ideal care looks like and what each employee's role is in shaping it. You don't have to have the answers. You just have to ask purposeful questions, over and over, until people know that you are looking for something other than business as usual.

Ask questions that create tension between the real and the ideal. Ask questions that stir emotional connections between people and their own potential. Ask questions that challenge the status quo. Then stay open to the stress and strain that such questions evoke. Listen to the sound of life beating in the silence and follow it.

When you create an environment of curiosity that connects people with the purpose of their work and their own potential, you open the door on their capacity to adapt, self correct, and flourish. Using the example of patient satisfaction surveys, one or more of the questions below can help you initiate this kind of inquiry.

An exercise in satisfaction

* Why do we send patient satisfaction surveys?
* What do we do with the results?
* What do we not do with the results?
* Who do we currently send surveys to?
* What perceptions do we want survey recipients to have?
* Which of our patients or recipients should not receive surveys?
* If we were on the receiving end, when would we not want to receive surveys?
* What do we want to convey to those people?
* What, if anything, is standing in our way?
* How does our survey process align with what we say we value?
* How do we know when the process is breaking down?
* What do we know about those breakdowns?

You will likely find that people throughout the system assume that someone else is responsible for catching the glitches. The primary care nurse assumes that the marketing clerk was tracking deaths and adverse outcomes. The marketing clerk was just doing her job by initiating survey mailings, unaware that the data she received included those who'd died or suffered a serious adverse outcome. Her boss, preoccupied with a dozen other marketing duties, assumed that finance or patient records had screened for such information, while the finance person or patient records clerk had no idea that marketing even sent out patient satisfaction surveys. It's not a question of blame; people are well intentioned and want to do good work. It's a question of focus.

In complex systems, many employees have little or no awareness of what others do. That's why alignment is such a powerful force. When we hold their attention on the deeper purpose, when we create opportunities for them to connect with others serving the same purpose, when we convey faith in their ability to figure out how to get and keep the dog wagging the tail, we create the conditions necessary for them to do the work themselves.

Focus on What's Going Well

To be aligned and working on purpose, people need information and lots of it. We'll talk more about this in Chapter 8, but for now, here are a few suggestions to help people get the information they need. Start by tracking, reflecting on, and publicizing *what works well*. The tendency of most managers, men and women alike, is to put energy into what's going wrong and figuring out how to fix or solve it. When we overlook or dismiss what already works well, we miss the great opportunities that successes present.

For example, when unsolicited letters arrive from patients or families, rather than just posting or circulating them, get everyone who had contact with that family talking about how they created a memorable experience. From those who gave care to those who delivered meals and swept floors, from those who transported the patient to those who maintained the medical records or handled registration, help each person become conscious and aware of how he or she contributed. Everyone needs to know what his or her own role was in making patients happy enough to write unsolicited letters. Yes, talking through successes takes more time than merely posting letters, but it is a time investment that will yield rich returns.

Your purpose in doing this is not to identify "best practices" in order to institutionalize them. That will simply lead you back into efforts to predict and control. Rather, you want to create and sustain a healthy tension between individuals and the environment. By shifting people's focus to the experience of the patient, drawing attention to their contributions, and fueling as much awareness, exchange, and reflection as possible about what's actually occurring, you encourage alignment, continual adaptation to the changing environment and, ultimately, great experiences for patients.

You can get similar results by exploring adverse events so long as you treat them as process or system failures rather than as people failures. Just remember to open the conversation neutrally with a line like "This process didn't work; let's learn why," and maintain a non-judging stance as people explore where the breakdowns occurred. Such an approach avoids blaming people—thus preserving the connections we value—and frees them up to see the importance of their role in creating a process that is purpose- and patient- focused. Note that addressing adverse events will be more productive if you first take the time to establish a pattern of identifying and discussing what's going well.

Use Small, Daily Practices to Stay Connected with the Big Picture

As I mentioned earlier, women are often process oriented and accustomed to multitasking and managing details. The more we focus on just getting the job done, the greater the likelihood of losing sight of the big picture. So in order to create alignment throughout your organization, you have to set your sights on the horizon and create practices for working big. Some simple practices that can help are in the box below.

Small daily practices for staying connected

* If you easily lose sight of the bigger picture, train yourself to put first things first by making purpose and values your anchor point.
    * Start each day by devoting 5 minutes to writing down one or two alignment activities for the day. These are specific efforts to connect daily activities with the organization's mission.
    * End each day by devoting 5 minutes to writing down what you did and how it helped connect you and others to the mission. This means verifying, not just assuming, that others made the connections.
    * Use your notes as an accountability partner. If you do them regularly, you'll soon be putting first things first.
* Get out and about. At least once a week, invite someone from another department to lunch specifically to learn what she does and to share your dreams of what can be.
* Once a week, take a few staff to visit another unit or department. Ask what's going well or what they take pride in. Be curious about life in their area. The farm won't burn down while you're gone.
* In every meeting you attend, listen for the threads of purpose. If you don't hear them, ask about them.

* Read a book on systems thinking. Peter Senge's classic *The Fifth Discipline* is a good start. Better yet, start a book club and make this the first book. Work through a chapter at a time. Yes, you have fires to fight and crises to handle. But in order to grow, you must protect time for the important but non-urgent activities that lead to high performance.

Do Not Overlook Your Own Internal Processes

Most healthcare organizations regularly gather employee opinion or employee satisfaction data. If your organization does so, then you already have some general information about where misalignments may be occurring. Just be careful how you interpret the data. If you find yourself responding defensively or wanting to explain or justify yourself, the data likely hit an emotional hot spot. Staying open and receptive to what's going on externally requires knowing how to stay present with and manage effectively what's going on internally.

A few years ago, I was invited to a senior operations meeting in which the results of a system-wide employee survey were being translated into action strategies. One theme was particularly bothersome to those in the room, namely that employees did not trust upper-level management to be working in their best interests. Many employees expressed trust in their immediate manager, but non-clinical employees in particular were critical of the motives of senior managers.

After some general discussion about possible "causes" and "solutions," which sounded to me like classic "fix-it" thinking, Sherri, the senior vice president for human resources made a remarkable pronouncement. She turned to her direct report and told him to revamp the hospital's recruitment, screening, and hiring processes to attract employees who would be more trusting and loyal! To my shock and dismay, no one in the room challenged her decision or seemed to recognize it as a firsthand example of what the survey results were telling them.

The feedback this group received was a perfect opening for the senior team to learn more about the perceptions of hospital staff and to clarify the gaps between what they, as an executive team, said they valued and how staff perceived their behavior. Imagine if the senior VP had said, "We have an opportunity here. Our employees, especially our non-clinical staff, don't trust that we're working in their best interests. What are we doing or not doing to generate that perception? And how is it affecting our ability to lead and to serve our patients?"

If she was truly interested in alignment, she might also have said, "I don't think we can answer those questions ourselves. So I suggest that we share the survey results—and our genuine concern—with employees and set out to get a really clear understanding of where and how we're missing the mark.

"I'd like to see us model a different way of showing up. I want us to convey to people a sincere interest in learning more about where our intentions are breaking down. I want us to ask questions, listen openly and non-defensively, and be grateful for every bit of feedback we get. Once we have a clear picture of how people actually experience our behavior, then we can revisit what we want and find ways to get ourselves aligned with what we say we value."

This kind of approach is one of being impeccable in word and deed, of aligning what we way we value with what we actually do. It is difficult to stay present and grounded when we're hit with something emotionally charged, something inconsistent with how we think we are or how we want to be known. It's easy to drift into a closed, defensive posture like this senior vice president and deflect attention away from the real issue: our own anger, anxiety, or fear. A title doesn't guarantee maturity. So whenever we get negative feedback, whether it's from feedback surveys, unsolicited letters or emails, or even a colleague, we need to attend to our internal reactions and guard against being pulled into a small, defensive corner. We can't hold a space for others unless and until we can stand the emotional heat ourselves.

| IN OUR RIGHT MIND

7

Nurture Not Knowing

THE RANGE OF WHAT WE THINK AND DO

IS LIMITED BY WHAT WE FAIL TO NOTICE

AND BECAUSE WE FAIL TO NOTICE

THERE IS LITTLE WE CAN DO TO CHANGE UNTIL WE NOTICE

R.D. Laing

The Tyranny of Being the Expert

Executive women disclose two common secrets to me in coaching sessions. The first is the fear of not knowing enough. The second is its first cousin, a sense that the answer is "out there"—in another workshop or conference, another article, another list of best practices, even another degree—rather than within. In our close relationships, it's easy to say, "I don't know." But when we step into work, bringing with us all of our assumptions about how we should be in a top-down world, we limit ourselves.

   Most of us devote years to becoming expert at what we do, believing that our professional success hinges on it. We don't speak up in meetings unless we're sure of 95% of the facts. We don't try new things unless we're 98% sure that they'll succeed. Like Katherine, the COO from Chapter 4 who felt tremendous pressure to avoid mistakes, we don't want to risk getting caught not knowing. Meanwhile, our male colleagues jump in with half the facts, make cogent and knowledgeable contributions, and get recognized for their efforts.

Part of this fear of not knowing enough is fostered by the hierarchical nature of organizations, where getting ahead is tied to having answers, solving problems, and speaking up. Part of it is also tied to how we think about our own success. My male clients typically attribute promotions and new responsibilities to their potential. They enter new positions and situations with a sense of competence and confidence about what they'll be able to accomplish. They have moments of self doubt, to be sure, but their self image as a competent person and their mental frame of succeeding *because* of their potential sustain them.

My female clients are more likely to attribute promotions and new responsibilities to their past performance. They enter new positions and situations with a sense of anxiety and doubt. They have moments of confidence, to be sure, but their story frames each new situation as another test of competence. So no matter how well they performed in the past, any new situation—be it a promotion, an unfamiliar problem, or a novel challenge—evokes anxiety and self doubt, which, in turn, can blind them to their own strengths.

My client Rhonda is a perfect example. In a coaching session one day, she was describing how terribly anxious and doubtful she feels when she has to chair executive meetings, even though she knows that she is able to "fake it" by looking and acting calm and confident.

I said, "And you call looking and acting confident 'faking it' because …?"

"Because it's not me," she said, quite directly and confidently. "Because I'm acting … because what I'm feeling inside is not what I'm putting outside."

"Isn't it interesting," I observed, "that you treat your *feelings* as ME and your *behavior* as NOT ME." She had never noticed the distinction before. As soon as she acknowledged that at any given moment, she was both anxiously doubtful *and* capable of behaving in a calm and confident manner, her story about herself began to change. Now she could expand it to include all of her experience.

So if you are one of the many women who think your success is the result of past performance and have difficulty trusting your potential and your capacity to adapt to whatever is thrown at you, then it's time to turn *not knowing* to your advantage. If you are caught in the grip of wanting others' approval and/or wanting to do everything perfectly, then your sense of competence is likely tied to doing the "right" thing or doing everything "right." You are probably running on a set of unexamined beliefs and assumptions you adopted long ago about *the way it is* in the workplace. As a result, you are likely missing the wisdom of your own experience.

The antidote, of course, is awareness. It can provide you with new perspectives and alternatives if you're willing to suspend judgment and be fully present to what is unfolding around you. In short, *not* being the expert can be one of your greatest strengths.

Every employee walking in the door of your organization wants to feel important and make a valuable contribution. As I've said before, part of your role as a leader is to create and hold a space within which that can occur. Unless you let go of the need to be the expert and trust in people's natural capacity to adapt to the challenges at hand, you'll be caught in the self-limiting trap of "expert" thinking.

So in this chapter, we look at several ways in which you can use "not knowing" to nurture an environment of awareness and adaptability. We start with personal life experiences and how they can serve as metaphors for finding new possibilities and perspectives. Next, we look more closely at how the Buddhist concept of beginner's mind can help you become aware of things that you otherwise may overlook. We close the chapter with some simple practices to use when the creative juices have dried up and you don't know what to do next. The whole gist of this chapter is that expert thinking, which values knowing over learning, competence over curiosity, and certainty over openness, is self limiting.

Make no mistake: in advocating a stance of not knowing, I am *not* advocating a lack of technical knowledge or expertise. Technical expertise is absolutely necessary for your success as a healthcare leader. It is just not sufficient for tackling the kinds of complex and recurring problems and patterns of unproductive efforts that now plague most organizations.

Let Life Be Your Teacher

Every activity, every interaction in your life is a seed for discovery. One simple way to tap your own adaptive power is to let experience be your teacher. When we approach personal experiences as metaphors, when we seek connections between what we're experiencing in one part of our lives and its relevance to other parts of our lives, new possibilities arise.

I took up rowing a few years ago. Not rowboat rowing, but 8-person team rowing in sleek, pencil-slim, 65-foot boats. The instructors opened the first class with a 10-minute video of seasoned rowers slicing through the water, pulling in unison at breathtaking speed. We were captivated by the images. Next came 10 minutes of basic terminology to familiarize us with the equipment. Then the instructors took us outside to teach us the basic rowing motion.

They put us on ergometer machines, or "ergs," and talked us through each of the 5-part movements of a rowing stroke. The movements were hard, but with the video images fresh in our minds, we had something to aspire to.

STEP OUT OF THE STREAM OF USUAL EXPECTATIONS
AND MINE YOUR OWN EXPERIENCE
FOR NEW METAPHORS FOR WORK.

I expected two to three 3-hour classes before we hit the water. Wrong. After 20 minutes on the ergs, the instructors took us to the boat rack, taught us how to carry boats to the dock, and talked us through rigging the oars and getting on board without harming the boat or ourselves. When we were properly seated, they gave the order to cast off. We were on the water—barely an hour into the first class!

I was stunned by the efficiency and effectiveness of their approach. They showed us what world-class rowing looked like, then gave us only what we needed to handle a rowing shell and ourselves safely before launching us into action. After that first class, we learned dozens of other terms and techniques, but not until when we needed them.

I recalled the orientations we used to give new physicians during their first week of residency. We put them through 3 days of mind-numbing presentations by the residency program directors, the program secretaries, the hospital CEO, the chief nursing officer, the benefits people, the security staff, and the librarian. They were instructed in the hospital's medical records, medical terminology, compliance, and patient safety procedures, and were introduced to the risk management team, the QA/PI and infection control coordinators, the MIS trainers, and the Institutional Review Board representative. We got them carded, sized for lab coats, I-9'd, and payrolled, then flooded them with forms for filing incident reports, research protocols, procedure logs, vacation and conference requests, and off-site rotation requests.

Our intentions were good. We wanted the new residents to feel welcome, so we flooded them with well-meaning information. In retrospect, I realized that our intentions were also self-serving. We wanted them to know the system—in order to make our jobs easier—so we inundated them with forms and protocols. As a result, we completely missed the boat. They were operating at a much different level. They wanted answers to just a few simple questions: *How do I keep from killing someone now that I'm the first physician of record? What do I do when I'm in over my head and a patient's life is at stake? When and where can I sleep?*

We addressed those questions, too. But they were squeezed between hours of droning on about things that were important to staff but meant little to PGY-1s drowning in concerns about their own adequacy as frontline physicians. How much different would their experience have been if we had focused on them and their patients rather than us and our procedures?

And, of course, weeks or months down the road, when they were settled in and needed to fill out forms and reports, get something from an ancillary department, or start a research project, they had no clue where to start. And, as you might predict, when they asked for help, their requests were often met with a sullen, "We told you that during orientation."

What are your new employee orientations set up to accomplish? And who are they designed to serve, your patients and new employees or your staff and systems administrators? Most large healthcare systems have an incredible maze of procedures and protocols that employees are expected to follow. Some organizations do what we did: they give new employees a near-toxic dose of administrivia during intense multi-day orientations and then assume that they will retain it all over time. Others get the basic paperwork done and then send the new employees off to whatever department hired them. What happens next is anyone's guess.

Orient People to What You Value

We all know the power of first impressions in shaping relationships, and the relationship between an employee and an organization is no different. How they're welcomed, the degree to which their orientation addresses their concerns rather than yours, and the amount of support they get in order to succeed early in their new role play a critical part in shaping their impression of your organization and their role within it.

So, too, does the nature of the information they get. I've been through several orientations. One in particular stands out because it was structured around the hospital's mission and values, not its policies and procedures. The human resource staff didn't run it; the vice presidents did, and each talked about the connection between their areas and the quality of the experience they wanted patients to have through the patient's direct or indirect contact with us. Sure, we had forms to complete and general information to review, but they were few in number and integrally linked to the mission and core values. Each section of the orientation included stories and examples of how the mission and values looked in action, not just on the clinical units but throughout the hospital. We even completed a series of exercises that clarified our own personal values and how they connected with the values of the organization.

That orientation was emotional and powerful for me. I left feeling deeply connected to the people in the organization and what they were trying to do. I felt part of something special. I knew what was expected of me and where to seek guidance when I was in doubt.

And what about the details, you might ask: the reports, the forms, the compliance requirements? The staff in my department brought them to my attention as they arose. Just like my rowing instructors, they taught me what I needed when I needed it.

So if you want a culture of service and deep commitment, then start from day one to shape the experience of each new employee coming in the door. Unless you are new yourself, adopt a stance of *not knowing* and take the time to sit through a new employee orientation. Pay attention to the information they are being given and the context within which it is framed. Is the focus on helping the employee succeed and contribute to the patient's experience, or is it on learning the system's rules and requirements?

When you sit down at orientation, spend a few minutes remembering the anxiety, anticipation, or ambiguity you felt when you were sitting in their seat. Use your personal or clinical experience to remind yourself of what happens when people are steeped in fear, anxiety, anticipation, or other powerful emotion: they have trouble hearing. So the first order of business is to create a safe environment within which *not knowing* is valued.

Pay attention to the energy level in the room. Are people engaged and asking questions? Are they alert and curious? Or are they sitting glassy eyed and silent? What might be more energizing? Notice your own energy level. What can it teach you?

Take what you've learned and use it to craft your own message for the people coming to your unit or department. Keep in mind that they want and need answers to only a few questions, especially in the early weeks of a new job:
* What do you expect of me?
* What's in it for me?
* How am I doing?

If you respond wearing a traditional manager hat, you'll likely answer those questions in terms of tasks, concrete rewards, and measures of performance. If you're wearing a leader hat, you'll likely start with a question that leads you both into an exchange of ideas around their role in fulfilling the organization's purpose and embodying its values, the importance of their contribution to the greater whole, and your personal interest in what supports their success.

Employees need both types of answers, although in the long term most will blossom more readily with the purposeful and personal guidance of the latter. Women know this intuitively already. We just lose sight of it when we're trying to do it the *right* way.

Take a View from the Outplacement Line

Even before new employees walk in the door, they get a taste of what your organization is like from your recruiting and hiring processes. How you treat relationships with potential employees speaks volumes about what your organization values. And since organizations comprise numerous interdependent parts and processes, how you recruit and treat new employees has a direct bearing on how they will treat patients.

Sampling these processes isn't as easy as sampling orientation. So use your imagination. Climb into a different set of shoes. Assume for a minute that tomorrow, you are "downsized" or "deselected" and have no job. You are no longer the unit director, vice president, or chief operations officer. Yesterday you were employed; tomorrow you're shell-shocked.

You shuffle through outplacement, wondering how this happened. You send out your revamped resume, second-guessing every decision you've made, every action you've taken—just in case there WAS something personal about being downsized.

You network with everyone you've ever met, keeping your voice upbeat and full of hope and smiles. You make calls. You wait. You send out more resumes and make more calls. You wait. Your patience starts fluctuating with your cash flow. Your friends ask how you like consulting or early retirement.

People you interview don't call back. They avoid your carefully crafted-so-it-doesn't-sound-too-eager e-mail. Days turn into weeks and weeks into months. You hear nothing about positions that people said "we want to fill in the next week or two." What do you do with the frustration? The fear? The powerlessness that arises when you can't push the river?

Now, slip back into your own moccasins. You still have your executive or managerial position and title. You're wondering how to get and keep good people. Jot down in your journal what you learned from standing in the shoes of someone who has been displaced, doggedly looking, and dangling. If you've actually been through the drill, write down what you recall most vividly about the emotional demands of that time.

Then compare your empathic wonderings or emotional recollections with what other displaced yet talented people have said. Below is a list I've compiled from working with people who've been through the outplacement line. I've tried to capture the tone as well as the content of the experience. What would you add?

* Be responsive. Like NOW. Applicants don't want to wait weeks for a preprinted card from your HR department saying, "Thank you we got your resume someone will be in touch sometime blah blah blah." Learn how your system actually works. Are you playing to talented applicants or to in-house schedules, targets, or cumbersome review systems? Organization that set high standards for responsiveness win lots of points with savvy applicants.

* Be specific. Applicants want only two things from an initial contact. First, are their skills a match for your needs? Yes or no. If no, then thanks for your promptness and directness; they're off to the next prospect. If yes, then what is the next step in learning about the position they might fill? Clean and simple. What is your organization doing to recognize a good fit, respond quickly and respectfully to those who are not, and hook the best people before someone else snags them?

* Follow through. Do the people who are hiring honor their own word? "You'll hear from us within a week" does not mean 11 days, next month, or when they get around to it. It means less than 7 calendar days. That includes holidays, sick days, and vacation days. Every unreturned call, every missed promise, every day of inaction is a chip out of your organization's credibility and a blow to your trustworthiness in the applicant's eyes—not to mention what it says about how you run your organization. Credibility counts.

* Follow through no matter what. "The department director was called out of town." "We haven't interviewed everyone yet." "The VP was sick for 3 days." "It's taking longer than we expected." Excuses, all of them. Applicants don't want excuses. They want information, even if it's only, "We've been delayed; here's our new timeframe." A promise fulfilled says volumes about your organization's credibility and your sensitivity to the applicant's situation.

These guidelines aren't proprietary information, or something a committee of eight must benchmark for six months before seeking someone else's approval to implement. They are simply emotionally and socially intelligent action anchored in empathy and respect for the importance of relationships even with people we do not know.

So step out of the stream of usual expectations and mine your own experience for new perspectives on the workplace. It could be anything: taking on a new role like parent or school activist or community volunteer; learning a new skill like speaking Japanese or baking Madeleines or playing a musical instrument; or resurrecting something significant from your past like a sport or a hobby, a relationship or an ambition. Then select and live with a question or two about it. You'll find some sample questions in below.

Let life be your teacher

* What does my experience with X have in common with what's going on at work?
* What distinguishes X from what's going on at work?
* What do I notice about this life experience that I've not noticed about work?
* How am I different when I'm doing X than when I'm at work?
* How do I withhold those aspects of myself in the workplace?
* If I brought them to work with me, what might be different?

New Possibilities Come from a Beginner's Mind

When I was taking rowing lessons, the instructors gave us a few minimal guidelines for how to row together and balance the boat. When we could do both, they gave us a great exercise in mindfulness, in being exquisitely attuned to what is happening in the moment. They had us row with our eyes closed.

It was a remarkable experience. Without visual cues, we had to tune in carefully to information from other senses:

* the sounds of oars clicking in oar locks, puncturing the water, and whooshing from back to front
* the physical sensations of being in or out of synch with others' movements
* the weight of the oar handle and the degree of tension or pressure with which we hold it
* the remarkable ease with which our bodies can move when we're focused and relaxed
* the fleeting yet riveting sense of being indistinguishable from the boat, the water, the crew.

It is hard to work with your eyes closed in the workplace. But you can create a similar sensation by assuming a stance of not knowing. It is a practice I mentioned earlier called beginner's mind. The term comes from the Zen master Shunryu Suzuki: "In the beginner's mind there are many possibilities. In the expert's, there are few" (2002, 21). Beginner's mind requires that you set aside your expertise in order to view the world with fresh, new eyes.

One way to begin is with some experiential practices like those on the next page. Try a few in order to have the experience of doing something from a beginner's mind. Then pay attention at work to things you normally take for granted. Look at a nurses' station or your office or the hospital lobby or cafeteria as if you were seeing it for the first time. What do you see that you normally overlook? How clean are the glass doors in the lobby or the tables in the cafeteria? How cluttered is the nurse's station or your desk? If you were a visitor passing through, what assumptions might you draw from what you see? How do those assumptions align with the perceptions you *want* patients, families, colleagues, or visitors to have as they wander the halls?

Practice beginner's mind

Here are some simple practices for cultivating a beginner's mind. Try one or two and see what happens.

* Pick a routine activity like brushing your teeth or eating with a fork, and switch to your non-dominant hand for a few days. Pay attention to how this feels and to how you respond to how it feels.

* Watch a video or a television program with the sound off to see how much you can discern the story line from body language, lip reading, and gestures.

* Take a common household or office object—a pair of tongs, for instance, or a lampshade—and create a list of at least 10 uncommon uses for it.

* Take a pair of dark glasses, cover the inside of the lenses with tape or petroleum jelly so you can't see through them, and sit in the lobby where you work. Listen to the conversations going on around you and imagine what the speakers look like.

By disrupting simple, everyday behaviors, you force yourself to experience them from a beginner's mind. Brushing your teeth with your non-dominant hand can connect you with the challenges of patients who have lost functional ability and must relearn activities of everyday living. Observing how you respond to the loss can heighten your appreciation of the level of frustration and powerlessness that patients often feel.

Watching a video without the sound helps you attend to the subtle nonverbal cues of others and to the ease with which we can misinterpret those cues.

Listing uncommon uses for a common object requires you to suspend what you already know about an object and think creatively rather than routinely—a practice that can be invaluable any time you are confronted with a recurring problem or with a group that has been together long enough to suffer from groupthink.

Imagining someone's appearance from the sound of his or her voice can reveal much about your own stereotypes and biases.

In short, a beginner's mind reconnects us with the mind of a child: curious, open, adventurous, and nonjudgmental. Those will serve us far better than the more common stances of being the expert, judging, and playing safe.

When you're in a meeting, lower your head, close your eyes, and just listen to how the discussion unfolds. Sit in the emergency department or surgery waiting room and do the same. What do you hear that you didn't hear before? What are the sounds of hope and fear, be they in the conference room or the waiting room? How do people express their hope and assuage their fear?

Ask your staff or co-workers to do the same, and then compare notes. In healthcare environments, it is easy to become inured to the sounds of joy and suffering, not just among patients and families but among co-workers as well. Remember the nurse in the unit that created a web of healing? Not until she began paying attention to healing did she realize how much suffering the staff were experiencing. What does listening with a beginner's mind reveal? And what does it suggest about next steps for orienting yourself and others to fulfilling the organization's purpose and adapting to the daily challenges you all encounter?

Pay Attention to What You Pay Attention To

A variant on beginner's mind is paying attention to what you pay attention to. Most of us experience lapses of attention. How often have you sat in a meeting and realized you missed the last few minutes of discussion? Or driven to work and realized you couldn't recall the last few miles? Your attention went elsewhere. It happens all the time. Similarly, our attention lapses when we fall into patterned ways of thinking and responding. Our automatic responses are usually laden with assumptions, expectations, and judgments.

Paying attention to what absorbs our attention is a powerful way to disrupt those automatic responses and learn more about our own belief systems. For example, the next time you're in a conversation with someone, pay attention to the silent conversation, the running commentary, that's going on in your mind. Pay attention also to the emotional charge that it generates. What are you telling yourself? *She's really on the ball ... he has no idea how to handle this situation ... why is he asking me for this? ... I can't get a word in edgewise.* Notice how the commentary and emotions change depending on your relationship with the other person. Your boss saying, "I want to see you right now" will likely evoke a much different internal response than a direct report making the same request. If this internal commentary is powerful enough to influence your behavior, write it down. I've done this for several years, and am always surprised at what it reveals.

Much of the fear and uncertainty we experience in the workplace is the product of this internal running commentary, not the external event. So if you want to discover how you hold yourself back and what conditions allow you to open up, pay attention to your own inner monologue. This is simply a variant on the exercises we talked about in Chapter 4 for clarifying what you value. For instance, consider the following:

* What are you assuming when you withhold a comment or opinion?
* What are you telling yourself when you do offer a remark?
* What's different about your internal monologue in each of these environments?
* How often is your monologue saturated with judgments?

When you're clear on what holds you back and what allows you to open up, you have the basics you need to reframe a negative monologue into one that's more self-enhancing. You also have the opportunity to *choose* how you want to respond. If

you need help surfacing that internal commentary, then team up
with a trusted colleague and use dialogue to observe and explore
your thinking and the emotional charge that it generates.

Practices like these are practices in staying present
to whatever is unfolding, and the capacity to stay present
is critical when you're leading, especially in tense and
emotionally charged situations. Most people react to negative
emotion in one of two ways: they back off or they lash out.
In both cases, the emotion is managing them; they are not
managing it. The more practiced you are at noticing your own
emotions and staying with them to see what they reveal, the
more aware you become of their energetic nature. They are
messengers, signals that something important is on the line.
Recall from Chapter 2 their Latin and French roots. They
move us. They *excite* us.

So when you listen to emotions with an open and curious
mind, when you witness how they ebb and flow with your
thoughts or your stories, you're grounding yourself in the
moment. You no longer are being pushed or pulled by them.
You have created a space for awareness and choice, and
now you can harness and direct their energy in positive and
adaptive ways.

As you get more comfortable with your own emotional
field, practice bringing a similar approach to group dynamics.
The next time you're in a meeting, pay attention to the
emotional tenor of the group. What is the energy level like?

Does it have a positive or a negative charge? What kinds of exchanges further the group's work? What disrupts or derails it?

WHAT DISRUPTS A GROUP'S PROGRESS
IS THEIR EMOTIONAL ATTACHMENT TO THE CONTENT
BEING DISCUSSED.

Listening with a beginner's mind—letting go of your own story of what's happening or what should or shouldn't happen, and merely observing what actually occurs—helps you grasp more clearly the dynamics at work in the room. What disrupts a group's progress is never the technical or analytic stuff; it is the emotional attachment people have to the content being discussed. They get attached to myriad things:

* Their own positions
* The need to look good or to impress others
* The desire to get a specific result
* The belief that their way is the "right" way.

Observing with a beginner's mind allows you to see patterns that you perhaps didn't see before. If you are willing to speak directly to what you observe—in an open, curious, and nonjudgmental way—you can often have a significant impact. As a mentor of mine once said, "If you can accurately describe what is going on, it will change."

Speaking to the group dynamic requires courage. We have been "dis-couraged" from inviting emotions into the workplace for years. But emotions are the source of our energy. Avoiding them simply drives them underground and inhibits the group's ability to make any meaningful progress. We need to cultivate the ability to surface the emotional issues accurately and without judgment, as described in the following section. This is what beginner's mind helps us do.

Seek First to Understand

This ancient wisdom urges us to suspend our own agenda—our own need to be heard and understood—and listen to others with openness and curiosity. Women are often good listeners when we choose to be. It's one of the ways we nurture relationships. When we seek first to understand, we're stepping out of the role of expert problem solver and into the role of witness and fellow traveler. By taking on the other person's frame of reference, we engage our empathic nature and create a safe space for strong emotions. When we can name it, we can change it.

I was observing a client, a chief nursing officer named Terry, in a meeting with several colleagues. They were having trouble agreeing on the meeting's direction. Different people were advocating different ideas, and people were getting frustrated at the lack of focus. When Terry finally spoke it was to summarize each person's position. "Jim, I think you're saying that we can't take any action until everyone is up to speed on this. Sally, you seem to think we need to get into action and people will come along in the process. Bill, you're not sure we have the right people in the room to move forward," and so on.

It was a simple reflective process, grounded in Terry's ability to tune into the emotional energy in the room, yet it was powerful. The group immediately began to soften. People felt heard. They felt supported.

During the break, Terry pulled the meeting organizer aside and said, "You still seem frustrated. What are you telling us that we're missing?"

The organizer, gesturing wildly, gave a lengthy, impassioned response that was a mix of history, intention, and interpretation. Terry listened for several minutes, then pulled from the detail a simple statement and an equally simple request. "So you're saying you have an approach you think will work and you want my support to try it."

"Yes!" said the organizer, "Exactly!"

"I can do that," Terry said, adding, "It'll be easier for me if you can stay calm. Are you willing to do that?" The organizer paused for a moment. "I *am* pretty worked up, aren't' I?" Terry nodded gently.

"Yes, I'll stay calm," said the organizer.

Terry took a long, cleansing breath. The organizer followed suit. They smiled at one another and returned to the room. The next 90 minutes were focused and productive.

Empathic listeners like Terry listen with a beginner's mind. In personal relationships, women often do this automatically. We listen for what's important to other people. We are sensitive to how tone of voice and physical presence affect others. We practice the very simple principle of seeking first to understand. When we are willing to slow down and attend to what is right here, right now, when we are willing to suspend *knowing* in favor of *learning,* we create possibilities that "being the expert" misses entirely.

It's tough to let go of being the expert. As I said earlier, most of us have spent years learning to become experts at what we do. Experts are highly valued in our culture. But being an expert can blind us to the most basic truths, like the reality of new physicians suffering through orientations created by experts, or of frightened patients and family members, or of colleagues who are seeking desperately to find a new home for their talents or to be heard amid a chorus of voices too busy to listen.

When we're working in expert mode, we also are not receptive to information that is inconsistent with our need to be seen as competent and confident. I suspect that was the case with the senior executive mentioned in the previous chapter who, upon learning that employees distrusted senior management, ordered her team to revamp the recruitment and hiring process to attract more loyal, trusting employees. Her inability to absorb and use negative information in a positive way reverberated throughout the organization.

So if you are among the many women who suffer from not knowing the answers, try going the other direction. Sit with your own fear and confusion. See what not knowing has to offer. Treat it as a process of discovery.

In my experience, getting grounded this way generates a quiet yet empowering sense of confidence, even in the midst of confusion and chaos. It allows us to stay connected to purpose and to offer up, as Terry did, the tension of the moment as an obstacle to a group's progress. Getting grounded this way also helps us hold an environment for change without feeling compelled to have the answers or to take the lead in the traditional sense of being the person in control. Quite the contrary. Our capacity to hold an agenda within the context of the group's purpose creates the container within which the *group* can do the work.

When You Are Stuck, Invent

As good as we are at attending to others, most of us struggle to slow down and attend to what's occurring in our own internal world. Many of my clients, for instance, feel trapped in a continual press for results. They buy their own hype about the dread consequences of failing to meet quarterly targets or standing their ground for something they know in their hearts to be true. They feel caught in a continual battle against time. They take no time to befriend the intricacies of their own ways of discovering and creating. And so they step back from their own knowing. They play small in order to stay safe.

The lesson here is simple: creating what we want is not a smooth, easy process. We have all had times when we've reached the end of our rope. The deadline is upon us. The creative juices have dried up. The horizon disappears behind a wall of frustration or self doubt. The inner critic steps to the pulpit and we begin chastising ourselves for losing focus or procrastinating or not having enough stick-to-itiveness. The painful slide toward despair is set in motion.

Beating up on ourselves does not work, nor does a forced effort to refocus and tough it out, especially when we're trying to get results through others. The only way around that wall is through it. We must sit with it and let the doubt, the confusion, the sense of impossibility swirl around us, without trying to control or direct or force anything.

A marvelous thing happens when we can let go of the need to force or control, when we can relax into not knowing and just allow the situation to unfold. New ideas start to flow. New directions make themselves known. Sometimes for me, letting go takes the form of telling myself *I have nothing to lose; I'm just going to sit with this while I mow the lawn.* Ironically, only when we can fully let go of our attachment to the outcome of something does a new path appear. And it always, always appears.

When my son Michael was in high school, he worked for weeks on a detailed pencil still life that he was submitting to a major art competition. He didn't complete it by the deadline. His usual style in these situations was to storm around in an anxious panic, predicting catastrophe and blaming himself. This time, however, he was the picture of calm. Down to the wire and with no time left to finish the drawing, he did what he often does when he needs to relax: he went skateboarding.

I heard nothing more about the drawing until several weeks later, when he came home from school, beaming, and told me that he had won a top national award. After the hugs and conversational details, I said, "I thought you ran out of time and didn't get it done."

"I didn't," he responded. "I just named it *Fading Objects* and turned it in." What a stroke of brilliance! He simply made the unfinished parts of the drawing an integral part of the work!

When I told my friend Virginia this story, she said, "I learned the same thing about weaving. When you make a mistake, you can go through the pain and tedium of unweaving it or you can treat it as part of the work."

What Michael and Virginia have learned is that being stuck, running out of time, even making mistakes are simply interpretations of the mind. They are the stories we tell ourselves about the circumstances we face, and we can either rail against them in frustration or reframe them as part of the act of creating something new. Obviously, this concept does not apply to medical errors or other adverse events affecting quality of care. But it has great application to how we think—and especially to how we *feel*—about our work, our relationships with others, and our roles in leading.

Over the years, I have struggled with the process of writing. "I hate to write, " I used to tell friends, "but I love to have written." Many times in the writing of this book, I've felt like I reached an impasse. I am out of ideas. I struggle with the words. I grind to a halt, not knowing where to turn next. Yet experience has taught me that hitting the wall is merely part of the process. When I cannot think my way to a solution, I must step into the confusion, experience the emptiness of not knowing, and abandon all attachment to the outcome, hopes as well as fears. This approach leaves me raw and vulnerable. Yet when I succeed, when I can let go of trying to force what I want and simply accept what is, the vulnerability gives me access to a deeper stream of knowing.

Taking this approach to the creation of anything—a book, a drawing, a new kind of work environment—requires patience and faith in our own creative spirit. We must learn to trust that even when the situation looks bleak, something new and exciting can pop up at any moment.

We give ourselves a respite when we can neutralize the notion of being stuck by thinking of it as a gestation period or a natural step in the process rather than as a gnawing problem to be solved. Similarly, we can create a break for ourselves by *not doing* or by doing something else so that the efforts we've already made can steep in the subconscious. How many times have you wrestled for days or weeks with a stubborn problem, thrown up your hands in despair, and then been awakened at 4 a.m. with a clear way forward, or had a sudden flash of insight while you were walking the dog or standing in the shower?

I have come to trust that when we can take the pressure off ourselves, our defenses come down and we clear a path for deeper ways of knowing. With the groundwork well laid and our energy spent, we need to allow time for the work to mellow and steep in another part of the brain. What we are doing here is finding ways to silence the left brain's chatter so the right brain's wisdom can emerge. We are honoring the fact that we are living organisms with a deep capacity to adapt, create, and renew.

So the next time you find yourself stuck on a thorny situation and with no visible options, try an experiment. Walk away. Give yourself permission to not know. And then give

yourself over fully to something else that you thoroughly enjoy.
Spend time with your kids. Read a good mystery novel. Go to
the gym. Row a boat. Walk the dog. And trust that when the time
is ripe, the right things will come.

8

Be a Hub of Information

IF WE FAIL TO RECOGNIZE INFORMATION'S
ESSENTIAL ROLE IN SUPPORTING SELF-ORGANIZATION,
WE WILL BE UNABLE TO SURVIVE
IN THIS NEW WORLD.

Margaret Wheatley

Living Systems Need Information to Thrive

When most of us women were growing up, we learned to value secrets. They were our stock in trade for cementing relationships. As adults, many of us continue the practice, sharing information either one-on-one or with small, intimate groups. Men typically treat information as power, while we treat it as privilege. They hoard it to protect their position; we hoard it to protect our relationships.

When we operate under either of these mindsets in the workplace, we scare ourselves with fears of what might happen if information were to escape our hold. It can be transformed into knowledge and knowledge, as we all have heard, is power. So we dole it out carefully to those we trust, treating it as private and confidential. It is not. Information is the lifeblood of organizations. Sure, information like patient medical records or employee personnel files requires a degree of protection but most operational information is not nearly as confidential as we suspect.

A common argument in top-down organizations is that if proprietary information is leaked, the results could be loss of competitive edge or market share. Information is protected with confidentiality covenants and shared on a need-to-know basis. But it is always changing, always morphing into new forms as it's filtered through human perceptions, expectations, and biases. Any report is already an outdated snapshot; "reality" has changed before the ink has dried.

High performing organizations use information the way any living system does. They let it flow freely with the knowledge that competitive edge does not arise from numbers and data, no matter how detailed, but from the capacity of their employees to use information in responsive and highly adaptive ways. Managers in these organizations trust in the innate capacity of individuals to organize in ways that sustain the identity and integrity of the whole. Employees are partners who understand the connections between their daily activities, the outcomes being measured, and the very success of the organization. They figure out on their own how to move the numbers without compromising other aspects of care or service and experiment with new ways of working. They do not need to be managed. They need to be informed.

Organizations that work this way are resilient because they nurture a workforce that continually adapts to whatever the larger marketplace is throwing at them. In the best service organizations employees actually anticipate and adapt to changes faster than management. Consider the following story, which Herb Kelleher, co-founder of Southwest Airlines, told in a business publication several years ago.

In an organization like ours, you're likely to be a step behind the employees. The fact that I cannot possibly know everything that goes on in our operation—and don't pretend to—is a source of competitive advantage. The freedom, informality, and interplay that people enjoy allows them to act in the best interests of the company. For instance, when our competitors began demanding tens of millions of dollars a year for us to use their travel agents' reservations systems, I said forget it; we'll develop an electronic, ticketless system so travel agents won't have to handwrite Southwest tickets—and we won't be held hostage to our competitors' distribution systems. It turned out that people from several departments had already gotten together, anticipated such a contingency, and begun work on a system, unbeknownst to me or the rest of our officers. That kind of initiative is possible only when people know that our company's success rests with them, not with me (Guinto 2006, 117).

Data are simply forms of measurement, but managers also protect other kinds of information on the mistaken assumption that making it public could threaten the organization's stability. Consider, for instance, that your hospital's executive team has decided to close a unit or discontinue a service line in six months. Rarely are such decisions shared openly and early with employees. I hear all kinds of reasons for keeping employees in the dark. Many use the paternal, "We don't want to worry people" or "What they don't know won't hurt them." Others fear that "People will start jumping ship" and the numbers will suffer. Behavior like this is based on pecking-order thinking, not nurturant thinking. It only serves those who are in control.

A more nurturing approach, and one consistent with humans as living systems, is to share as early as possible both the information and your concerns about its impact on people. Danette, a client of mine, did exactly that when one of her units was marked for closure following a merger. She gave employees the truth along with opportunities to talk through their reactions. She held regular meetings to answer questions, encourage people to grieve and, later, celebrate what they had achieved. She also talked with staff on other units, openly anticipating and addressing their fears and encouraging them to help those being displaced.

She made this decision—which ran counter to what upper management expected her to do—because she imagined herself in her employees' shoes. "Here's what I asked myself," she said. "Would I want be told at the last minute and have to deal with all the emotional turmoil of grieving while I'm panicked about finding something else? Or would I rather get the news early, have time to work through the shock, and then search for a good fit?" For her, the answer was clear. The wisdom of her choice was born out in the unit's waning days: all but two staff members stayed to the end. And all had new positions waiting for them. Morale across her units stayed high because of how she nurtured and supported people through the process.

When information flows freely and people know what's happening, what's working, and what's not, they are quite capable of acting in intelligent ways. That is what the great service organizations have learned and the wannabes have missed.

Witness Southwest Airlines, which has posted a profit every single year since 1974. Their primary approach to service is simple: they rely heavily on "making sure everyone knows when things are running well and when they're not" (Guinto, 2006, 120). That is information sharing, and it occurs every day and across every level, from senior executives to front-line managers and employees.

The remarkable thing about Southwest is that it shares information not just with employees but with competitors as well. For example, the airline used to sponsor *Southwest Airlines Day,* which was an opportunity for executives from other companies to go to Dallas and learn firsthand how Southwest served its customers and managed its employees. They finally stopped when Colleen Barrett, their president emeritus and a confessed "communication freak," decided "enough was enough. People ought to know the story by now" (2006, 116).

YOUR COMPETITIVE EDGE IS NOT IN
YOUR FINANCIALS, METRICS, OR STRATEGIC INITIATIVES;
IT IS IN YOUR EMPLOYEES' CAPACITY
TO ADAPT TO THE CHALLENGES AT HAND.

Even though information about Southwest abounds and the elements of their success have been documented in countless articles and books, other airlines simply cannot create a similar environment. Southwest soars on a set of simple guidelines, a deep respect for employees' abilities, and a continual press to make sure that everyone knows when things are and are not running well. The combination seems too soft, too simple to work. But Barrett argues that Southwest's success really is that straightforward:

> I think the biggest mistake that Southwest wannabes make is that they think that everything we do is a secret or a program. ...I can't tell you the companies over the years who have called or have come in wanting to learn our secrets. And we've been very open over the years about what we do. It's not like we have trade secrets (126-127).

The take-away from Southwest's story underscores what I said earlier: your competitive edge is *not* in your financials or scorecard metrics or strategic plan initiatives; it is in the capacity of your employees to adapt to the challenges at hand. What Southwest's competitors fail to understand is how powerful a clear purpose, trust in your employees, and lots of information about what's working and what's not can be when you put them into practice every day.

The healthcare organization I mentioned in Chapter 3—the one that lived with SPIRIT—was similar to Southwest in both its approach and its success. The senior team entrusted front-line managers with detailed financial and operational data that I have rarely seen shared beyond the executive ranks. They also taught managers how to read and interpret the data, and managers were expected to use it, in turn, with front-line employees. More importantly, the senior team actively sought information from employees throughout the organization as a way of staying well connected and informed themselves. As a result, the organization thrived.

Share Openly and Purposefully

When we protect and hoard information, we leave front-line and even supervisory-level people working in the dark. For example, few hospital employees know how their organization makes money. Some managers guard it as highly proprietary; others assume that employees are not interested. I've even heard a few declare that it is too complex for most employees to understand. Yet when employees are educated about the processes by which net margins are created, they not only "get it," they naturally adapt their behavior in ways that reflect a deeper grasp of the organization's needs and a greater commitment to its survival.

When the only information staff nurses hear is "Last month was a bad month; you need to work harder," they have nothing to guide them. But when they understand that during cyclical downturns in volume, staffing and supply inventories need to change as well, then they can adapt accordingly. Armed with education and information, they can self-organize in ways that anticipate and adapt to normal cyclical changes.

THE VALUE OF INFORMATION
EMERGES FROM PEOPLE'S INTERACTIONS WITH IT
AND WITH ONE ANOTHER AROUND IT.

Since hospitals are living systems, their units and services are interdependent. So the more opportunities employees have to witness and experience the connections between their own efforts and those of other departments, the better. When floor nurses see a flooded emergency department during a diversion, they gain a whole new appreciation for the importance of expediting appropriate patient discharges and bed turnarounds. When staff understand the complexity of patient flow—registration processes, unit capacity, bed availability, transport services, and so on—they are on the road to thinking in systemic rather than silo-like terms. They learn to see the bottlenecks affecting throughput, and can partner with one another in experimenting with new ways of moving patients smoothly from the emergency department to the house.

Similarly, when physicians get information about hospital reimbursement arrangements and the financial implications of their orders, they gain a whole new appreciation for how their orders affect the institution. Given ample information and some guidance in how to interpret it, they are quite capable of deciding when a particular lab test or consultation is unnecessary for a patient's diagnosis and can be done on an outpatient rather than inpatient basis.

When outcomes measures were first being tracked in one of the healthcare organizations I worked with, leaders debated for 6 months whether or not to make public the mortality and morbidity statistics of staff cardiologists. Opponents were concerned that publicizing such data would embarrass physicians and create dissent between the administration and the medical staff. Proponents argued that access to information was essential for healthy self-correction. The proponents won out. And they were right. Within months, the outlying cardiologists' morbidity and mortality statistics began coming in line with those of their peers. All they needed was information; their desire to do well did the rest.

So look at your own department or areas of responsibility. Live with one or two of the questions below for a while to learn more about your own practices with information. Pay special attention to when and how your words and your actions differ.

An exercise in information sharing

* Who do your staff serve, indirectly as well as directly, and what assumptions have you made about the information they need to serve those people? Think not just in terms of patients but also of people in other departments. How can you test the validity of those assumptions?

* How can you increase the flow of information that broadens and deepens your staff's understanding of the importance of their work within the larger system? What information can you use to illustrate their influence and impact?

* How often and what do you share from managers' or executives' meetings with everyone who reports to you? What are the potential consequences for not sharing?

* If you are more than one or two levels removed from the front line, what expectations and networks do you have in place to assure that your direct reports are sharing information with those at the front line?
* What information do you gather from staff and take back to managers' or executives' meetings to expand their awareness and understanding of what goes on in your area?

If you are in the majority, which means that information transfer stops at your doorstep, then try a one-month experiment. Gather your staff together, share the information you are getting relevant to a key aspect of serving patients or customers, and invite them to question it, scrutinize it, and apply it to their own work lives. Then meet regularly to reflect on what they are observing and learning. Chances are good that when they get a steady flow of useable information coupled with opportunities to apply it and learn from it, they will shift the focus of their attention in ways that improve performance and generate novel and effective alternatives.

There is one caveat to this experiment, however. Share the information face-to-face. Do not rely on memoranda or emails. The value of information emerges from people's interactions with it and with one another around it. Remember, we are living creatures working in highly complex, interdependent systems. We need opportunities to exchange ideas and build on the synergy created by those exchanges.

Memoranda and emails are static; people scan them for what's important and can easily overlook key information. Personal interaction is dynamic. It directs our attention, helps us pull meaning and significance from information, and strengthens and expands our relationships in the process.

When people begin talking, you likely will encounter differences. They'll have different perspectives, assign different interpretations, and identify different gaps between what they are being told and what experience tells them is true. When this occurs, dig deeper. Assume a stance of not knowing. Ask more questions than you answer. Welcome gut reactions and employee experiences as new information.

The danger is in ignoring information that does not fit with your current view of reality.

Make Information Meaningful

In order for information to be useful, it must be meaningful. Nurses cannot effectively self-staff until they understand the limitations of productivity standards and the influence of acuity and census levels. They cannot anticipate, track, and respond quickly and effectively to subtle trends until they have ample data and a solid understanding of the interplay of key variables during cyclical downturns. Marketing people cannot know why patients shouldn't receive satisfaction surveys until they know the importance of being sensitive to a family's loss and who in the house has that information. Cardiologists cannot know to change their practice patterns until they have meaningful data about how their performance compares with that of their colleagues.

I said in Chapter 3 that when you are guided by a strong, internal sense of purpose rather than by the need to conform to external expectations, you begin to work differently. What seemed like an overwhelming to-do list begins to shake out into natural priorities: those that further your intentions and help fulfill your purpose, and those that do not.

The same is true for information. You likely have volumes of information passing across your desk. So think strategically about what is important and what is not. Remember, the measurable results that most organizations track are not the same as the dynamic results that most leaders want. We have been led to believe that if we can just find the right metric or the right ratio, the results we want will follow suit. It does not happen that way. In fact, pursuing the numbers typically shifts our attention away from what we most want: greater personal accountability, engagement, and adaptability in the moment.

As usual, start with the end in mind: what you want for those you serve, how you want to work together and treat each other in the process. Then think about what informational measures might serve as markers for the journey. You can also look at the volume of memos, charts, ratios, and percentiles that cross your desk, and ask yourself this question: *what does each of these tell me about engagement and teamwork, adaptability and creative responses to the unexpected, quality of care and patient experiences?*

Look at every piece of information in terms of its value in furthering your intentions, helping people understand their impact, and deepening awareness of what is essential for serving patients. Try classifying information into one of the Four I's:

* *Imperative* for success
* *Important* but not essential
* *Interesting* but not important
* *Irrelevant.*

Then talk with your staff. They probably have little knowledge of what passes across your desk, so educate them. Ask them what information they think is important that isn't currently available. Have them do a similar ranking, and compare notes.

Remember: conversations are important for making information meaningful. Take the time to explore each other's reasoning, not just express opinions, so you create a pool of shared understanding (see Chapter 9 for a set of communication skills that help greatly with this). Remember to work from questions rather than answers. And pay particular attention to how you respond when others' opinions differ from yours. Are you open and curious, or do you shut down or defend? This information is "imperative" for your own development.

Conversations broaden people's awareness of the complexity of the system and bring more wisdom to bear on defining the relative importance of information. They also give you an idea of what each person knows and doesn't know, which is useful when you are mentoring or developing people.

Many times, employees lack experience with concepts that seasoned managers take for granted. Again, we are back to exploring our own assumptions, this time about other people's behavior. How many times have you assumed that an employee should be able to do something and then been disappointed when the results were poor? How would you approach the employee if you assumed that he is operating from a different point of reference and perhaps has little experience with what you consider common knowledge?

How often have you assumed that a staff physician whose office was emailed a spreadsheet of reimbursement rates for diagnostic codes knew how to translate it into the costs associated with each order written or with each delayed discharge? How would you approach the physician if you assumed that she has little time to decipher complicated spreadsheets but wants to help contain costs for her patients while preserving quality of care?

You need the thinking and engagement of every single employee, so invest your time in creating opportunities for people to interact with, draw meaning from, and see the connection between the information they get and the mission or purpose they're pursuing. Nurture their curiosity and they'll grow in exciting, unpredictable ways.

Information Is Only Useful If It Moves

How we think about organizations determines how we structure them, which, in turn, conditions how information flows through them. In hierarchical organizations, information typically flows from the top down. Those at the top have ready access to lots of information as well as frequent opportunities to exchange and discuss it. They sort and select what flows to the next level, where information is again sorted and selected.

While this process is going on, information is also flowing through human networks, which means that people at each level are operating within their own contexts and adding their own meanings. In organizations with communication bottlenecks or breakdowns, important information frequently does not even reach the front lines in a useable form. As a result, great intentions at the upper levels don't get translated into meaningful information that guides and aligns behavior at the front lines.

When a good friend of mine went to a world-renowned hospital for surgery on an abdominal aortic aneurism, I saw "world class care" on brochures in the lobby and posters on the walls. I asked the receptionist what "world class care" meant. She wasn't sure, and she wasn't curious enough to pick up the phone and get an answer.

Later in pre-op, I mentioned the brochures and posters to several staff and asked what "world class care" meant. Their responses ranged from a wordless look of confusion to "I have no idea" to "Beats me. It's probably something the marketing department cooked up."

Staff on the post-surgery floor sang the same song. One shrugged, two shook their heads, and another said, "I wish I knew. They sure don't treat *us* that way."

I concluded that someone higher up had great intentions and had made a significant investment in glossy brochures and posters, but those intentions never made their way to the front lines. Why not? Probably because the information about world-class care was being treated as a *thing,* a commodity to be launched after much senior-level discussion and with lots of brochures and brouhaha, but without anyone thinking to weave it into the fabric of employees' everyday lives.

As a result, I encountered the dead end of the dream, after it had been sorted and filtered through numerous levels of management and then interpreted by those at the front lines, who seemed to be hearing it for the first time. Small wonder that "world class care" at one level of the organization translated to confusion, cynicism, and resignation at another.

Since organizations are networks of connections, they have the potential to be broad webs of inclusion if you get information flowing freely within them. What if the people who aspired to providing "world class care" in this organization had done what organizations like Southwest Airlines do: move information frequently and in all directions about what is working well and what is not? What if they had said, over and over, "Let's gather examples of what world class care looks like," and then made heroes of those who provide world-class care? What if they were so serious about providing world-class care that they aligned their hiring, orientation, development, and communication systems to support every effort to deliver it?

If you are at the other end of the spectrum—getting volumes of information that is not in a useful or useable form—then assume a stance of not knowing and begin asking others when and how they use it. Or ask those who issued the information to help you extract the meaning and relevance of it for you. In short, don't assume that you are the ignorant one.

* * *

Pushing to get information moving through ever-larger circles is a personal challenge for many women, and runs counter to how most organizations operate. Yet it is one of your high leverage points for getting people aligned and working on purpose. Information is not important until people can interact with it and pull meaning and new possibilities from it. So position yourself at the center of an information network.

If need be, examine and challenge the common female assumption that information is confidential. Try a new assumption: information is essential for people to grow and adapt.

When you provide information that people can use to make sense about how their unit, their department, or the organization is doing and how they can influence the outcomes, you set the stage for greater teamwork, innovation, and creative responses to the unexpected. When you help people get information about their own performance that helps them self correct and grow, which the next section is about, you set the stage for greater trust, personal accountability, and engagement.

So whether you are a senior executive, a front-line supervisor, or an individual contributor, treat information as the currency of change. If you have trouble sharing information, try the practices on the next page.

Become a hub of meaningful information

* Examine your own assumptions about information.
    * Make a list of what you consider confidential, privileged, and public information.
    * Write down the reasons or rationale for your assignments.
    * For confidential and privileged information, identify the consequences to you for sharing it and the consequences to those you serve for not sharing it.
* Spend a week observing and jotting down what you actually do with information.
    * What do you share and what do you not share?
    * When you withhold information, what is your story?
    * What are you telling yourself? If you're whispering the common refrain "I don't have time," step back and ask yourself is it really a matter of time or a matter of focus? If it's the latter, create a practice or two that help you stay mindful of what's most important.
    * Consider a third possibility: it's a matter of fear. When we anticipate serious consequences, the mere idea of taking a course of action that runs counter to our assumptions can evoke fear. If you notice a pattern of withholding due to fear, then try the next practice.
* Test your assumptions.
    * Your purpose in doing this is not to change or alter or improve anything. It is merely to gather information that will help validate or disprove your assumption.
    * Pick an assumption with a modest consequence and write down what you fear will happen.
    * Share your intention with a trusted colleague along with a request for post-action feedback.
    * Then do the thing you fear.

- This next step is critical. Gather data about what actually happens in the wake of your action. Then work with your colleague to compare your fear with what actually occurred.
- Chances are, your imagined consequence either didn't occur or it occurred in a very mild and tolerable form.

* Share the information with those you lead. It is a powerful form of meaningful information for others.

* Keep data and metrics in clear perspective. They are not the ends you seek; they are merely measures of your progress. When they become the center of your attention, they distract you from your purpose and intentions. Use them to reflect your success, not direct your efforts.

What We Call Feedback Rarely Is

In order for people to grow, adapt, and perform at their best, they need information about their own performance. One source of information—feedback—has earned a bad reputation over the years. The word first came into the language to describe the self-correcting information built into mechanical systems and electronic circuits. Information was fed back into a system as a means of regulating system performance.

Thermostats, for instance, feed back information in order to maintain a set temperature for a room. Notice that the flow of information is circular. But notice also that the nature of thermostats, like other mechanical systems, is to maintain the status quo, not to encourage growth, change, and adaptation. When we use feedback in organizations, we should be aiming for growth, adaptation, and innovation, not for control.

As humans, we get feedback hundreds of times a day. Every time I type 'fedeback' or 'feedbak' into the computer, my word processing program immediately underscores it with a red, wavy line. I then click the right button on the mouse and get an alternate spelling plus options to ignore it, auto correct, or search for other options in the program's dictionary. I'm operating within a web or circular loop that includes me as the typist, the words that I type, and the software program that translates my keystrokes into visible characters. My desire to create readable prose prompts me to correct spelling errors as I go, and my interactions with the keyboard and software make it happen.

FEEDBACK IS CRITICAL FOR LEARNING;

JUDGMENT IS NOT.

Unfortunately, what we call "feedback" at work rarely is. In true top-down style, those higher on the food chain are expected to "give feedback" to those lower. So the information flow is linear and unidirectional. And the feedback that gets delivered is usually negative; it is the underbelly of reactive, fix-it thinking, designed to keep things stable and under control. You know the drill: a hundred things are going right in your area, and your boss or the senior vice president hones in on the one or two things going wrong.

Of course, we rarely call workplace feedback "negative." We usually dress it up by telling ourselves that it is *constructive criticism*. This is the "I'm-doing-this-for-your-own-good" approach to whacking people. I find nothing constructive about criticism. It hurts. It shuts people down, whether they show it or not. It demoralizes them. And because it can cut to the quick of their sense of competence or worth, the scars stay fresh for years. One executive I know, who prided himself on his relationships and ability to work well with people, was told by a relatively new boss, "You're just not a team player." The remark pierced his soul and hurt him deeply. His level of engagement took a nosedive. That was years ago, and he still bristles at the mention of the boss's name.

Nearly every woman I have met dislikes, worries about, and avoids giving negative feedback. Small wonder. It threatens relationships, dissolves connections, puts us in that distasteful one-up position, and leaves everyone feeling badly.

Feedback is critical for learning; judgment is not. How we frame feedback determines how we use it, so let's look at some ways to reframe our understanding of it.

Let's start with the common assumption that workplace feedback is something one person gives another. This is a linear, not a circular view. Whether we are correcting mistakes or praising progress, *telling* people something about their performance often does little to nurture their ability to self-correct.

However, if we assume that people already have a natural capacity for self-correction, as Tim Gallwey did, then new possibilities open up. Now we can become partners in helping them learn how to get meaningful feedback moment-to-moment and monitor their progress internally. Now feedback becomes information flowing between person and environment, fueling adaptation and creative change, rather than someone else's opinions, belatedly delivered, about how an employee's performance missed the mark.

This view of feedback is much more consistent with women's natural preferences to help one another than it is with men's typical style of jumping in to fix it. Most of us actually give feedback all the time, not in the form of advice or judgment but in the form of listening, empathizing, questioning, and encouraging.

Recall, for instance, a time when you were wrestling with a thorny personnel issue or were trying to decide whether to apply for another position, and you sought out an understanding friend or colleague. Chances are, just voicing and having another person witness your situation led you to a new insight, a decision, or a clear course of action. When we listen deeply to others, we naturally respond with a continual flow of non-verbal and minimal acknowledgements and prompts. And the sheer act of mindful listening and support creates the kind of environment in which others can discover their own answers and direction.

If you do not practice deep listening already, try it. The next time one of your kids or friends or direct reports is struggling with a situation, simply give them your undivided attention, then listen and follow their lead. Offer nothing more than an occasional summary of what you are hearing. Put your own agenda aside and strive instead to appreciate and understand their experience. When you do that fully, they likely will experience a shift. Their focus and energy will move away from the struggle and toward a resolution that works for them.

I find that what often stands between people and good performance is not a lack of skill; it is the interference that comes from what other people are telling them or what they are telling themselves. If they are bored, stressed, overwhelmed, or doubtful, their self-talk interferes with their ability to focus on what is interesting, engaging, promising, or challenging about the task at hand. When we step into our feminine power to create safe havens by listening, empathizing, questioning, and encouraging, we help quiet the interference. By helping people feel seen and heard, we help them reconnect with their true self and what it knows.

The Best Feedback Comes from Within

Chances are good that you have children or nieces and nephews. Remember when they were babies first starting to walk? You didn't give orders or critique their progress. You didn't say, "Now grab hold of that table edge and pull yourself into an upright position ... Okay, good, now put your left foot ahead of the right" or "You're not coming along fast enough. We need you walking by your first birthday." You also didn't give them technical feedback: "When you let go of the table, you didn't have your weight evenly distributed, which is why you fell."

Why? Because you knew and believed, *deep down*, in their capacity to walk.

So you encouraged every effort to get into a standing position. You said, "Yes! Yes! You can do it! C'mon!!" You offered your index fingers for them to hold onto so they could get immediate feedback from their bodies about what it takes to balance. You let them step and fall, step and fall, step and fall, encouraging every approximation of walking. You created a supportive environment, and their capacity for self-correction did the rest.

You can use a similar process at work if you start from a deep faith in your own and others' capacity to learn. The self-observation exercises throughout this book are designed to help you get the kind of feedback you need to peel back the judgments and work from the core of who you are. They start with awareness, that mysteriously curative action I've talked about earlier.

With physical activities, we naturally absorb and use feedback. Sometimes it comes at us gently, as when a rowing shell tilts to one side. Sometimes it comes at us full force, as when eight novice rowers lean quickly to the opposite side and the boat rapidly rolls past the centerline in response. With mental activities, we usually have to slow down, suspend judgment, and merely observe what is happening, stripped of our stories about the situation. When we do so, we open ourselves to feedback in the moment. And feedback creates new possibilities.

Beth, the client I talked about in Chapter 1, is a prime example of how this works. She got so anxious about meetings starting on time that she consistently jumped in and usurped opportunities for Carl, one of her direct reports, to take the lead. Only when she was willing to slow down and observe what was actually occurring in the moment—internally as well as externally, physically as well as mentally—did she discover that her own anxiety was the obstacle standing in Carl's way.

She also realized that she was expecting Carl to behave *as she would* in situations.

The awareness of what she had been doing was sobering because she had never thought of herself as a "do it my way" kind of person. Yet here it was.

The gift of awareness is that it creates new choices, which, in turn, open the way to new behaviors that generate new outcomes. You may recall that when Beth realized what she was doing, she made some significant changes in both her beliefs and her behavior. The process took mindfulness and courage. She practiced being more aware of the anxiety that arose when things were not going her way, and then reframing it. She also practiced different ways to allay it. She began testing and letting go of the assumption that her way was the "right" way. She started asking about, identifying, and building on her staff's strengths, which required that she be mindful of her habitual style of hammering on weaknesses and consciously choose a different approach.

In short, when Beth learned to observe her own experience with beginner's eyes, she discovered how her own take-charge style was a major block to developing others. When she learned to suspend criticism, work with the end in mind, and engage her direct reports in getting feedback they could use to self-correct, their individual talents began to emerge.

Feedback is important fuel for change. Change occurs one action and one person at a time. A small gesture can have a great impact. A slight shift in perspective can reveal a new world. As one executive coaching client said, "What I notice most is that everything is the same, yet everything is different. I'm the same person ... but people respond to me differently, they seek me out, they're more engaged and committed."

Be a Fellow Traveler, Not a Critic

Here is a technique that's very effective at helping people get feedback and learn how to self-correct. You can use it with direct reports, colleagues, people senior to you, your kids, your friends, and just about anyone who wants to accomplish something important to them. There is just one caveat. In order for it to be effective, you must have a genuine desire for a mutual, positive exchange. That is your purpose. If you want to put someone in his place or get someone to do things your way, then do *not* call it feedback. Call it control.

Feedback needs a context, so engage people in conversations about what they are trying to achieve. The box on the next page summarizes some basic steps. Help people clarify their thinking rather than give them solutions. Consider, for example, someone who is struggling to learn how to delegate. You might ask for their working definition. For some, delegating means, "Here, take this and do it." For others, it means micromanaging every facet of the activity. Sometimes, just clarifying what a word means will produce new ideas or choices.

* Identify what they are trying to accomplish
* Clarify the "why," the purpose or reason they're doing this; when appropriate, offer distinctions that create purposeful choices
* Explore how they are currently approaching the effort
* Ask them what they wanted and didn't get or what they got and didn't want
* Help them articulate the logic or reasoning that informed their actions
* Invite emotion into the conversation as valuable information about how they are framing the situation
* Suggest a self-observation exercise to become more aware of what actually happens in the moment so they begin separating their experience from their stories about the experience
* Help them reflect on the results, distill the learning, and apply it
* Trust in their capacity to adapt in self-enhancing ways.

Help people clarify their purpose: *why* do they want to delegate? Are they trying to unload tasks they don't like or are bored with? Or are they trying to develop someone's potential? The answer has a direct bearing on what they delegate and how. Clarifying their purpose is another way to create choices they may not be aware of.

It may be useful to explore *how* they delegate. Are they throwing tasks at people without giving any direction or clear expectations? If so, then try some open-ended questions about what they think employees need in order to perform well. Offer your own experience with being given new tasks and no direction, or ask what they need when they've been in that situation. Are they prescribing all the "how's"? If yes, then offer a distinction between a process focus and an outcomes focus, or suggest experimenting with what happens when they offer "what" and "by when" instead of "how." By exploring each other's perspectives, you create a dialogue and powerful opportunities for greater awareness, your own as well as theirs.

Many times, people's personal styles get in the way of their effectiveness. Remember that what drives our behavior is our mental model. In situations like these, you might start by asking one of the following questions:

*   What did you want in this situation that you didn't get? Or
*   What did you get in this situation that you didn't want?

As the person contrasts what he wanted with what he got, help him articulate the thinking or logic that informed his actions. Keep your questions neutral and listen for leaps of logic or unfounded assumptions. Sometimes in the course of discussion, a person discovers his own answers ("I assumed that …" or "I guess I should have double checked with…"). Other times, you may see something he does not. When that happens, merely draw attention to it ("Sounds like you took his comment personally…" or "So when you did X, she did Y …"). By being a fellow traveler rather than a critic, by observing rather than judging, you create and hold a space within which the other person can discover what's true for him.

Self Awareness Is the Starting Point

What you are doing here is using a mutual exchange to expand awareness, both yours and theirs, of the relationships between events and our thinking about them, without judgment. It is a common coaching technique, and one you can use yourself. Here is an example.

One woman I coached, Charlotte, frequently bristled about all the slights she suffered in her interactions with male colleagues. They ignored her ideas. They excluded her from important meetings. In her words, they "disrespected" her. She had a powerful—and self-reinforcing—story to explain what she was experiencing: they felt threatened by her. And she was unwilling to back down and be "a doormat" in order to help them feel more comfortable.

While her story worked to explain what she was experiencing, she often felt angry, hurt, or both. One day, I asked, "Would you like an observation?" When she said yes, I told her I was struck by how often she interpreted men's behavior as personal attacks. She had never looked at it that way. We explored a few examples and then created a coaching exercise for her.

She agreed to pay attention to and jot down what she was telling herself whenever she felt slighted by a male colleague. She also agreed to observe and jot down what she experienced in her interactions with women. By observing herself in action in several situations, she discovered that she assigned entirely different intentions to women's behavior than she assigned to men's. She also discovered a whole set of expectations she had—that she had not been aware of—about how men *should* respond to her.

When we began experimenting with new and more self-enhancing ways of thinking about men's behavior, Charlotte began to see how her own thinking was fueling her anger and leading her to react in negative ways. For instance, she was working with Brad, a male peer, on a new ob-gyn service line product with a tight roll-out timeline. She came to one of our coaching sessions so angry with Brad that she was near tears.

He was "barging ahead," she claimed, by excluding her from two key meetings the previous week with one of their largest ob-gyn practices. Her story came pouring out: he was clearly intimidated by her knowledge of the product line and he wanted to be the star who pulled this off, so he "deliberately" scheduled the meetings when she was out of town.

"Yes," I said, "that story is one possible explanation for why he excluded you. Now give me three more possibilities, including at least one that assigns a positive intention to his actions." After several minutes and a coaching reminder of her experience with female colleagues, she generated a new explanation: given the timeline, Brad might have been trying to keep the project on time and on track by not waiting until her return to schedule the meetings. The shifts in her energy and mood were palpable.

As a next step, she agreed to try an experiment. Rather than hammer Brad with accusations, she agreed to thank him for ushering the project along in her absence. More importantly, she also agreed to prepare for the conversation by practicing the delivery of those words from a place of true gratitude. Neither of us knew Brad's reasons for scheduling the meeting, but after Charlotte offered him genuine thanks for forwarding the project, she began feeling much more like a respected peer in conversations with him.

I call this the iceberg approach: the content of someone's words or actions is the observable tip of the iceberg; beneath the surface are the emotions driving the behavior, and at the base of the iceberg are the deeply held beliefs generating those emotions. In the workplace, we rarely explore anything beneath the observable tip. But our ability, as women, to dip below the surface and have conversations on the emotional level is sometimes exactly what a situation requires.

So when you pick up on something that you think is holding someone back, put it out as an observation. Maybe you have a director whose credibility is low because she will not make decisions without everyone's approval. You might say, "Other people's approval seems really important to you." If she affirms your observation, then you can follow up with a question like, "What would it take for you to trust your own judgment?" Note that the focus isn't on the negative *getting rid of* her need for approval but on the positive *moving toward* self-confidence. If she disavows your observation, then you can explore how she views her behavior and offer—as one possible interpretation— the connection you see between her approach and her credibility.

Maybe you have a direct report who blames everything on other people. You might say, "It seems to me that you feel like a victim of everyone else's actions, and it leaves you feeling powerless." If your observation is on target, then you can ask, "What would it take to get you into the driver's seat?" Again, your focus is on creating self-enhancing thoughts and behavior rather than eliminating what is self-defeating. If she does not see a connection, then engage her in how she does feel, and look for ways to link her thoughts and feelings to her behavior and the outcomes she is getting.

In both cases, you are listening not just to the content but also to the emotional message underlying it. Women are often remarkably intuitive at grasping the emotional tenor of a situation, yet we tend to support rather than challenge the other person's experience. We can—and often need to—do both. When the person feels understood, you have created an alliance, a trusting base from which to work.

When people sense that you're working in their best interest, you can help them get information to self-correct. Beth wanted to feel effective as a leader and had to discover first what was driving her frustration with Carl. Charlotte wanted to feel more respected by her male colleagues and had to learn first how she personalized their behavior. Both needed to find out more about how their own stories were driving their behavior. In situations like these, the best feedback does not come from outside; it comes from within.

Your role in offering feedback—your purpose—is not to "fix" anything. It is to help the other person get useful information to self-correct. So you must be able to offer neutral rather than judgmental observations of their behavior.

If you do not already view feedback this way, then start a list of examples from your own life. Look for times when you disengaged judgment and merely paid attention to the challenge at hand. How did you learn to use the Internet, play tennis, create a thriving garden, crochet, or solve Sudoku puzzles? Treat your own experiences as metaphors for figuring out what feedback might be effective at work or for someone else.

As I mentioned earlier, what often holds us back is our negative self-talk. So welcome feelings as well as behavior into the discussion since they often are in the driver's seat. Use self-observation exercises and visions of what people want to increase their awareness. And above all, trust in their capacity as living beings to adapt to new information in self-enhancing ways.

9

Let "What" Lead and "How" Will Follow

LEARNING FROM EXPERIENCE IS A FACULTY
ALMOST NEVER PRACTICED.

Barbara Tuchman

LEADERS ARE MORE POWERFUL ROLE MODELS
WHEN THEY LEARN THAN WHEN THEY TEACH.

Rosabeth Moss Kantor

One of the fascinating qualities of human beings is our capacity to translate simple guidelines into highly complex and adaptive behaviors. Take rowing, for instance. In Chapter 7, I mentioned that our instructors gave us some minimal guidelines for rowing together and balancing the boat. Eight people, each wielding a 14-foot oar in a 65-foot boat less than 30" wide, could reach remarkable speeds when we followed a set of three simple yet purposeful guidelines, even though we were novices at the sport.

This chapter expands on the idea that when people know *what* they want to create, they can be brilliant at figuring out *how,* especially when they have a few purposeful guidelines to point the way. We begin by revisiting rowing as a simple illustration of the power of purposeful guidelines and look at how stellar service organizations use guidelines to help employees best serve customers.

The idea of guidelines is easy to grasp and readily transportable to healthcare, but it takes effort to translate intention into action and a sustained way of doing business. So we look at the experience of a telemetry unit that worked hard to transform their approach to patient care within the constraints of a traditional management structure. As their story illustrates, *not knowing* can pose numerous difficulties for care providers accustomed to working around rather than through everyday problems—and it can produce remarkable results.

Their story also introduces another important theme: translating what we know into effective action requires practice, practice, and more practice—something traditional hierarchies do not foster. So the second half of this chapter looks at what practice means, the importance of protecting time for learning, and three forms of communication that support people's efforts to figure out how to get the results they want.

Purposeful Guidelines Accelerate Learning

The thrill of rowing comes when you're slicing through the water at high speed, your body stretching and pulling in unison with the person ahead of you, the boat responding rhythmically to a beat of surge-recover-surge-recover. From the shoreline, rowing looks like it takes years to master. But as I learned, when you combine a strong desire, a picture of what great performance looks like, and a few guidelines for getting started, even beginners can have a high degree of success. And when you bring learning like this to work, the lessons multiply.

ROWING GUIDELINE NUMBER ONE is to match the speed and movement of the person directly ahead of you. The boat goes nowhere fast if everyone is moving at her own pace, so the person in the last seat, the coxswain, sets the 'rate' or number of strokes per minute, and everyone else matches that pace.

GUIDELINE NUMBER TWO is to stay centered over the boat's keel or centerline. The natural tendency when a boat starts tilting is to lean quickly to the other side. When eight people with 14-foot oars in hand do that, the result is immediate and dramatic. With practice, rowers learn to make small corrections simply by squeezing a butt cheek or lessening the pressure of a foot. As each rower finds her own center of balance, she begins to correct automatically. It's much like learning to ride a bike.

GUIDELINE NUMBER THREE is to stay relaxed and focused. A tense grip on the oar not only drains energy, but also makes the movement forced and choppy. If a rower's attention drifts, it can throw off her rhythm and result in a tangle of oars and body parts. When each person is fully present in mind and body, the movement comes naturally and the crew slides into a rhythm that's effortless and effective.

When each crewmember matches the speed and movement of the person ahead, balances over the centerline, and stays relaxed and focused, the boat slices through the water with remarkable speed and precision.

These guidelines easily generalize to any small group effort. Learning to move in unison is equivalent to aligning with and working from a sense of shared purpose. High performing teams become so attuned to one another's styles and intentions that they perform at levels far beyond what any individual could likely achieve alone. Watch a great trauma or critical care team. While each person moves independently, they work as one, absorbed in the moment, concentrating fully on the task at hand, and guided by a shared sense of why and what.

Staying balanced is equivalent to learning how to self correct. Paying attention to when and how we react to what we don't want—the boat leaning to starboard, for instance, or a dip in employee or patient satisfaction scores, or a thwarted expectation—lets us experiment with lighter, gentler forms of correction until staying balanced becomes a natural, un-self-conscious process. Staying balanced is a never-ending process; the boat, the department, the organization, are continually tipping and tilting. Continual change requires that we continually adjust. And continual adjustment requires that we stay open and receptive to what is unfolding in the moment.

Being relaxed and focused is equivalent to what athletes call working in the zone and what psychologists call flow. They're prerequisites for excellence, be it on the river or in the workplace. When we're engaged in something we thoroughly enjoy and the challenge at hand is matched by our competence and skill, we naturally slip into a state of concentrated yet effortless focus. We're in the zone. Stress, which occurs when the challenge exceeds our skill, and boredom, which occurs when our skill exceeds the challenge, put us outside that optimal zone and thus interfere with our ability to relax and focus.

Notice that all of these guidelines are about relationships: with other rowers or team members, with the boat or department or organization, with ourselves at play or at work. The party line tells us that work is about *tasks:* outcomes, activities, to-do lists, measurable progress against goals, and so forth. Experience reminds us that work is about *relationships.* What we do, how well we do it, when we do it, and why are always anchored in relationships.

Purpose-driven guidelines evoke our capacity to self-organize, self-correct, and adapt to whatever we encounter in the moment. We don't need to know *how* before we step into action.

We do need to know *what:* what mission we are fulfilling, what tradition we are upholding, what dream or big possibility we are realizing. In fact, *not knowing how* allows us to tap the full power of our adaptive and creative abilities.

Working Models Already Exist

Companies that are devoted to creating great customer experiences have learned the power of working from a few purpose-driven guidelines. In Columbus, Ohio, a restaurateur named Cameron Mitchell has a simple guideline for every employee's behavior, and every employee I've ever asked knows and lives by it. "The answer is yes," goes the guideline, "What's the question?"

Cameron opened 10 restaurants in Columbus in a dozen years, and all are thriving. Two of them, the *Columbus Fish Market* and the *Cap City Grille* are within walking distance of each other. One night while dining at the *Fish Market*, I asked our server about the guideline. She smiled and said, "It's posted in huge letters in the kitchen and it means we do whatever it takes to give you what you want."

"What if I want meatloaf?" I asked, knowing it wasn't on the menu.

"We don't serve that here," she said with another smile, "but we'll gladly send someone over to *Cap City* to get it for you." She paused, and then asked, "Why? Are you hungry for meatloaf this evening?"

The purpose of Mitchell's guideline is to create as much space as possible for employees to serve each customer in highly personalized yet consistently purposeful ways. Employees don't have to memorize a thousand prescriptive "how to's." They simply have to use the guideline, their desire to do good work, and their best judgment.

Guidelines are broad, simple standards that flow from an organization's mission or purpose and give structure and direction, not directives, for people's actions and interactions. They are high leverage principles that put service and patient or customer experiences rather than scorecard indicators at the center of employees' efforts.

Nordstrom, the Ritz-Carlton, and Southwest Airlines are three more organizations that show what's possible when managers trust in the self-directing capacity of people who are committed and aligned. Each excels at *creating great customer experiences*, which is significantly different from *providing customer service*. The former puts the CUSTOMER at the center of activity; the latter puts the in-house PROCESS at the center of activity. Each of these great service organizations excels at the former, while their competitors typically get lost in the latter.

GUIDELINES ARE BROAD, SIMPLE, STANDARDS
THAT GIVE STRUCTURE AND
DIRECTION—NOT DIRECTIVES—FOR
PEOPLE'S ACTIONS AND INTERACTIONS.

Nordstrom, for instance, is known for its fanatic attention to satisfying customers. Its salespeople are free to sell merchandise to customers from any department in the store, which means that if you can't find what you want in one department, your salesperson may well go in search of it in other departments. Salespeople are also free to accept returns even when the merchandise wasn't purchased at Nordstrom or was damaged by the customer. The degree of freedom extended to Nordstrom salespeople would make most managers shudder. But from Nordstrom's perspective, these front-line people—not the managers—control the business. According to Jim Nordstrom,

"'People will work hard when they are given the freedom to do the job the way they think it should be done, when they treat customers the way they like to be treated. When you take away their incentive and start giving them rules—boom! You've killed their creativity" (Spector, 1995).

Ritz-Carlton's motto, "We are ladies and gentlemen serving ladies and gentlemen," captures the essence of the kind of experience that each staff member is expected to create for hotel guests. I once heard a professional speaker tell about his first stay at a Ritz-Carlton. The morning after he arrived, he was returning from a long run. As he approached the hotel's entrance, sweaty and scantily clad, he saw a uniformed doorman approaching. "Given my appearance and the fact that this was a luxury hotel, I figured he was going to ask me to use the side rather than the main entrance," the speaker said. "So you can imagine my surprise when he greeted me by name, handed me a fresh towel, and said, 'I hope you had a great run!'" Needless to say, the speaker stays at the Ritz-Carlton whenever he can.

Southwest Airlines is dedicated to "Living the Southwest Way," which means working with a warrior spirit, a servant's heart, and a fun-loving attitude: three simple guidelines that help employees deliver the level of service for which Southwest is famous. Warrior spirit came out of the airline's early legal battles and economic hardships, and "has provided the 'wings' upon which Southwest could grow and thrive" (Barrett, 2006). The servant's heart is a variant on the Golden Rule. And stories about employees' fun-loving attitude abound among frequent fliers. Just recently, I was on a Southwest flight and, as we were landing, the attendant announced, "Thank you for choosing Southwest Airlines. If you're traveling in the future, we hope you'll think of us. And if you've already booked with one of those bankrupt airlines, we offer our condolences."

These companies, and others like them, understand the importance of organizing their identity—their mission, values, orientation, training, in-house systems—around those they serve. They are devoted to creating great customer experiences, while their so-called competitors are busy trying to figure out how to provide (yawn!) customer service. These high performers can be models for you to aspire to, living examples of what's possible when people are clear on *what* and have the freedom to define *how*. Keep in mind, though, that leading from purposeful guidelines is not a quick fix, as the healthcare example in the next section illustrates.

***

Before we move to that example, let's make a distinction between the *purposeful* guidelines of companies like these, which shape the entire experience of the customer, and the *process* guidelines that most healthcare systems use to shape the quality of clinical care. The two can compliment one another, but they have different impacts on customer and patient perception and satisfaction. Below are two examples from personal experience, one from the airline industry and the other from healthcare, to illustrate the distinction.

In June 2008, I boarded a Southwest Airlines flight in Baltimore. It was about 5 p.m. and a storm was blowing in from the west. We were delayed for over an hour at the gate and for three more hours on the tarmac. Instead of arriving home at 6 p.m., I arrived nearly five hours later. I understand that nature is unpredictable, so I was okay with the delay.

A week later, I received a letter from Southwest apologizing for the delay and acknowledging that they have no control over Mother Nature and air traffic controllers. The letter went on to say that they *do* have control over how they respond to such events, so they were issuing me a "Luv" coupon good for one year. It was equal to half of my airfare! Whoa, was I pleasantly surprised!

The other example occurred just a few weeks after this flight and involved my mother's hospitalization, which I mentioned in Chapter 6. I think she received adequate care, but I cannot say that she received adequate service. In addition to the incidents described in Chapter 6 regarding a walker and portable toilet, the following happened.

It was day ten of her hospitalization. At 9:30 a.m., her physician called to say that he had just finished her discharge orders and she should be "Good to go in hour." So I arrived about 10:30. For the next six hours, we waited, asked questions, waited again, watched the shift change, asked more questions, and waited some more. We finally pulled away from the hospital at 4:45 p.m., seven and a quarter hours after her physician completed the discharge orders!

I think of the difference in these scenarios as one of focus and full engagement. A four-plus-hour delay with the airline—which was due to Mother Nature—got me a personal letter and a voucher for free travel. A seven-plus-hour wait to take my mom home—which was due to dysfunctional in-house processes designed by human beings—got me a day of lost income, a backlog of missed messages, and not so much as a peep of acknowledgement from anyone within the healthcare system.

More importantly, my 92-year-old mother spent the day sitting on her hospital bed, dressed and ready to leave. She ate a belated lunch that I bought at 2:00 p.m. from the fast-food restaurant in the hospital lobby because for some mysterious reason the discharge orders reached dietary in time to cancel her lunch. By the time she finally arrived home that evening, she was exhausted.

Imagine for a moment the impact of such experiences—over 53 hours waiting for a walker, 19 waiting for a bedside toilet, 7 waiting to go home—on patients and family members who know nothing about healthcare systems. Even if they enter your system believing they'll get great clinical care, experiences like these affect their perceptions.

We all know that in a layperson's mind, lengthy delays or poor food service easily translate to questions about clinical care, just like unprofessional staff behavior in the halls can translate to concerns about similar unprofessional behavior in the operating room. As my mom said when we were driving away, "It's a good thing I didn't get *really* sick while I was here. I'd be dead and turning stiff as board long before they even knew I'd kicked the bucket!"

Here Is a Working Model from Healthcare

While hospitals are not in the retail or hospitality business, the notion of starting with "what" and "why" and turning people loose on the "how" is still transportable to the care and nurturing of patients and families. When we trade the traditional control-comply mindset, with its hard-wired assumptions about being experts and having answers, for a more collaborative and empowering stance, we naturally do what the great service organizations do: we put customers—or patients—at the center of activity and the power to generate appropriate, creative ways to serve them into the hands of those at the front lines.

In concept, the process is simple. In action, it requires addressing challenges that most care providers are not accustomed to, as outlined in the example below. If you're interested in the details of doing this kind of work, I encourage you to read the full article from which this example is drawn (Braaten and Bellhouse, 2007).

In 2004, a telemetry unit set out to improve their unit's reputation and to win back the confidence of referring physicians. They had to learn to work entirely differently, so they began by learning how to make small, meaningful changes at the bedside. If you've done process improvement work, some of what they did will be familiar.

Their first step was to slow down and document how work actually unfolded on the unit, using detailed drawings. They found that the mere act of slowing down and observing what actually occurs yielded some eye-opening discoveries. For instance, in one hour, one nurse interacted with 17 people around 13 issues, and changed locations 27 times. Only 42% of her time was spent on patient care (2007, 163).

Learning to see what is actually occurring requires that we suspend what we *think* we know about how work unfolds and rely instead on *actual observation* over time. It is just like the self-observation practices I've encouraged you to use throughout this book, in which you observe and write down what's actually occurring in the moment. I guarantee that it will reveal more than you *think* you know.

When the telemetry nurses slowed down and observed what actually was happening, they uncovered another challenge. They were so accustomed to work-arounds that *they had trouble even identifying problems.* They needed a point of contrast, something that signaled, "Hey, this is not going well." So they turned to a very concrete description of *ideal* patient care. It comprised five clear, specific, and "purposefully binary" conditions, quoted below:

* "Exactly what the patient needs, when and where they need it

* Customized individually
* Immediate response
* No waste of any resource
* Safe—physically, emotionally, professionally, and spiritually – for all" (2007, 163).

Once they knew what the ideal looked like, they could see when and where current care was falling short. Here's the kernel of gold: when providers do not know what ideal care looks like, they won't recognize it, *even when they have it.*

The telemetry unit's ideal functioned as a purposeful guideline. It helped them recognize work-arounds and process breakdowns and it drew their attention to how those were affecting patient care. Seeing the gap between real and ideal deepened their commitment to quality care and lessened their tolerance for sub-optimal conditions.

When the staff could identify process problems, they encountered another obstacle: they thought they knew how to solve these problems. It was a natural but faulty assumption, and a variant of the *knowing-doing* dilemma I've talked about earlier. Knowing that problems exist—even knowing them intimately at the local level—does not automatically translate to being able to solve them.

That's because process problems spread out like webs over both time and space. Recall from Chapter 1, for example, the numbers of people involved in getting a single patient through a single surgery in a single hospital. When we limit our thinking to what's right here, right now, we miss the very complexity that is fueling the problem.

So the telemetry staff had to slow down and take a stance of *not knowing.* They took a single problem and learned how to observe it, illustrate it, and eventually drill down to the root cause of it. Then they had to find solutions that were simple, cost effective, and easily implemented at the point of care. Basically, they needed solutions that required few or no additional resources.

Meanwhile, another dynamic was arising. The process the telemetry staff was learning—contrasting ideal care with real care, then using bedside observation to formulate and experiment with small, continual changes at the point of care—was much different from how the rest of the hospital operated. And since process problems are systemic, the effects of their efforts were being felt in other parts of the organization.

Their hospital, like many, rewarded employees for figuring out how to work around systems problems, not for drawing attention to them. With this new approach, managers were being informed regularly about less-than-ideal conditions. That, in turn, meant that managers had to redefine their roles from being fix-it specialists to being partners in exploring and resolving breakdowns. It was not easy, especially for managers who "viewed their worth by their ability to rescue staff from problems" (2007, 165).

As an aside, this story also illustrates another important point. The process the telemetry staff used appears to be an example of getting rid of problems they did not want—the "fix-it" mentality I've cautioned about in several chapters. The distinction is this. They examined how existing processes were breaking down within a larger context of defining and providing ideal care for their patients. Rather than grounding themselves in trying to fix problems, they shifted to a clear vision of ideal care. That is the power of purposeful guidelines: they keep us focused on *what can be.*

There are at least two key challenges in doing this kind of work, especially if you are transforming from a fix-it orientation to the pursuit of something that deeply matters. The first is to hold a space for short-term problem solving *in the midst of* holding forth a clear purpose and a vision of the ideal. Again, it is a matter of "yes and" rather than "either or." Awareness is critical: when you're aware of the difference between fix-it thinking and pursuing an ideal, you have a wider perspective and, in turn, more choices. You can take a step back and ask yourself, *Is this a short-term problem to solve or is it part of a broader, more complex process that we must balance by staying true to our purpose?*

The second challenge is to create and hold an environment for ongoing learning and adaptation. You might know a lot about what needs to happen, but translating what you know into effective action requires practice, reflection, and the continual testing of results against intentions. In short, learning and adapting require skills that traditional top-down organizations do not foster. Those skills are the subject of the rest of this chapter.

People Learn by Doing

Everyone knows that great performance, be it athletic or aesthetic, requires practice. Imagine sitting through a high school soccer game watching teams that never practiced or paying big bucks to see *The Nutcracker* with dancers who hadn't rehearsed. The idea is ludicrous, yet we tolerate it at work every day. We send employees to daylong or weeklong training programs or conferences that energize them with new information and ideas, but on Monday morning we give them no time or chance to practice, experiment, and play with new ways of being and doing *as part of their job.*

Whenever we're learning something new, we pass through a range of competence that moves from beginner through expert to master. If you're a clinician, think back to when you learned how to give injections. Your first several sticks were probably painful for the recipient, no matter how many oranges or pigs' ears you practiced on beforehand. Remember the first time you drove a car or gave a public presentation? With each new task, you had to pass through an awkward beginner phase, with all its attendant anxiety and uncertainty.

IF YOU WANT A HIGHLY ADAPTIVE

AND RESPONSIVE WORKFORCE,

YOU MUST MAKE LEARNING

MORE IMPORTANT THAN KNOWING.

Most business organizations are performance- rather than practice-oriented. In such environments, the unspoken expectation is that people should be good at new things right away. In cultures with a low tolerance for mistakes, people learn quickly to stick with the tried-and-true rather than suffer the embarrassment and vulnerability of exposing their lack of mastery.

Given this performance-based mentality, most organizations treat development and performance separately. Managers are expected to manage performance while the human resource or organizational development departments are expected to train and develop. The two rarely meet. As a result, employees get the beginner's basics—usually in the form of a training course— with little or no opportunity to practice what they learned in real time and integrate it into how they work.

Throughout the book, I've suggested personal practices to help you become more self-aware and develop your potential. If you're part of the minority who actually *do* the practices, then you're already mining the benefits. If you want people to grow and develop, if you want the spirited engagement and creative energy that come from people learning and working at the edge of their skill levels, if you want a highly adaptive and responsive workforce, then you must declare practice an endangered species and protect it fiercely. You must make learning more important than knowing.

Practice Has Different Meanings

We usually think of practice as a way of mastering a skill. Most of us can recall hours spent sitting at a piano or with violin in hand, going through boring repetitions of scales and chords. In work situations, we've all been through training seminar role-plays in which we're asked to practice certain communication or conflict management skills. But these sessions separate practice from actual performance.

Learning the basics of a new skill is fairly simple. What's difficult is translating that skill into powerful performance. Running scales teaches us nothing about performing a Chopin etude. Conflict management role-plays are useless unless we can call forth and use the principles in a tense situation. And that means we must go through the awkward stage of getting comfortable with new behaviors. We must practice regularly and in real situations.

Practice is also a way to awaken and realize who we are, a way to deepen our awareness and discover what is true in life. Practice in this sense is experiential; it allows us to reconnect with ourselves. It is an exercise in awareness, a form of focusing our full attention on something important to us.

With music, the goal of this form of practice isn't to see how many scales or chords we can play. It is to gain a deeper appreciation of the interaction between fingers and keys or bow and strings, to hear how a slight change of finger position evokes a wholly different sound, to meld with the instrument in ways that heighten our awareness and call forth our own creative powers.

With work, the goal is similar: deeper appreciation, heightened awareness, greater creativity. Rather than talking through a disagreement with the aim of "winning" the argument or proving the other person wrong, we might set out to deepen our understanding of the other person's perspective or experiment with finding common ground. We might experiment with how a shift in tone or word choice can evoke a wholly different response, like Gallwey did with the AT&T operators (see Chapter 2) or search for points of shared interest that inspire new metaphors to move us forward as a group, like the high touch surgery and rehab units mentioned in Chapter 3.

This form of practice works with any kind of situation. If you're in a boring meeting, for instance, pay attention to your boredom. Sit with it. Listen for what's missing. Watch other people; you're likely not alone. Then just imagine saying something like, "I don't feel engaged in this; does anyone else feel the same way?" What kinds of reactions does just *imagining* this evoke in you? Sit with the reactions and see what else wells up.

By attending to the inner world of experience as well as the outer world of activity, you can learn much. Consider, for instance, Teresa, one of my clients who had a performance review that she thought went well. Feedback from her boss was very positive and useful. Then a month later, she got the numeric ratings for her performance and learned that her pay increase was actually below the mean.

She was bothered for days by the discrepancy between the positive tone of the meeting and what seemed like a below average pay raise, especially since she had met or exceeded all of the performance criteria for the year. She wanted to talk with her boss, but didn't know how to approach the conversation.

In our coaching session, we began with a question of purpose: what did she want from the conversation? She struggled with the answer. On the one hand, she wanted to know if her boss really viewed her as below average. On the other hand, she was nervous about the possible outcomes. What if the boss *did* see her as below average? What if the conversation became confrontational? Questions like these not only triggered deeper concerns about her ability to read the boss accurately and to trust her own assessment of her performance, but they left her ambivalent and fearful about even raising the issue.

So we took a few moments to explore her fear. How did she imagine the boss would perceive her inquiry? What if she heard that her performance wasn't as good as she thought? How would she likely react? Then we reframed the fear as a sign of how important this issue was to her.

Examining it gave it less power and reframing it in a way that neutralized its negative charge renewed her interest in getting the truth about how her boss viewed her performance, even if might not feel good. Soon she was free to concentrate on what she really wanted from the conversation. With a clear sense of purpose and a new perspective on her own nervousness, she felt confident in her ability to create a meaningful conversation.

This session introduced Teresa to the practice of attending to her inner world in a different way. Staying with the experience—the fear, the confusion, the uncertainty—and exploring it without judging it allowed her to focus on what she wanted rather than what she didn't want. It also gave her a practice she can use regularly to find her way through and beyond feelings that previously had held her back.

Her experience is not unusual. As women, our deep desire to preserve harmony in relationships can lead us to behave in ways that are inauthentic. We nod agreement in meetings in order to appear supportive and then pursue our own course in private. We say "yes" when everything in us wants to say "no" and end up feeling overwhelmed and guilty. We tolerate poor performance and then get overextended by trying to do the work ourselves. And when the resentment sets in, as it always does, we deliver the final blow to ourselves: we complain to others that we are powerless.

So when you think of coupling practice with performance, think not just of skill development but also of deepening awareness in ways that connect people, yourself included, with present experience and the potential to make a difference. Test the waters with something minor, like boredom or disengagement. When you sense it in yourself, acknowledge it—and perhaps even speak it. When you sense it in others, speak up in a neutral and non-confrontational way. At the very least, you'll find out if you're a lone ranger or one of many. If you *are* the lone ranger, then you have a beautiful opportunity to observe what fuels your own disengagement. And if you're not alone, then you've created a chance to clarify a meeting's purpose and identify what's necessary to get everyone more emotionally engaged.

As your confidence and skill grow, move to more sensitive issues: the person whose bad behavior is out of synch with organizational values, the poor performer who has an excuse for everything, the lack of alignment between what leaders say they want and what they reward or acknowledge.

Without practice, the kinds of skills that leaders most need in order to hold attention on "what" while people figure out "how"—skills like listening actively, staying calm and effective in the midst of powerful emotions, holding courageous conversations that deepen people's awareness and commitment, learning from experience—never get the time and attention they need.

Protect Time to Bring Learning and Doing Together

In problem solving organizations, there is always another fire to fight and never enough time to learn something new. We're always addressing yesterday's "mistakes," so it's easy to get stuck on the treadmill and find ourselves feeling increasingly powerless and ineffectual. Moreover, we can't "solve" or "fix" ourselves to something we want that doesn't yet exist.

When we're solving problems, we're engaged in cause-effect thinking. By contrast, when we're envisioning what we want and taking action to realize it, we're engaged in possibility thinking. I said previously that in healthcare, a good vision is hard to find. That's because most vision statements are vague, sweeping ideals: become a world-class hospital, or be #1 in patient care. What does "world class" or "#1" look like? If people can't envision it, they can't create it. When the telemetry unit staff set out to work differently, they began with a picture of ideal care that was so specific they'd know it when they had created it.

Creating gets people into action and learning through trial and error. They build on what they learn. It's much messier than the orderly process of planning because at each turn, people have to figure out what to do next. There is no precedent, no pre-existing solution, no clear formula for "how." So they need different skills than traditional problem solving skills. They also need a holding environment that supports exploration, differences, and a balance of *doing* with *reflecting, learning*, and *adapting*.

The urgent will always drown out the important, which is reason enough to protect time for practice and reflection. So consider building it into your own work calendar.

Select a time to meet regularly, when the only agenda is one of reflection and learning. You want to balance blocks of performance time with blocks of practice time. The former is devoted to experimenting with new behaviors in the course of daily activities and gathering information on the impact of those behaviors. The latter is devoted to reflecting on the results and learning so that you can create more refined approaches.

Experimenting is a way of testing the efficacy of something you've not tried before, so it requires a beginner's mind. You have to suspend your stories and preconceptions about things, even things you're "expert" at. Experimenting has little value unless it's coupled with reflection, which is the purpose of practice time. Reflect on what worked and what didn't, and use what you learn to decide what to try next.

Even if you don't have much experience with practice per se, women's conversational styles are easily adapted to the task. When a friend or colleague is struggling with something, we often ask questions rather than give advice, support rather than confront, suggest rather than command. All of these are great skills for encouraging practice.

You just need to be aware that practice involves a degree of openness that most people aren't familiar with, especially in cultures that expect people to have the answers. This openness operates at two levels. The first is a personal level of awareness about our mental models: our own beliefs, assumptions, and self-interests. Since our thinking about situations determines the results we get, developing the skills to become more aware of our beliefs, opinions, and perspectives and how they influence our results is the first step to being able to generate new courses of action for ourselves.

Once we've tried something different, we must be open to reflecting on what we did in ways that yield new learning. This is the second level of openness, and it requires that we explore each other's perspectives and responses to actions. In short, practice time creates opportunities to explore the edges of both our current and alternative frames of reference in ways that greatly increase our ability to get the results we want. In the next section, we'll talk about a useful set of skills for doing that.

The Fox TV series *House* captures this spirit of learning and working at the edge. Each week, Dr. Gregory House, a curmudgeon who specializes in diagnostic medicine, and his colleagues tackle an unusual case. Within 20 minutes, they have a working diagnosis that always misses the mark. They confer. They disagree. They experiment. They learn.

House knows more because he's more experienced, but he's often baffled, too. And when that happens, he makes his thinking transparent. He thinks out loud, asks questions, gets ideas from his colleagues, and records their responses on a white board. Then they go back to the patient, the library, or a quiet place to try a different approach, gather more information, or reflect on what they've missed.

That's the process of working at the edge, of practice as a way of deepening awareness and learning from self and others: dialogue, disagreement, experimentation, reflection, inquiry, and, at times, being stuck. Yes, *House* is made for TV, so the drama is exaggerated. But the process is invaluable for anyone who wants to master complex adaptive learning in action. And if you think about your own life, you likely already have a model that you can use.

Build Practice Sessions Around Three Forms of Communication

In most organizations, people set goals and expect results. Rarely do they take the time to explore how goals are met. During practice time, we dig deeper to examine what's working and what isn't. Practice time gives us a chance to slow down and explore the differences between what we intended and what we got.

Before we look at some basic skills for practice sessions, let's address the time involved in holding such sessions. As I've said, many of the personal practices in this book are a matter of focus rather than of time. Practice sessions, however, do require time. So if you're concerned about how to fit in more activities, I invite you to consider the following.

* Practice sessions help people to learn from experience. The more people learn, the more they grow and contribute. Yes, giving them the proverbial fish takes less time in the short run, but once they've mastered the art of fishing, many will start finding new fishing holes and reeling in results that none of you could have imagined.

* Second, when people grow in competence, they grow in confidence. Practice sessions help them do both. Confidence fuels their willingness to try new and different things, which fuels their competence, which builds their confidence ....

* Third, the skills necessary for practice sessions are also the skills of effective communication, which is at the top of most people's wish lists when I ask them what they'd like to see more of in their organizations. When you create opportunities for people to explore beliefs and assumptions in a safe setting, the effect carries over. They start paying more attention to clarifying what's said

in conversations with other people. They start asking questions rather than assuming they know the answers. They start appreciating the value of different perspectives. Effects like these lead to fewer misunderstandings and stronger bonds because they're anchored in the emotional reward of feeling heard and understood.

* Fourth, practice sessions help you create a learning environment. When people are reflecting, learning, and growing in positive ways, they respond with greater commitment and enthusiasm to their everyday work. Work becomes an ongoing opportunity to develop their potential, not just a way to earn a paycheck.

Since the purpose of practice sessions is to learn from experience and figure out new "how's," the process is accelerated when people are skilled in at least three forms of basic communication:

* framing their remarks in order to create a shared context for thinking through events and perspectives,

* advocating their positions and opinions in ways that make their thoughts and feelings transparent to others, and

* inquiring openly and receptively into others' views in order to develop a pool of shared understanding.

These are the common skills of what is called "action inquiry." It is a strategy for increasing our effectiveness at creating the results we want by inviting us to examine our own mental models in real time as we pursue a course of action. Action inquiry invites us to pay attention to how our thinking shapes the results we get and to test the validity of our assumptions and interpretations so we can enhance our effectiveness. Below is a brief description of these skills and some suggestions for when to use each.

Framing: Every Picture Needs It

The next time you're in a meeting, pay attention to how it begins and unfolds. Most likely, the chairperson will start with the first item on the agenda, assuming that people know the meeting's purpose. Pay attention to the flow of conversation. Are people working from a shared understanding of what the meeting is about? Do they respond to, explore, and build on one another's ideas as they work toward a purposeful end? Or do they make comments that seem disconnected or veer off on irrelevant side trips into exceptions and personal interests? Do they disengage via silence or say things like, "I don't understand why we're talking about this"? Pay attention to your own inner voice. Do you find yourself wondering, *Where's she going with this?* or *Why did he bring that up?* If yes, then the group probably lacks a shared frame.

To frame a situation (a meeting, an agenda item, even a comment in conversation) is to state the purpose and what you're trying to accomplish. At times, it may also require you to put your assumptions on the table for examination. Framing is one of the most frequently ignored skills of effective communication.

In large organizations, it's tough to stay focused on what matters because business is highly complex and our attention shifts quite easily from the big picture to the demands of the day. Framing is a simple way to focus people's attention at the start of a meeting or conversation and keep it focused.

Recall, for instance, the senior executive meeting I mentioned in Chapter 3, in which a subordinate, the facilities planner, presented a master list of space requests for the next year's capital budget. Several executives zoomed in on the details, tossing out questions, making additions, and so forth. The group spent 20 minutes sidetracked in details until the president, frustrated by everyone's inattention to keeping patient care services in-house, interrupted with a directive.

Imagine, for example, that the facilities planner had said, "We've developed a facilities budget for next year based on our new service lines, the relocation of the lab, and projections for administrative space. The budget is higher than we anticipated because of Corporate's decision to decentralize staff three months ago.

"We need a decision about whether to submit this to Corporate as is—in which case I expect that it'll be returned to us—or alter our service line goals now, in which case I think our best bet is to start by revising our plans for the new endoscopy suite."

Such a statement frames the purpose, outlines the dilemma, and gives the group two options, along with the planner's assumptions about each course of action. Now those who are listening know what the planner wants from them, why, and how their decision might be received. Below are some other examples of ways you can use framing in meetings or in practice sessions with a group.

Using framing to get and stay on purpose

* Set the tone and direction of conversation with a clear frame. "We've been experimenting with sentinel events and inventory supply in recent weeks. I suggest we examine what we've learned about involving patients in helping us identify potential sentinel events, and then address the supply experiment."

* Frame the meeting with a question about what the group wants to accomplish by the end of the meeting. Merely reaching a shared understanding of the purpose of a meeting can do wonders for keeping a group on track. If you write the answer on a white board or flip chart, it's even more powerful.

* Use framing to reframe a conversation or discussion when it's getting off track. Say something like, "We started with X and it feels like we've shifted to Y without reaching any agreement on X. Does anyone else see it that way?"

* To deepen the group's learning, shift from content to process with a new frame. "It seems to me that we keep getting sidetracked. I don't think it adds much to our meetings, so I'd like to look at when and how it happens."

* Consider framing your first practice session around the setting of ground rules for participation. Since the purpose of practice sessions is to deepen awareness and learning, think about the basic principles you want to work by. For instance, you might decide that each individual, not just the group leader, is responsible for keeping the group focused, signaling a shift in subject matter, questioning the process, and summarizing key points to assure a shared understanding. Or you might decide to divide and rotate activities like these – premature shifts in focus, process ambiguities or breakdowns, periodic summaries of who, what, and when – among individuals in the group.

Advocacy: That's My Story and I'm Sticking to It

Advocacy is the second basic communication skill. Most men are great at it, at least on the surface. They put forth an opinion, a perspective, or a course of action, or they listen to someone else's opinion and then offer up their own. Think of the dozens of meetings you've been in with people who are masterful at making a case for their position and getting others to buy in. That's advocacy. But to be effective as a practice and learning tool, advocacy requires that we go beyond the basic stating of our position or a course of action to making our own thinking transparent to others. It requires us to share the data, perspectives, assumptions—and sometimes the feelings—that formed our position in the first place.

The nature of advocacy is that it starts and ends in our own world. If we want to build practice fields for learning, we have to share that world, invite others into it, and be willing to adjust our point of view or adopt a whole new view.

According to Peter Senge, even when people meet to exchange each other's views, they don't learn much because, "As each side reasonably and calmly advocates his viewpoint just a bit more strongly, positions become more and more rigid" (1990, 198). The tension escalates as each person senses a growing threat to his or her position. Breaking the cycle requires curiosity about the other person's position combined with the willingness to face the limitations of our own position. Senge summed it up like this: "When operating in pure advocacy, the goal is to win the argument. When inquiry and advocacy are combined, the goal is no longer 'to win the argument' but to find the best argument" (1990, 199).

Effective advocacy offers up our own internal reasoning for review and invites others' perspectives so that we avoid being limited or even sabotaged by our own assumptions or misinterpretations. Here's an example. One of my clients, Kate, asked for help in creating staff meetings that were engaging and energizing. I talked with her employees, who agreed that meetings were tedious and boring, and we agreed that I would survey them to gather more information about their current meetings and how they wanted staff meetings to operate. Less than 50% of them responded.

Kate interpreted the low response rate as a lack of caring and commitment, and planned to open the next staff meeting with a statement to that effect. Then she caught herself.

"I've made some pretty big assumptions here, haven't I?" she said during a coaching session.

"I think so," I replied. We talked through the assumptions and then I asked, "How do you want to handle the staff meeting?"

She decided to tell people about the response rate, acknowledge her initial reaction to it, and offer a few other interpretations that she generated during our conversation. She wrote these on a flip chart and then asked the staff to build on her list. The exercise took about four or five minutes.

The responses were revealing. Each person had a different perspective on the low response rate. More importantly, one brave soul ventured some skepticism about "management" really being willing to take action based on staff input. His confession led to a few other employees voicing similar doubts. Kate listened attentively and other staff began opening up about feeling micromanaged and undervalued. When they were done, she said, "What I realize in listening to you is that what you describe as micromanagement, I describe as techniques I've learned to track lots of complex projects as efficiently as possible. I see now how you interpret that as being micromanaged. I probably would feel that way, too."

By making her initial interpretations and feelings transparent to the group, she created a safe environment for them to acknowledge their own beliefs and feelings. By listening openly and then comparing her own intentions with what staff labeled as micromanagement, she initiated a conversation that began to dissolve the discrepancies between her perspective and theirs.

In the end, her willingness to be so forthcoming in revealing her own inner world drew deeper, more authentic responses from her staff. The result was an unexpectedly lively, engaging, and productive exchange. She gained a new appreciation for how different people had different interpretations of her actions and for the need to "think out loud" about what was driving her. Many of her staff gained a new appreciation for the complex demands on her of balancing multiple people's needs and expectations. Some additional pointers for advocating effectively are listed below.

Getting the most from advocating your point of view

* Be explicit in describing how you came to your position. Include both external and internal sources—ie, data that you took into account, assumptions that you were running on, even feelings that played a part in forming your perspective.

* Ask others if they see any leaps of logic in your thinking or any misplaced personalizing of others' intentions.

* When people offer differing perspectives, be open and curious. Suspend judgment so you can step beyond questions of right or wrong. Ask what they used as the basis for their perspective so you can learn about other data sources. You're out to expand your view and, if possible, to discover similar or shared interests that can help you both move forward. Even if you discover that your core beliefs are at odds, you can still deepen your appreciation that others are as committed to their beliefs as you are to yours. That lesson alone is valuable.

Inquiry: "Reality" Is Relative and Every Relative Has His Own Reality

Inquiry is the process of questioning for the purpose of understanding another person's reasoning and assumptions. As a form of learning, it is rarely practiced, primarily because most of us believe that our own views and beliefs are "true," that they accurately reflect "reality," and that they are obvious since they're grounded in real data and experience.

What we fail to realize is that we all pull information selectively from events in the environment—we literally take in different data. We then assign our own interpretations to the data we select, draw conclusions based on those interpretations, and then respond based on our conclusions and assumptions. We lump the whole process together as "reality," without ever teasing apart the myriad mental steps we took between the event and our response to it.

Inquiry is the process by which we look *at* those steps rather than look *through* them as if they were the lens of "truth." Inquiry as a means of learning is only effective when we're genuinely interested in mutual understanding and are willing to change and be changed by what we hear. So staying open and receptive is important. When you find yourself wanting to jump in and "correct" someone else's perspective, use it as a signal that one of your own beliefs is being challenged. Shift your attention and listen more actively. It will help the other person feel heard and, in turn, be more willing to explore deeper assumptions.

Below are some guidelines for using inquiry to balance the more familiar stance of advocacy. Note that these guidelines apply not just to practice sessions but to any conversation in which you're unclear about the other person's reasoning.

Chances are good that this approach is familiar to you from your personal relationships, but it recedes into the background when you're at work and someone is questioning one of your actions, decisions, or positions.

Balancing advocacy with inquiry

* Use inquiry when someone holds a position different from yours or when his actions don't make sense to you. "What leads you to that conclusion?" or "Help me understand what led you to that course of action" are good openers. They're neutral and non-threatening. They offer the other person a chance to voice his perspective, which always feels good, and give you a glimpse of the thinking that is underlying his decision or opinion or behavior.

* Once you have something to work with, validate your understanding of the other person's position before moving on, with a statement like, "So what I think you're saying is…" or "Am I correct in hearing you say that …." If you missed his point or misconstrued his reasoning, you'll likely know from his response. If you assume that you understand without verifying what you heard, you risk building the conversation on a house of cards.

* If his reasoning still isn't clear to you, then inquire more deeply, with questions like, "What specific information led to your conclusion?" or "We seem to be operating from different data. What did you rely on?" Because inquiry digs into the other person's mental frames, and because most of us treat our beliefs and worldviews as sacred, tread carefully, especially with people unaccustomed to this kind of communication. Consider, also, making your strategy explicit by telling the other person that you're seeking a deeper understanding of his position, not trying to third-degree him. When people know our intentions, they are much less likely to assign their own interpretations to our behavior.

* Make your own reasoning transparent. Early on, you might say something like, "I'm asking these questions because we have different perspectives and don't agree on how to proceed. I really want to understand how you see this, so I need your help." Offer the data informing your perspective or the interpretations you assigned to it. "I'm basing my opinion on the downward trend I've seen in our quality data" or "I'm assuming that the downward trend in our quality data is the result of ...."

* Inquiry is also helpful for examining the validity of your own perspectives, as Susan did with her transcriptionists. The challenge here is to frame questions in ways that encourage other people to disconfirm rather than rubber-stamp your assumptions and reasoning. It's tough to do since most of us have spent years learning not to disconfirm others' ideas, especially the boss's. You might say, "Here's my opinion and how I reached it. What flaws or leaps of logic do you see?" Or "I value your perspective. Here's my rationale. What do you think I might be overlooking?" In this way, you make it easy for others to offer differing perspectives.

Balancing advocacy and inquiry is a dance of sorts, a give-and-take in which people express their own views and inquire about others' as well. Its real value is in helping people surface and discuss their assumptions and examine how those drive their decisions and actions. Because it can touch us at deep levels, it can also evoke strong emotions, so tread gingerly at first.

I suggest that you avoid using *why* questions in general when you're starting to engage people in inquiry. They cut right to the quick of people's intentions and often trigger a defensive response if they're not well tempered by a neutral frame of curiosity. Think about the times when you asked your child, "Why didn't you do your homework?" or asked your spouse,

"Why did you buy that?" or asked a subordinate, "Why did you miss the first planning meeting?" Such questions don't invite open discussion; they invite defensiveness and can derail your efforts to generate greater mutual understanding.

"What" questions typically get you more information with less pushback. Practice them within the context of a relevant situation. For instance, questions like the following give people working scenarios within which to begin surfacing and testing their assumptions.

* "What data do we have about our patients' experiences with endoscopy?"
* "What do we suspect but have no information to confirm regarding our community screening program's impact on primary care referrals?"
* "What do we need to know that we don't know now about the steps it takes to deliver meds to a single patient when and where the patient needs it?"

Put It All Together in Practice Sessions

Leadership is a performing art. Your role, like that of athletic coaches, conductors, and stage directors, is to help people develop their potential and deliver the best performance possible. Just as directors and athletic coaches combine practice sessions with performances, you must do the same.

Active listening, framing, and a balance of advocating and inquiring are basic tools to help you and your performers to learn, grow and evolve. They take time and effort to master, so consider learning more about them before trying to use them in the workplace.

Peter Senge's work on learning organizations (1990, 2006) and Bill Torbert's on action inquiry (2004) are good starters. So is Michael Marquardt's work on action learning (2004). Don't give up when you feel like you're fumbling. This is difficult work. Surfacing deeply engrained mental models requires practice and a disciplined approach, but it will yield an ensemble that's far greater than the sum of its parts.

Set an intention to practice. Block out time on the calendar, perhaps during a staff meeting, to explore each other's viewpoints for the purpose of creating a pool of shared meaning. As people's understanding deepens, use these same skills to define one or two initial experiments. Then gather data, reflect on the results, and keep the momentum building with another iteration.

There is no single right way to create a practice field. The "how" will unfold as you get deeper into it. So chip away at your current mental models. Inquire and explore. Begin nurturing the abilities to self-correct, to refine what you know, and to improvise in the midst of fresh awareness. And get others into action with you. Partnership and collaboration will generate energy and adaptive innovation much faster than solitary endeavors.

10

Trust the Power of "Once Upon a Time ..."

THE UNIVERSE IS MADE OF STORIES, NOT ATOMS.

Muriel Rukeyser

Stories Are Our Frames of Meaning

Our work—indeed, our lives—are built on and steeped in storytelling. Stories are how we make sense of things. Of course, at work we don't call them stories. We dress them up in professional language like 'case study' or 'example' or just plain 'conversation.' But if you listen closely, you'll hear stories everywhere—in the hallways and bathrooms, around cafeteria tables and shuttle stops, over dinner and breakfast, under the breath and in full earshot of the boss. Whether they're one-liners or extended narratives, stories are woven deeply into the fabric of our everyday lives.

Stories are how we pass on what we know. They help us understand how and why things change and what we might do to make a difference. They are the currency of character: they tell us whom we can trust and they tell others who we are. They show us how to handle life out of balance or warn us of what dread things lie ahead if we're not mindful. They reflect what we value and can inspire us to move forward despite setbacks and suffering.

A few years ago one of my clients, Joel, lost 25 percent of his business when a large client failed to renew their contract. I heard about the loss from several managers and knew there was fear and trembling among the ranks. A competitor had gone through the same thing and stayed afloat by laying off several workers. People feared the same would happen here.

I was at the all-hands meeting when Joel told the rest of the company about the loss. "Yep," he said. "We're losing our biggest account. And that's ok. We didn't lose it because of quality of service. We lost it because of a merger. What it boils down to is this. With that fat account we were comfortable. Like a wolf that's been domesticated, we learned to eat from the bowl and didn't bother to go hunt. Well, the bowl's no longer full. And we still know how to hunt. So let's get out there.

"And remember, we built this company on our own strength, not on one client," he added. "I think they'll come back to us with renewed appreciation for what we do. Maybe we'll be able to take them back. And maybe our bowl will be so full that we won't. It's up to you."

By creating a story that reframed how people thought about the loss—from disaster to opportunity—Joel shifted how they felt, not just about the situation but about their ability to survive. The story assuaged their fears, renewed their confidence, and energized them to take positive action. Eight months later, they had two record-breaking quarters under their belt and were oversold for the first three quarters of the year while their competitors were struggling to stay afloat.

STORIES CONNECT US WITH OURSELVES.

Stories are compelling in ways that are impossible for policy manuals, to-do lists, and job descriptions. Good stories cut to the quick of what we believe and most value. They have characters we know personally or metaphorically and care about. They have a moral or a message. They pit people against problems and give us a glimpse of what it takes to survive. They capture the complexity and often the conflicting or contradictory nature of our circumstances. They give us hope. They give us direction. They give meaning and purpose to our work and our lives, whether we're bricklayers building a cathedral or healers easing the suffering of others. And they do all of this with remarkable efficiency because of one critical element: emotion. Stories connect us with ourselves.

Cultivating both the stories we tell and the way we tell them—combining purposeful content with emotionally evocative delivery—is the art of storytelling. Bringing impersonal facts to life in narratives of experience is something most women do daily in our one-on-one conversations. Honing our natural storytelling abilities into effective strategies for pulling people together is the focus of this chapter. Pointed and well told stories pave the way for us to influence others without having to resort to the more common tactics of telling, controlling, and power-playing.

Facts Inform; Stories Influence

When we want to effect a change, we accomplish little unless we're able to influence people. I said earlier that logic makes us think but emotion makes us act. Influencing starts with shifting how people feel about whatever's at hand. Stories are powerful for effecting such a shift because they create a context within which facts take on personal meaning and significance. Here are some examples.

One of my clients, Molly, asked for help in creating a presentation for her hospital board. Her goal was to get support for an area-wide organ donor program. Steeped in data and limited to a 15-minute time slot, she was struggling with how to narrow the numbers and gain the board's approval for the program.

I asked, "What's the most memorable donor case you can recall?" She told me about a young father who had recently died in the hospital following a heart attack. Thanks to the awareness and sensitivity of the hospital staff, his corneas, kidneys, and liver gave three recipients a new lease on life.

She grasped the story's power and opened her presentation with a compelling narrative about the man, his family, and the lives of those he touched. She then linked it to a few well-chosen facts and some short stories of other patients awaiting transplants. No PowerPoint, no spreadsheets, no glossy one-pagers from the marketing department. Just a handful of stories delivered in a way that captured everyone's attention and spoke to the heart. She got approval for the program before she left the room.

Sometimes putting one situation within the context of another can illuminate its significance in ways that logic can't touch. I was coaching a physician, Judith, who was the newly-elected president of her medical staff. She had never held a leadership position and was apprehensive about the responsibility. "I'm not leader-like," she told me often. "And I *hate* to talk in front of groups."

Her first talk, of course, was a doozy: a presidential address to the medical staff. Her work was complicated by the fact that an aggressive competitor had recently acquired the hospital and fear and distrust were running high among her physician colleagues. She had a vision for the future but she knew the medical staff had to move beyond their fears before they could imagine a different future.

Judith was at a loss for how to do that effectively. So I asked her about times in her own life when she'd been fearful of what was coming next. She recounted a phenomenal story from childhood. Her father was working in another town. She was home with her siblings and mother when a raging storm triggered a flash flood. Their house was destroyed and they barely escaped with their lives. The family lost everything and had to start over in another town. She was only eight or nine at the time but could vividly recall the fear, anxiety, and mourning that came in the wake of the flood.

So here was a remarkable story about having to start anew while grieving a major loss that spoke poignantly to the struggles of her colleagues. She seized upon the idea and used the story as a metaphor, ending with a call to the physicians to put aside their differences and unite in preserving the identity of their hospital. She was flooded with handshakes, calls, and emails for days afterward. The self-effacing woman who hated to talk to groups had connected deeply with a tough audience by offering what we all want and need: a frame for our plight that renews our hope and asks us to contribute to something greater than ourselves.

Listen to the Song of Life

In order to hone your storytelling skills, start by listening differently to people at work. Pay attention to the stories they tell about the organization, the tasks at hand, and the people they work with and serve. Become an avid observer. Invoke your female instinct for hearing the hidden as well as the overt message, the emotional as well as the rational.

Begin collecting stories. Jot down snippets of dialogue. Make a list of the metaphors that people use in talking about work or one another. Listen also to the stories people tell themselves and each other about "the way it is" or about their motivation to take one course of action over another. We usually think of stories as narratives of events and actions but the most common stories are the ones we create to explain why we do things and why we can't. There is always a story within the story.

As you listen, be curious. What do people's stories say about the culture, their work, and the storytellers themselves? Notice how their stories limit or create new possibilities for them, like the quality assurance person who continually complains, "No one respects what we do" or the chief executive's admin who says "I'm the stoker and the caboose; I make sure my boss has what she needs and nothing important gets left behind."

Pay attention to your responses to their stories. Which ones pull you in? Which ones repel you? What do your responses reveal about what you value? Experiment with stories. What do you observe, for instance, when you present a set of facts to one group and a story that illustrates the facts to another group? What do you notice when you change your own story about a situation?

The more you listen for the story within the story— what stories are saying about the storyteller, the work, the culture—the more aware you'll become of the power of stories to influence.

"What" and "How" Stories Tell Us about the Culture and the Work

Several years ago I worked at a large Catholic health care system. It was located for more than 75 years in what had become a poor, crime-ridden inner city neighborhood. During those years, it evolved from a small hospital and school of nursing to a vast complex of buildings and garages comprising several city blocks.

In the 1970s all the buildings were painted pale beige at the behest of a former nun-turned-CEO who wanted to create a unified and coherent whole. From the first brush of that beige paint to the present day, not so much as a single line of graffiti ever marred those hallowed walls despite blocks of run-down and boarded-up buildings sprawling in all directions. The story is a testament to the high regard the neighboring residents have for the hospital and the church. When I worked there, staff told the story with great pride and drew from it a personal sense of respect and significance.

What are the stories of pride and respect in your organization? Gather and spread them. They speak to what's going well in subtle yet powerful ways. When you share stories about people's pride in the organization, others begin telling stories of their own.

Listen carefully and you'll hear dozens of stories about the culture of your organization and the lessons people draw from everyday events, especially from people in support roles and frontline positions. Their stories are especially important because these people are the face of your organization. They'll treat customers and patients as they are treated.

Knowing the "what" stories gives you options. You can use them to reinforce people's commitment and pride. You can use them to draw attention to important points. You can craft new stories to reframe people's perspectives and redirect their energy like the business owner who inspired his people after the loss of a major client or the medical staff president who reframed a painful merger in ways that helped the staff coalesce into a unified group.

* * *

"How" stories give us guidance in how to do the work, fit in, get things done, and get along. They capture valuable lessons, stand as caveats, and remind us of our shared humanity in gentle uplifting ways.

The Gallup Organization conducted a study of nurses that involved patients' reports of pain following injections. What they found was that a nurse's skill level at giving injections wasn't nearly so important in influencing a patient's pain level as what the nurse told the patient. The "average" nurses usually said something like, "'Oh, don't worry, this won't hurt a bit'" and then "plunged in the needle with businesslike efficiency" (Buckingham and Coffman, 1999, 93-94). But the "best" nurses took a different approach. They warned the patients that the injection was going to hurt a little but they'd be as gentle as possible.

That's the power of story, even a one-line story. It conveyed the truth, framed the caregiver's concern, and created an emotional connection that actually lessened the patient's perception of pain. It also spoke volumes about how the best nurses viewed their patients and their work.

Annette Simmons, author of *The Story Factor,* tells this story-within-a-story. "If you tell a manager to 'stop criticizing employees,' she may counter with, 'How else do I let them know they are making mistakes?' …However, if you tell her, 'In Washington, D.C., last week, I had a Haitian cab driver who shared his grandfather's favorite saying with me, '"The man who beats his horse will soon be walking,"' you call her attention to a larger, deeper context" (2001, 33).

"Stop criticizing" is analytic, left brain control. The "grandfather's favorite saying" is intuitive, right brain synthesis. When we use stories in this manner, we shift from giving orders to conveying norms, from reinforcing the hierarchy to underscoring that we're all in this together, from masculine competition to feminine collaboration and community.

Story can imbue a simple message with a universal meaning. A former client of mine, a department director in a huge and impersonal system, had a sign above her computer. It was a continual reminder, she told me, of her real job: keeping herself and others motivated and working on purpose in a high stress, high-pressure organization. It was the story I quoted at the start of Chapter 6 by Antoine de Saint Exupery, author of *The Little Prince*:

IF YOU WANT TO BUILD A SHIP,
DON'T DRUM UP THE MEN TO GATHER THE WOOD,
DIVIDE THE WORK, AND GIVE ORDERS.
INSTEAD, TEACH THEM TO YEARN FOR
THE VAST AND ENDLESS SEA.

With this story as her guide this director excelled at motivating people within and beyond her department.

You can bring any story into the workplace if it makes a point. So listen to your own life for stories that can help people see their situation in new ways. Here's an example.

One day, my son and I were doing spring clean up at my

mother's house in the country. He found a small toad in a flowerbed and picked it up. In response to his touch, the toad contracted so much that it looked like a little clump of dirt in his hand. We were fascinated by its ability to camouflage itself so completely. He put it back on the ground where it remained inert-like for several seconds. Then he gently touched it. It leaped into action, stretching to nearly five inches in length and covering eight feet in three long leaps.

The following week I met with a senior hospital executive who acted as if she were the lowest person on the totem pole. I told her the story of the toad. It drew tears to her eyes.

"That's me," she said soulfully. "I play small. My whole life has gotten really small. And the only time I stretch is when I try to get away from something that scares me." The story captured perfectly how she presented herself in the workplace and the toad became a metaphor for the importance of redirecting her life and work.

Trish, another client, was trying to get a small group to compromise on a heated issue regarding staffing. Rather than tell them what to do, she decided to tell them a story about an interview she'd seen on television. She, like I, was an avid fan of *Inside The Actor's Studio*. James Lipton, dean of the Actor's Studio in Manhattan, was talking with Steven Spielberg about the scene in *Indiana Jones* when a bad guy is brandishing a scimitar in anticipation of a duel with Indy. Spielberg explained that Harrison Ford was sick the day they were to film the scene and only had about an hour of energy in him. Spielberg jokingly said, "Then why don't you just shoot the guy?" To Spielberg's surprise, everyone on the set laughed.

"'So,' he told Lipton, 'we scrapped the duel, did four takes with the gun, and Ford went back to the hotel to sleep. Compromise'," he said, "'often makes your work better.'"

Nearly everyone in Trish's group recalled the scene, so she asked, "If it works for Steven Spielberg, how can we make it work for us?" The group found a solid compromise within the hour.

Notice that without the punch line, this story wouldn't have been nearly as effective. We women use stories to invite people in, not necessarily to make a point. In conversations with each another, we intuitively understand the dynamics at work. But when we use stories at work, especially in mixed gender groups, we must take care to keep them short and purposeful.

If you listen, you'll hear "how" stories everywhere: how to get along with the surly IT director, how to get a wheelchair for a discharged patient in less than 45 minutes, how to work around delays so patients aren't stacked up in the hallways, how to expedite a request to attend a CEU conference or get a lax resident to respond to a page.

From these stories you can learn volumes about what's working and what isn't in your organization and use the information to shape strategies for getting greater alignment. Ask staff for stories about how people are embodying the organization's values or fulfilling its mission. Doing so draws attention to what's working well and gives others ideas about how to do the same. It shifts the focus from negative to positive, from what we don't want to what we yearn for.

Use your own stories to shape and influence how other people perceive and respond to situations. For instance, one of my clients, an operations VP, told me one day, "I called my physician's office for an appointment and got a voice message saying they're open from 8 to 3 and please leave a message. I was frustrated and hung up.

"Then I called the BMW dealer to schedule service for my car. I got a human being—a friendly human being. She offered me a loaner and asked if I needed to have the car picked up or wanted to bring it in myself. *My car gets better service than I do!*"

The experience jolted his awareness of how healthcare is often set up to serve its own rather than those needing care. At the next staff meeting, he used the story to jump-start a conversation about how to become more patient friendly.

"Who" Stories Reveal Character and Intention

"Who" stories take us to bedrock, to the core of a person's identity. Some of them tell us about other people. Some tell others about us. "Who" stories reveal character and motive, strengths and limitations, potential and lost opportunity. They reveal what we value and what we believe. Their power lies in their ability to bring character to life and engage us in ways that connect us emotionally to one another and to what we know in our hearts.

The next time you're in a hospital elevator or a family waiting area, listen carefully to the stories people tell about their doctor. Eight times out of ten you'll hear, "He's the best in town" or "I've heard she's the best there is." These are the stories we carry with us to assuage our anxiety and allay our fears about all the terrible what if's that our brains can fabricate. We desperately need to trust someone in whose hands we're entrusting our lives or the lives of those we love.

Think about it. We don't sue the family doctor who delivered our babies and soothed our nerves when the kids had high fevers or held our hands when our loved ones were dying. We don't sue the person who, we believe, is acting in our best interests. We sue people we don't know. We sue people we think don't care about us. We sue people with whom we have no emotional connection.

If you want a culture that values patients' experiences, then press staff to listen to patients' stories. It's a simple yet powerful way to honor and acknowledge the individual. When our stories are heard, we feel a connection, and when patients feel connected, they leave with powerful stories about the quality of care they got.

If your patient satisfaction scores are low, talk with staff. You may well find that they're so absorbed in tasks and internal goings-on that they can tell you little about the aneurysm in 436 or the liver transplant in 620. Shift their attention from the task to the person and you create an entirely different expectation of what's important.

If you want stellar customer care, take a tip from Southwest Airlines president emeritus Colleen Barrett. "To me" she says, "it isn't a matter of just getting the message out to our people that we want good customer service. ...It's a matter of creating heroes out of the people who do customer service well. ...We do it [create heroes]," she sums up, "because it's the easiest way to show people what great customer service is" (Guinto 2006, 121-122).

How does the airline create heroes? By sending senior managers into the field to talk about employees who are providing great service, by publishing customer letters in-house, by celebrating every achievement, by profiling a Star of the Month in the monthly in-flight magazine. In short, Southwest creates heroes *by telling people's stories.*

Here's an example. One month, the airline profiled Becky Price, a ramp agent and avid fisherwoman in Ft. Lauderdale/ Hollywood. The story told about her work, her family, and her love of fishing, and ended with an invitation to the reader: "Being a ramp agent is no easy job, so next time you land in Ft. Lauderdale/Hollywood on a beautiful day perfect for fishing, look out your window and give Becky a big thumbs up for the great job she is doing out there!" (Jones, 2006, 22). Imagine the impact on Becky— and her colleagues— of having dozens or even hundreds of passengers giving her a thumbs-up as their planes taxi to and from the concourse.

"Who" stories often reflect qualities that we value and want to emulate. They guide us in figuring out how we want to be known. Tom, for example, is nearing retirement and continues to be enthused and engaged in developing the young people in his marketing department. One day, I asked him what he has learned about developing others.

"I follow a simple rule," he said. "*Nine roses for every thorn.* I learned it years ago and it's invaluable. I focus on the roses—on what's beautiful and creative and coming into being in someone—at least nine times before I deliver a thorn. Works wonders." I was so impressed by him that I still use his story to get others focused on the rose rather than the thorn.

Tom stands out for another reason. He was part of a large group I was coaching and he was the only person who invited me to his office to meet the people he works with. In his words, he wanted me to see him in his "home environment." After a short meeting in his office, he started the tour. He wanted me to meet everyone. At each desk, he introduced the person by name and by some notable talent, contribution, or accomplishment. And at each desk, he introduced me in equally glowing terms. The experience was memorable. People, myself included, admire and respect him because of how we feel in his presence.

People like Tom, Colleen Barrett, and the medical staff president whose childhood home was lost present us with great opportunities. Their authenticity and ability to align who they are with what they do creates an environment in which we—if we are willing—can test the limits of our own talent. They give us a chance to become what we are capable of becoming, and the stories they tell about us provide the platform from which we can move forward.

So begin observing yourself in action with others. Pay attention to your behavior: to the stories you tell, the nonverbal messages that accompany them, your level of presence and authenticity in the moment. Then ask yourself questions like those highlighted below.

The story network

---

* How do I think people feel in my presence?

* How do I want them to feel?

* How are my answers colored by the stories I tell myself about these people?

* How are my answers colored by my stories about my own behavior?

* Based purely on my words and actions, what stories do I think people tell about me?

Your response to each of these questions is another story and your effectiveness as a leader is highly influenced by the degree to which your stories of who and how you are correlate with how others experience you.

I am not talking about the stories you tell other people that begin, "When I was 24, I took a job ...." I am talking about the stories you tell yourself about your own life. Stories that justify or explain your behavior and attitudes and expectations. Stories that support the decisions you make and the actions you take or fail to take. Stories that keep you in self-enhancing or self-defeating cycles and that open or close the doors of opportunity.

For some women, these stories take the form of a defining moment that set the course for an entire career. They may even define the kind of person the storyteller was to become. "My mother died of breast cancer when I was 16," the director of an oncology unit told me. "I vowed then and there to devote my life to caring for people with cancer."

Other stories are very short—just a few words. As an executive coach, I hear them all the time. They have very long histories and usually very sad endings. The formula for creating one is simple. Just complete one or both of the sentence roots in the self-limiting exercise below with a word or two of your own choosing. Stories like these form when people meet a Y in the road—a choice to follow their hearts or the caveats of caution—and they choose caution.

When stories become self-limiting

I am not [pick one] …	I am too [pick one] …
creative	boring
adventurous	cautious
courageous	dull
well-read	quiet
politically savvy	outspoken
good with	self-conscious
numbers	unsure of myself
details	ignorant of the issues
accounting	worried about offending others
politics….	afraid of being wrong

Diane, for example, was a long-time employee of a large organization with great benefits. She was more than a dozen years from retirement but was obviously frustrated and feeling dead-ended in her work. I asked why she stayed.

"People have no choice," she said. Her use of the word 'people' caught my attention. "Most of us CAN'T leave."

"What do you mean?" I asked. "I don't see anyone holding you against your will."

"I've talked with LOTS of people. They're all like me. They can't leave."

"Why not?" I inquired.

Here came her first line of evidence.

"BECAUSE," she insisted, shaking her head at my idiocy. We sat in silence for a few seconds before she added, "*You don't understand!*"

"Golden handcuffs?" I asked. She gave a slight roll of the eyes, dropped her gaze to the table, and went silent. I waited. Fifteen seconds. Twenty-five.

"A lot of people here feel the same way," she said, still staring at the table. "Job security. Retirement. If you have a family, *you can't leave.*"

Ahhh. Now we're getting to the prison walls. Like many, Diane was imprisoned by her own beliefs about those metaphoric golden handcuffs. She saw no options beyond the one she was living. Her spirit was withering, her energy unconsciously directed at sabotaging the system that she thought had stolen her life. People like Diane trade commitment and courage for compliance and the illusion of security. They keep telling themselves the same sad story about their life and become bitter and disappointed in the process.

Other people live by different stories. Consider Eleanor Roosevelt's quip about women being like tea bags: you never know how strong they are until you put them in hot water. Or Steven Spielberg's remark that, "Every movie and every one of my seven kids marks a chapter in my life. The question is how many chapters I can get out of this book."

So venture onto the high wire. Dare to create a culture of caring by bringing patient stories into your meetings and conversations. Model the way by setting aside 30 minutes a month, a small fraction of your time, to listen to a patient or family member. A simple, compassionate inquiry will open the door to remarkable stories. Then dare to fuel others' commitment by asking for and exploring stories of patient service. Make the telling of stories a ritual for pulling people together around a shared purpose and for strengthening their connections through a set of shared values.

Use Metaphors to Create New Opportunities

Roosevelt's and Spielberg's use of metaphor—a form of story that likens two dissimilar things— is a great way to create new ways of understanding everyday things. Think about how the common military and sports metaphors for work both shape and reflect how we behave and what we expect.

What if we switched from military and sports metaphors to metaphors of gardens, rich in allusions to growing, nurturing, cultivating, thriving, blossoming, and renewing? Or metaphors of webs, woven with images of connections, networks, symmetry, balance, and center-out design. How different would our work worlds become if we filled them with allusions to cultivating compassion or weaving webs of inclusion rather than battling disease or leveling the playing field?

What if we used metaphors to give people options that

they wouldn't otherwise exercise? One of my clients, an operations VP, was having difficulty getting the emergency department nursing staff to call when they needed help. Their tendency was to close the department and divert patients to other facilities—a costly and, in many instances, unnecessary action. He had tried several times the direct approach of asking them to call for help, but the diversions continued. A man of metaphors, he finally said to them one day, "Look, if you think it's going to rain even as far off as Fiji, call and give us a heads up. We'll be there to help."

A few weeks after this conversation, he and I were meeting and his phone rang. He checked the caller ID and saw that it was one of the emergency department nurses. He hit the speaker phone button and said, "Hello?"

"This is Fiji," said a female voice. "Clouds are rolling in."

Maybe you have a story about expecting one thing and getting another or about struggling to save face or overcoming adversity or rising to the occasion. Whether they are about toads or teabags, powerful metaphors are about things that matter to people. In that regard, they carry a double wallop: they convey messages about situations *and* about who you are as a leader.

Screenwriting teacher Robert McKee believes that "the measure of the value of any human desire is in direct proportion to the risk involved in its pursuit." He says that we create stories as metaphors for meaningful life, and to live meaningfully is "to be at perpetual risk" (1997, 149).

So our challenge—to live meaningfully in the workplace—requires the perpetual risk of caring, with its attendant vulnerability, in a public place and often in the face of myriad messages and metaphors to the contrary. It takes courage to speak from the heart when others are working from the chin up. Story can open the way. The Haitian cab driver, the medical staff president's childhood, the toad and the dirt, the clouds rolling in over Fiji: they by-pass reason and pierce the heart in ways that logic can't touch.

Hone and Practice Your Storytelling and Presentation Skills

Storytelling involves two elements. The first is the ability to *craft* an effective story; the second is the ability to *deliver* it effectively. An effective story has characters we care about and a message that's important. It can capture both the complexity and the simple truths of life. You can learn to craft stories by working with a book like Annette Simmons' *The Story Factor,* joining a group like Toastmasters, or even taking a creative writing class. With a little practice, you can create stories that teach, inspire, and move others in ways that strategic plans, goals and objectives, and satisfaction surveys cannot.

The second element is the ability to be an effective storyteller. For this, you need strong presentation skills, not just at telling stories but also at getting and focusing people's attention on what's important. Because women use conversation differently than men, our speaking styles can obscure the real message and undercut our credibility in mixed gender situations. For instance, many of us unconsciously rely on mechanisms like these:

* Wrapping tough messages in diffuse language to soften their impact
* Using a hundred words to explain a ten-word idea
* Talking faster when the other person's attention is drifting so we get everything said before the other totally checks out

* Talking in the high, breathy pitch of a schoolgirl when we're excited or nervous.

We also use different non-verbals than men. We tilt our heads more than men, which suggests submissiveness or uncertainty. We keep our hands and arms so close to our bodies that we appear small and insignificant or we gesture so quickly and wildly that we look scattered and unfocused. We have a hard time keeping eye contact when asking tough questions or giving direct messages.

Few people, male or female, are comfortable speaking before an audience. Yet so much of our credibility hinges on how we present ourselves that learning some basic presentation skills is well worth the investment.

As always, start in the world behind your eyes. When I moved into an executive position and had to give reports at medical staff and hospital board meetings, I was terribly worried about how those audiences would judge me so I over prepared. I jammed in lots of content, scripted every word, and rehearsed endlessly. The result? I came across as stiff, intellectual, and aloof.

When I began speaking for a living, I joined an organization of professional speakers and learned quickly that they had a different view of audiences. "People desperately want you to do well," a wise colleague told me one day, "no matter who they are. They want to be entertained as well as educated. They want to feel like the time they invested in listening to you was worthwhile. So treat them as friends rather than foes." Just that simple shift of perspective gave me license to loosen up and relax.

What do you tell yourself about audiences when you have to give a presentation or report? How confident are you that what you have to offer is of value or that you even have the right to be seen and heard? I've been amazed at the number of senior-level women who secretly fear that others' ideas are more valid or important than their own or that others will judge them harshly. Self-doubt will undermine you more quickly than even the harshest critic. So get to know your own internal stories and invest the energy in rewriting the ones that hold you back.

What do you tell audiences by way of your language (both body and verbal), the speed and pitch of your voice, your posture and movements? Observe yourself and others in action. Become a student of your medium as well as your message. Whose speaking styles do you admire and what makes their delivery so compelling for you? Who has good ideas but never seems to get heard? How do you present your own stories, points, and ideas? Below are some behaviors—meek paired with strong—that can expand your self-awareness and your effectiveness.

Meek or strong: what's your style?

* Do you use the language of fogballs and mindless phrases to cover your anxiety ... or the language of assertion and powerful pauses to pull others in?

Fogballs and mindless phrases	*Assertion and powerful pauses*
* It seems to me that perhaps we should...	* We want to ...
* Maybe another way of approaching this is to consider ...	* Let's approach this as ...
* Well, uh, the reason we're, uh, here today is, um, to review the, you know, the JCAHO site visit results ...	* We're here to review the JCAHO results ... [pause]

* Do the speed and pitch of your voice rise with your anxiety … or do you consciously alter them to make different points and keep the audience engaged?

* Do your shallow breathing and self-consciousness lead people to request that you repeat yourself or speak louder … or do you remind yourself to breathe deeply and speak from the belly, which gives you volume and self-assurance?

* Do you keep your hands on the podium and make occasional small gestures that get lost beyond the first row … or do you extend your arms and make broad, clear movements that direct the audience's attention and reinforce your point?

* Do you stand in one place … or get out and connect with your audience?

* Do you automatically smile and nod your head even when it's not appropriate … or do you consciously adjust your body and facial expressions so they are congruent with what you are saying and feeling?

Remember that awareness is curative. Know how you are. Know what you want to accomplish. Then lighten up and practice being the way you want to be. What do you have to lose?

I once heard a professional speaking coach, Dan, talking about the differences in how men and women move on the speaking platform. He observed that men take up a lot of space: they walk back and forth and use big gestures and strong body language. Women take up much less space: we stay within a small area and use subtle gestures and meeker body language. When Dan asked us women to stand and practice filling more space, many of us felt awkward and exaggerated because we were conditioned from years of experience to play small, not stand out, not draw attention to ourselves. This always costs us in terms of credibility.

After working with Dan, I started paying attention to how men and women move off as well as on the platform. I saw precisely what he had been talking about. In meetings, men are usually either leaning forward with both arms on the table, elbows extended left and right, or they're leaning back with their arms and legs outstretched. Women are usually sitting upright, arms and legs tucked in, or they're leaning slightly forward, hands in laps or quietly taking notes. In hallway conversations, men often stand in the traffic zone while women hover near the walls.

Don't misinterpret me. I am not asking you to walk and talk like a guy. I *am* asking you to be aware of your physical presence, how it influences your credibility, and how you can alter it to be more effective. You can have the greatest stories in the world, but unless you can deliver them in a direct and confident way, their impact will be diminished.

How we present ourselves tells the world a lot about how we feel about ourselves. Because we have operated in a man's world for years, many of us continue to play small and by the book. We can change that. By telling purposeful stories that engage people emotionally, by pulling groups together with shared stories about fulfilling the mission and connecting with patients and one another as people, by speaking from the heart about what we know to be true of human experience, and by delivering our messages in ways that get heard, we can usher in a way of leading that emphasizes purpose and community, shared norms and service to others.

11

Savor Your Self Doubt

THERE IS NO PASSION TO BE FOUND IN PLAYING SMALL,
IN SETTLING FOR A LIFE THAT IS LESS
THAN THE ONE YOU ARE CAPABLE OF LIVING.

Nelson Mandela

IF YOU THINK YOU'RE TOO SMALL TO HAVE AN IMPACT,
TRY GOING TO BED WITH A MOSQUITO IN THE ROOM.

African Proveb

Our self esteem flows from the judgments we make about two aspects of our nature: our competence or the ability to handle what life throws at us and our self worth or the ability to respect what we want and need for ourselves in order to be happy. I often call them the "do" bucket and the "be" bucket. We need to feel confident about both in order to develop a healthy sense of esteem. Otherwise we suffer from feelings of inadequacy, insecurity, guilt, and ultimately remorse for a life not fully lived.

Several years ago, I was leading a program on creating a resilient organization. The participants were all top leaders in their organizations and most were women. I posted a list of self-reflective questions for the group. The last question was, *How can you use your self doubt creatively?* One woman in the audience started waiving her hand.

"That's the one," she said excitedly, jabbing an index finger toward the list. "That's where I get stuck." Others nodded in agreement.

So I asked them, "What is self doubt like?"

Another woman called out, "It's the fear that people are going to find out I really don't know what I'm doing!" Heads nodded around the room. A chord had been struck.

Intense self doubt is so common that psychologists have given it a name: the impostor syndrome. It's especially common in people who strive to be great and perfect at what they do. Their fears of looking foolish, making mistakes, not knowing or being enough, or being wrong or incompetent slip into the driver's seat and take control.

"How can you possibly use self-doubt creatively when it's so debilitating?" someone asked.

I answered with a personal story.

In the process of writing this book, I sometimes was very clear about my purpose: where I was going and what I wanted to say. Other times, I started to think that what I'd just written or wanted to write was obvious or repetitive or just plain stupid and naïve. I felt like Humphrey Bogart and Kate Hepburn in *The African Queen*: mired in the weeds, getting more and more lost, jumping out and dragging the boat forward, then giving up in despair and lying on the deck exhausted and depleted. The inner critic was whispering in my ear. *You don't have anything new to say. People already know this stuff. You're never going to get out of this. It's too hard. Forget it. Go do something* easy *like weed the garden or wash the car.*

Self doubt dragged me to the dark side of my soul. I felt increasingly alone, adrift, and cut off from my own powers. It consumed me and I just wanted to escape.

One day when I was in a particularly deep pit of self doubt, I called a fellow coach who offered a series of thoughts and questions.

"Perhaps your work on this book is a metaphor for your clients," she began. A metaphor, I thought. "Say more."

"When self doubt is overwhelming you, how do you refocus and get back to what's most important?" she asked. "What's the process you use?"

I had no immediate answers.

Then she added, "If you did know, what might your experience offer others who are struggling with the same challenge of staying focused?"

Those few questions kindled my curiosity and redirected my attention. I knew intellectually that self doubt is a universal dilemma, that we all occasionally question whether we have what it takes to create what we want in our life and work. And I knew that in the midst of our confusion and frustration, it's easy to lower the hammer of disapproval and reduce ourselves to a piddly pile of self doubt. It is essentially a form of suffering that we bring upon ourselves.

When I'm in its throes I lose perspective. I become so constricted that I cannot see beyond it. Through my coach's questions, I was able to disengage from it emotionally, step outside my self-absorption, and observe the experience through a much broader lens. I started to frame it as an opportunity rather than an obstacle and then as something everyone experiences when trying to create something new.

I began to wonder, how do I get beyond self doubt? I decided to live with the question for a while, to observe myself from an outside perspective and see what kinds of answers emerged. Here is what I learned.

When I'm writing and self doubt attacks, I close down the computer. I turn my attention to something I'm good at and enjoy, which gives me a chance to reconnect with my confident side. I call a friend or invite someone to dinner. Sometimes I take myself to dinner. When I grant myself the time to reconnect with what I do well and with people whose company I enjoy, I tap into the whole of who I am and return to the work with different eyes.

Sometimes I reread a chapter or passage and know intuitively that it's off the mark. It needs to go. I read another chapter or passage and an inner voice says, Yes, you're on the path. This is carrying you forward. In both cases, it's not my intellectual brain at work; it's a deeper form of knowing that lets me hold the whole picture and see in a flash whether and how a particular part fits.

When I shift perspectives, I also see how differently I hold others' self doubt—as a small part of who they are—compared with how pervasive my own seems to feel. It renews my energy. I remind myself that moving through self doubt requires those qualities we too often believe we have no time for: patience, presence, the suspending of judgment, the curiosity and willingness to reflect on the ways in which our own experience might be representative of what others experience, too.

When we can trust that self-doubt is an inevitable part of creating, we can pay attention to it in different ways. It is no longer a personal deficit; it now becomes a sign that what we're mired in is our own frame of reference, our own self-imposed blinders. Other frames are out there, as the camera shows us in the African Queen. As Bogart and Hepburn lie exhausted and defeated on the deck, the rain begins to fall. It's a discouraging end to an impossible journey. But as the camera pans back, we see how close they are to Lake Victoria. It lies just beyond the marsh grass. The waters rise. The weeds disappear. The boat drifts freely into the lake. And when they awaken, the path to fulfilling the purpose of their journey is clear.

So savor your self-doubt as a path to new awareness. The next time it lowers a cloud of gloom over you, try one or more of the exercises below.

Find your way back

* Do something you're really good at and notice how it feels. Remind yourself that this confident side is as much or more a part of you as the doubting side.

* Reach out to your network. Call a close friend and inquire about her life. Or ask her about times when she has been riddled with doubt and observe your responses to her. Notice when and how you hold her suffering with compassion. What allows you to do that? What would you have to let go of to hold your own suffering with similar compassion?

* Help your kids with their homework or take a personal day and volunteer to help at a rehab unit. It will balance your perspective and remind you of the power of patience in working with people who are struggling.

* Create a different story about your situation, one that reframes it into a larger perspective. Imagine yourself in a hot-air balloon gazing down at a dense clump of trees. This is the forest you're lost in. Then gaze beyond to the sky and the open spaces stretching toward the horizon. Those are the whole of you.

Befriend the Inner Committee

We all have an inner critic that imposes judgments on us. Some of us have a whole inner committee. Self judgment is the fuel for self doubt. When we judge ourselves, we beat others to the punch. Each judgment evokes a negative emotion and when we tighten the lid on that emotion, we give it power.

The voice of perfectionism stops me dead in my tracks. For another woman, anger erupts at inopportune moments. The flaws of a third surface when she least expects it. Shame pushes a fourth to play small in those moments when she could step into her own greatness. Judgment is like a pressure cooker. If the steam can't escape, the emotional pressure builds until it has enough force to blow the top off.

So the antidote to self doubt isn't to ignore it or let it consume us. The antidote is to witness and accept it—to become more aware of when and how it operates and what it has to tell us about the judgments of our inner critic. And remember, witnessing and accepting it means nothing about our desire or willingness to change it. Acceptance simply means that we can see it for what it is: a temporary state that occasionally arises and disrupts our ability to move forward. The more we can see self doubt as a natural form of self protection, the more we can use it as an opportunity to grow.

So rather than treating self doubt as the enemy, give yourself permission to suspend judgment and treat it as an object of curiosity. Ask yourself questions like the ones my coach asked me. How do you get through it? What might your response say about the experience of being human? What's universal about it?

Try this simple exercise. Make a wish list of how you'd like to be: the qualities, values, and behavior you want to embody. Now assume for a moment that your wish list is filled with possibilities that *already exist in you.* Then observe yourself in action for a while. When and how do you hold yourself back from expressing those possibilities? What fears or judgments are standing between you and who you are capable of becoming?

Next, consider what it would take for you to let go of those judgments. Experiment with letting go. Start with something minor: your impatience with how easily you're distracted or your intolerance for turning in a less than perfect report. Observe how you actually do the work and try stripping your observation of all disapproval.

For example, I used to criticize myself for procrastinating on projects and causing a lot of undue stress for myself and those around me. When I stripped away the judgment and simply observed how I approached a project, I saw that my natural process was to let ideas steep beneath the surface until I was down to the wire, then kick into high gear and do what needed to be done. The pattern had never failed me, but the stress of self criticism had been costly. Stripping away the judgment left me with the same set of facts and an entirely different emotional response.

With this new perspective, I was freed up to redirect my energy from self criticism and doubt to experimenting with my own natural process. The discovery taught me first-hand that change begins with the acceptance of what is. Only when we can acknowledge and accept how we are, warts and all, can we let go of what has been holding us back and play with other ways of being.

If you cannot let go, then create a different practice for yourself. Observe when and how you hang on to your self judgments. What parts of you are they protecting? How do they keep you safe? Whose voice do they really represent? Learn all you can about your holding on by witnessing it from a distance.

When you disengage from it emotionally and take a broader perspective, you create a space for choice. You can hold on or you can let go.

Bringing your self doubt to work can be a powerful way of creating a safe space for others, provided you do it mindfully and with purpose. Airing fears and doubt to allay your own anxiety can jeopardize your credibility. But voicing them as normal responses to challenging situations and using them to make a connection with or for someone else speaks to a universal experience. Sharing your own experience in self accepting terms helps others feel less alone and gives them license to do the same.

If you're among the minority who try to deny any insecurities, then take another look. Truly confident women recognize and hold their own frailties with a high degree of compassion and acceptance. Whether you see it or not, presenting a well defended face to the world hides a deeper sense of self doubt that others will see. In the presence of those who look to you as a role model, authentic self disclosure and an accurate self perception will enhance your credibility far more than a mask of invulnerability.

Take a Lesson from the Actor's Studio

I'm an avid fan of the cable television program *Inside the Actors Studio*. Each week, James Lipton, dean emeritus of New York's Actors Studio Drama School, interviews a famous actor or director. I love the passion with which these artists talk about their craft and the courage with which they tackle their fears and doubt. Yes, they are famous, but they are still mortals wrestling with the same insecurities as the rest of us. And the lessons they offer give a glimpse of the greatness in each of us that lies just beyond our doubt.

When Lipton interviewed Dustin Hoffman, the actor talked about the difficulty of "finding the character" of autistic savant Raymond Babbitt in the movie *Rainman*. Hoffman had researched autism, but when the filming began he still hadn't "found" the character.

The cast and crew did three takes of an early scene followed by some improvisation. At day's end, director Barry Levinson called Hoffman over to see the improv takes. Levinson was laughing. Hoffman told James Lipton that he was convinced he'd blown the day and was ready to resign. Then he viewed the takes. Raymond was responding with a terse, gutteral "Yeah!" to every statement by his flashy brother Charley, played by Tom Cruise. Hoffman had no idea what else to do so he went with this gut reaction.

"And that was it, that was *the place*!" he exclaimed. He'd found the character in an improvised moment.

"A take," Hoffman told Lipton, "is the actor's time to fail. Every art has a failure quotient" and for Hoffman, having to film without finding the character put him on the verge of failing. But "Failing isn't the worst," he added. "Putting something out there that's safe so you don't get hurt or because it worked before—that's a sin. You've failed yourself. Put something out there that's '*Oooh, oooh in that place*' with somebody. That is worth everything."

When he let go of the worry and fully embraced the moment, he put something out there that was '*oooh, oooh in that place*' with the other character and it worked brilliantly. Yes, he was talking about film but his words apply equally well to leadership. It is a performing art. When women leaders put something safe out there so we don't get hurt or because it worked before, we are failing ourselves.

As any artist knows, the greatest challenge is learning to honor our own strengths. I find it reassuring to hear masterful artists like

Dustin Hoffman confess to the small voice of insignificance and uncertainty. I find it inspiring when they choose to step into their fear rather than back away. Melanie Griffith once told Lipton that every time she starts a new movie, she's so scared she can barely recall her own name. "You do the homework," she said, "and then you have to put it all aside. That's the scary part." Similarly, Tom Hanks admitted that every time he steps onto a new set, he fears that he'll be discovered as an impostor. Yet he continues to step onto new sets and deliver award-winning performances.

Every day we have the choice to play small or to put something out there from the core of our own being. As women, we bring valuable strengths to our organizations. Our nurturing nature, our capacity to form and sustain strong relationships and networks, and our desire to help others develop are precisely what today's healthcare organizations need.

So the next time your gut suggests a courageous course of action and your head overrules it in an effort to play safe, think like an actor and trust your gut. Get out of your head and engage others from the heart. Invite them to bring all of who and how they are to what they do. Step through the doubt and put something out there that's *"oooh, oooh, in that place"* with someone. In short, don't fail yourself. Who knows? It may lead straight to your own greatness.

Cut a Crooked Line

One of my clients, Melissa, was talking about the difficulty she has letting go of her need for things to be perfect. One day she and her two little girls were invited to a neighbor's house for some cake. The neighbor had made a heart-shaped gingerbread cake and asked the girls if she should cut it straight or crooked. "Oh," they squealed, "cut it crooked!"

"It about broke my heart," said Melissa. "Never in a million years would I have thought to cut it crooked! I would've cut it symmetrically, no questions asked." She paused for a moment before saying, "And at that moment, I realized that *I need* to *cut a crooked line*. I need to give my kids more latitude for finding their own ways of doing things and myself more latitude for daring to color outside the lines or cut a crooked line."

And so it is with leadership, whether we're leading our own brood or the people we spend our working hours with. When we suspend judgment and work from our deepest longings, we find new ways of *being* despite our fears. It is a journey, this process of stepping into our own power, not a quick fix.

So learn to savor your self doubt as a source of wisdom about the human condition. The poet Marianne Williamson describes the struggle eloquently:

> Our deepest fear is not that we are inadequate.
> Our deepest fear is that we are powerful beyond
> measure. It is our light, not our darkness, that
> most frightens us. We ask ourselves, who am I
> to be brilliant, gorgeous, talented, and fabulous?
> Actually, who are you not to be? You are a child of
> God. Your playing small doesn't serve the world.
> There is nothing enlightened about shrinking so
> that other people won't feel insecure around you.
> We are born to make manifest the glory of God
> that is within us. It's not just in some of us; it's
> in everyone. As we let our own light shine, we
> unconsciously give other people permission to do
> the same. As we are liberated from our own fear,
> our presence automatically liberates others (1992,
> 190-191).

Buried deep within each of us is a place of self acceptance and love. It is a place to which we occasionally retreat and within which we can believe in our own innate goodness and worth. Marianne Williamson knows it. And if you were to be nakedly truthful, so do you.

Many of us have been well trained to deny this part of ourselves. Yet it continues to call to us even in the dark hours of doubt, whispering softly in the background that we are capable of great things. When we choose to pursue the life, the work, the kind of environment that matters most to us, we become models who can light the way. It does not mean that we are more or better than others, merely that we are all in this together.

References

Anderson, Bob. "Leadership: Uncommon Sense." http://theleadershipcircle.com/site/main/position-papers.html

Barrett, Colleen. (June 2006) "Corner on Customer Service: 35 Years of LUV." *Southwest Airlines Spirit,* v. 15, no. 6, 16.

Block, Peter. (1987). *The Empowered Manager: Positive Political Skills at Work.* San Francisco: Jossey-Bass Publishers.

Braaten, Jane S. and Dorothy E. Bellhouse. (2007) "Improving patient care by making small sustainable changes: a cardiac telemetry unit's experience." *Nursing Economic$* 25, no. 3: 162-166.

Buckingham, Marcus and Curt Coffman. (1999). *First, Break All the Rules: What the World's Greatest Managers Do Differently.* New York: Simon & Schuster.

Butterfield, Paula and Ernest Mazzaferri. (1991). "A new rating form for use by nurses in assessing residents' humanistic behavior." *Journal of General Internal Medicine* 6:155-161.

Butterfield, Paula and James Pearsol. (1990). "Nurses in resident evaluation: the participants' perspectives." *Evaluation & the Health Professions* 13: 453-573.

Buzan, Tony with Brian Buzan. (1996). *The Mind Map Book: How to Use Radiant Thinking to Maximize Your Brain's Untapped Potential.* New York: Penguin Group.

Collins, James C. and Jerry I. Porras. (1994). *Built to Last: Successful Habits of Visionary Companies.* New York: HarperBusiness.

Deutschman, Alan. (May 2005). "Change or Die." *Fast Company* 94: 51-62.

Gallwey, W. Timothy. (2000). *The Inner Game of Work: Focus, Learning, Pleasure and Mobility in the Workplace*. New York: Random House Trade Paperbacks.

Gladwell, Malcolm. (2000). *The Tipping Point: How Little Things Can Make a Big Difference*. New York: Little Brown and Company.

Goleman, Daniel. (1995). *Emotional Intelligence: Why It Can Matter More than IQ*. New York: Bantam Books.

———— (1998). *Working with Emotional Intelligence*. New York: Bantam Books.

Guinto, Joseph. (June 2006). "Mom Knows Best: 16 things Colleen Barrett knows about how to please customers and things you should know about her." *Southwest Airlines Spirit* 15, no. 6: 118-127.

———— "Wheels Up." *Southwest Airlines Spirit,* v. 15, no. 6, 109-117. HFMA Educational Report. (March 2006). "Tackling the Capacity Crisis: Successful Bed Management Strategies." See http://www.hfma. org.

Jones, Melanie. (June 2006.) "Star of the Month." *Southwest Airlines Spirit* 15, no. 6: 22.

Kouzes, James M. and Posner, Barry Z. (1987). *The Leadership Challenge: How to Get Extraordinary Things Done in Organizations*. San Francisco: Jossey-Bass.

Lipton, Bruce. (2005). *The Biology of Belief: Unleashing the Power of Consciousness, Matter and Miracles*. Santa Rosa, CA: Mountain of Love/Elite Books.

Marquardt, Michael J. (2004). *Optimizing the Power of Action Learning: Solving Problems and Building Leaders in Real Time*. Palo Alto: Davies-Black Publishers.

McKee, Robert. (1997). *Story: Substance, Structure, Style and the Principles of Screenwriting*. New York: HarperColllins.

Reichheld, Frederick F. (2001). *Loyalty Rules: How Today's Leaders Build Lasting Relationships.* Boston: Harvard Business School Press.

Senge, Peter. (1990). *The Fifth Discipline: The Art and Practice of the Learning Organization.* Revised edition issued 2006. New York: Doubleday.

Simmons, Annette. (2001). *The Story Factor: Secrets of Influence from the Art of Storytelling.* Cambridge, MA: Perseus Publishing.

Spector, R. (1995). *The Nordstrom Way: The Inside Story of America's #1 Customer Service Company.* NY: John Wiley & Sons, Inc.

Suzuki, Shunryu. (2002). *Zen Mind, Beginner's Mind.* New York: Weatherhill, Inc.

Tannen, Deborah. (1990). *You Just Don't Understand: Women and Men in Conversation.* New York: William Morrow and Company, Inc.

————. (1994). *Talking from 9 to 5: Women and Men in the Workplace: Language, Sex, and Power.* New York: Avon Books.

Torbert, Bill. (2004). *Action Inquiry: The Secret of Timely and Transforming Leadership.* San Francisco: Berrett-Koehler Publishers, Inc.

Wheatley, Margaret J. (1999). *Leadership and the New Science: Discovering Order in a Chaotic World,* 2d ed. San Francisco: Berrett-Koehler Publishers, Inc.

Williamson, Marianne. (1992). *A Return to Love: Reflections on the Principles of A COURSE IN MIRACLES.* New York: HarperCollins Publishers.

Yeats, William Butler. (1974). *The Collected Poems of W. B. Yeats.* New York: Macmillan Publishing Co., Inc.

Zander, Rosamund Stone and Ben Zander. (2000). *The Art of Possibility.* Boston: Harvard Business School Press.

Dramatis Personae

Note: the client stories are true; the names are not

Index

meaningful, 198-201
networks, flowing through, 201, 203
and new employee orientations,
    169-71
only useful if it moves, 201-0
about patients or customers,
    sharing, 156, 189-90, 192-3, 197,
    203
as power *vs.* as privilege, 189
as proprietary, 190
and self-awareness, 213-17
Inner Game of Work (Gallwey), 46-8
inquiry, 116, 240, 249-52
    and advocacy, 246; *see also* action
        inquiry
Inside the Actors Studio, 264, 286
intention(s)
    acting with, 119
    another person's, 221
    assigning to others' behavior, 214-
        15
    behavior and, 43, 48-9, 69
    defensive response and inquiring
        about, 251
    defined, as universal force field 63
    furthering your, 198-9
    vs. misaligned systems, 149, 152-4
    personalizing other's, 248
    positive, 49, 215
    purpose and, 67
    sharing, with a trusted colleague,
        204
    testing results against, 232
    translating into action, 220
    "who" stories and, 266-72
internal commentary, 178-79
interpretations, 18, 38, 198, 246-51
"in the moment," xii, 12-13, 15, 17-19,
    38, 97, 199, 210, 221, 229

J

journal, 23-4, 32, 37-8, 46
judgment(s)
    feedback *vs.*, 207, 209
    about feminine behavior in
        patriarchal environments, 35
    holding space *vs.*, 213
    self, 284-5
    suspending, 11, 99, 131, 165, 180-2,
    210, 213, 282, 289
    trusting one's own, 216

K

Kelleher, Herb, 190–1
Kennedy, John F., 77
knowing
    vs. doing dilemma, 230
    "how," 136, 223
    vs. learning, 182, 234
    translating into action, 16, 220
Komen breast cancer movement, 132
Kouzes and Posner, 101–2, 292

L

leader(s)
    assumptions about being the, 20
    credibility as, 77
    as fellow travelers, x
    helping individuals to work on
        purpose, 64
    help people adapt to complex
        challenges, x
    inner personal work of, xvi
    intelligent use of emotion by, 40
    intentions, 69
    managing vs. leading, 36–8
    organizational purpose, breathing
        life into, 59, 73
    purpose vs. vision, distinguishing,
        76
    as visionary, 78
    what they actually do, 34–5
    what they want vs. what they
        reward, 237
    who is the, 31–4
leadership
    and alignment, 143
    as authority and control, 37
    as a community endeavor, 25-6
    and emotions, 39
    historical perspective on, x
    as influence and adaptation, 37
    The Leadership Circle, 20
    and living systems, 25-27
    and loyalty, 110
    vs. management, 37
    new models of, ix

About the Author

My career resembles a meandering river, flowing from one discipline and venture to another. I started college with intentions of becoming an artist, then switched midstream to pursue a couple of degrees in English literature. Mixed into those years were short-term stints as an employee in bureaucracies large and small, which kept driving me back to the classroom.

In the early 1980's I became a psychologist and practicing psychotherapist. Several entrepreneurial ventures supported me during those years. Without realizing it at the time, I was learning important lessons about the nature of work and the influence of work environments on people.

In the mid-80's, my son was born and I took a position in a large academic medical center. I began working my way through the ranks, got an executive Masters in Healthcare Administration (eMHA), and later became the first woman to direct the graduate medical education (GME) programs in the country's largest osteopathic training hospital.

In 1998, I started my own business as a leadership coach and professional speaker. I was scared. By then I was a single parent with a mortgage, a house and family, a newly widowed mother, and an uncertain career that needed to support both college and retirement. I was also inspired. I'd been swept out in a corporate housecleaning and it had given me my calling: I wanted to partner with people to create more humane, compassionate, and courageous workplaces.

As if by magic, people who were two, three, sometimes six steps ahead of me and on a similar path began appearing in my life. Some invited me to join them in organizing an active chapter of the International Coach Federation. Others guided me into the world of professional speaking, which has taken me across North America and allowed me to meet thousands of hard-working professionals, many of whom are health and mental health providers.

I wrote a column for executive women in healthcare for two years, became one of a few dozen coaches selected by the Federal Executive Institute to work with senior executives in the federal government, and have had the good fortune to coach in Notre Dame's Executive Integral Leadership and eMBA programs. As the t-shirt says, Life is Good.

At the time of this writing, I'm experimenting with a number of approaches for convening different kinds of conversations with people. Inspired by the work of people like Christina Baldwin, Peter Block, Juanita Brown, Ann Linnea, Toke Paludan Moeller, Harrison Owen, and Meg Wheatley, I continue to stay on the steep side of the learning curve. New ways of working together are emerging and I want to be on the crest of the wave.

About You and Your World

I love stories. If you have a story that speaks to what you've read in this book and want to share it, you can reach me at the following.

Peppernight Press
P.O. Box 164024
Columbus, OH 43215
www.peppernightpress.com